NEW MEXICO'S ROYAL ROAD

Trade and Travel on the Chihuahua Trail

NEW MEXICO'S ROYAL ROAD

*Trade and Travel
on the Chihuahua Trail*

by Max L. Moorhead
Foreword by Mark L. Gardner

UNIVERSITY OF OKLAHOMA PRESS : NORMAN AND LONDON

By MAX L. MOORHEAD

Commerce of the Prairies, by Josiah Gregg (editor).
Norman, 1954.

*New Mexico's Royal Road: Trade and Travel
on the Chihuahua Trail.* Norman, 1958.

The publication of this volume has been aided by a grant from
THE FORD FOUNDATION

Library of Congress Cataloging-in-Publication Data

Moorhead, Max L.
    New Mexico's royal road : trade and travel on the Chihuahua Trail
/by Max L. Moorhead ; foreword by Mark L. Gardner.
        p. cm.
    Includes bibliographical references (p.   ) and index.
    ISBN 0–8061–2651–5
    1. New Mexico—History—To 1848.   2. Royal Road of the Interior Lands.
3. Santa Fe Trail.   4. New Mexico—Commerce—Mexico.   5. Mexico—
Commerce—New Mexico.   6. Chihuahua (Mexico : State)—Description and
travel.   I. Title.
F799.M794   1994
382'.72160789'0903—dc20
                                                    94–35293
                                                    CIP

2   3   4   5   6   7   8   9   10   11

Contents

Illustrations

Foreword

HISTORIAN MAX L. MOORHEAD (1914–1981) is probably best known for his outstanding work as the editor for the University of Oklahoma Press edition of Josiah Gregg's *Commerce of the Prairies.* First published in 1954, and still in print, it is the edition most relied upon by scholars interested in the famous overland trade between the United States and Mexico. Moorhead followed up this achievement in 1958 with an equally noteworthy piece of scholarship—what might be considered his own *Commerce of the Prairies.* It is the book in your hands, *New Mexico's Royal Road: Trade and Travel on the Chihuahua Trail.*

A pioneering work in its own right, *Royal Road* was acclaimed by many, including J. Frank Dobie, who wrote in a 1959 review, "The title of Mr. Moorhead's final chapter, 'The Significance,' applies to his whole book." Founded on impressive archival research, *Royal Road* traces the history and physical route of the Chihuahua Trail (or as it was known in

Spanish colonial times, *El Camino Real de Tierra Adentro*) from Juan de Oñate's colonizing expedition to New Mexico in 1598 to the end of the Mexican War 250 years later. Most of *Royal Road*, however, is devoted to Moorhead's particular area of interest: the caravan trade between the United States and Mexico that flowed over both the Santa Fe Trail and the Chihuahua Trail during the Mexican period, 1821 to 1848.

This overland commerce, Moorhead informs us, was considerably larger and more complex than scholars previously had realized. Perhaps this is obvious to Borderlands historians today, some thirty-five years after the publication of *Royal Road*, but it is a point worth repeating, because a limited view of what Moorhead correctly labels the "so-called Santa Fe trade" still persists.

Beginning in 1822, just a year after the commencement of legal trade between the United States and Mexico, some Santa Fe traders began hauling their goods to Chihuahua City, 580 miles south of Santa Fe, via the Chihuahua Trail. By the early 1840s the majority of the goods carried over the Santa Fe Trail was intended not for the markets of New Mexico but for those of Chihuahua and other Mexican towns beyond. Thus, Moorhead tells us, the famous Santa Fe Trail became an extension of the older and longer *Camino Real*, and if we look at the origins of some of the merchandise taken down these trails, we find that this trade route stretched even farther eastward, reaching out across the Atlantic Ocean to Europe.

Moorhead provides us with an exceptional account of the nuts and bolts of the overland trade—customs duties, wagons, draft stock, smuggling, routes, business techniques, and trade goods—as well as its impact on northern Mexico and Missouri. Additionally, he includes several footnotes with thumbnail sketches of some of the prominent players in that commerce, each a valuable nugget of research. While scholarship in the

decades since *Royal Road* first appeared has both comple-
mented and corrected some of Moorhead's findings, his book
remains the best scholarly examination of the pre-Mexican
War trade over the Santa Fe and Chihuahua trails. In at least
one instance, historians are just now following Moorhead's
lead: he points out in *Royal Road* the significant role of native
Mexican merchants in the overland trade, an important aspect of this business that scholars have begun to illuminate
only in recent years.

It is particularly appropriate that *Royal Road* is being
reissued at this time, for interest in both the Chihuahua Trail
and Santa Fe Trail remains high. The Santa Fe Trail was
designated a National Historic Trail by Congress in 1987. The
Santa Fe Trail Association, a non-profit organization of over
1,200 Trail enthusiasts, publishes a quarterly, *Wagon Tracks,*
and holds biennial symposia to re-examine and promote that
trail's history. In 1988 the Camino Real Project was founded to
study and champion the Royal Road. Funded by numerous
grants and donations, it has produced an archaeological inventory of the route, a traveling exhibit, a volume of scholarly
essays, and a map brochure and has brought about the place-
ment of forty-three highway markers in New Mexico and the
State of Chihuahua, Mexico.

Trail scholars and aficionados will welcome the reap-
pearance of *New Mexico's Royal Road.* It is a necessary compan-
ion to Josiah Gregg's *Commerce of the Prairies,* and like Gregg's
work it can be considered a classic as well—an example of
history at its best.

Mark L. Gardner

Preface

THIS BOOK is the outgrowth of a suggestion made many years ago by Professor Herbert E. Bolton at the University of California. The famous "Santa Fé trade" of the nineteenth century was, he postulated, not so much the interchange of goods between Missouri and New Mexico as it was a very extensive commerce which was merely channeled through the ports-of-entry of those two frontier states but which involved a large part of both the American and Mexican nations. In 1947, I decided to test this hypothesis by reducing it to a simple statistical problem in volume and value. By examining the customs records in the archives of New and Old Mexico, I could, I thought, ascertain quite easily but also exactly just how much of the merchandise from Missouri passed on through the city of Santa Fé and down the Camino Real to the interior centers of Mexico. This was my original intention, but two unforeseen developments eventually destroyed both its simplicity and its practicality.

In order to interpret with some degree of intelligence the statistics of this primitive international trade, I began work by familiarizing myself with its general background and setting. These less quantitative circumstances, however, soon became so absorbing in themselves that I was unable to tear myself away from them and return to the central problem. Then, when I finally got into the customs records, I found that they were not only incompletely preserved but also sometimes falsified, and that smuggling and embezzlement had been so obviously prevalent as to render the figures useless for the purpose of my proposed analysis. By this time I was too deep into the problem to abandon it without sacrifice and too engrossed in its ramifications even to desire my release.

And so I allowed myself to be led on and on, into the myriad circumstances surrounding an insoluble problem. In fact, my neat little project threatened to become a career. I found myself delving deeper and deeper into the past. I became absorbed in the blazing of the original trade route, in place names along the trail, in carts, wagons, horses, mules, burros, and oxen, in personalities, business methods, government restrictions, and international war.

What has at long last emerged is not the statistical analysis originally contemplated, but rather a much broader and deeper essay. It is a narrative and description of the origins, development, inner workings, and significance of the commercial, cultural, political, and military traffic on the oldest major highway in what is now the United States.

In bringing the story to light, I am deeply indebted to the American Philosophical Society at Philadelphia for a generous grant-in-aid which made possible my travel to, research in, and micro-copying from Mexico during the summer of 1950; and to the University of Oklahoma Faculty Research Fund for the support of these and other phases of the project. For kind and effective personal assistance in making materials available, my appreciation is also due to a large number of friends and associates, especially the following: Miss Estelle T. Weeks, in the National Archives at Washington, D. C.; Dr. Arthur J. O. Anderson, Miss Evelyn Bauer, and Mr. William Reed, in the Museum of New Mexico at Santa Fé; General and Mrs. William J. Glasgow, at El Paso, Texas; Srs. León Barrí, Jr., and José Carlos Chávez, of the Sociedad Chihuahuense de Estudios Históricos at Chihuahua, Mexico; Dr. Albert William Bork, of Mexico City College; Sr. Luís G. Cevallos, of the Archivo General y Pública de la Nación at Mexico City; General Juan Manuel Torrea, of the Archivo de la Secretaría de Relaciones Exteriores at Mexico City; and to the entire staff of the libraries and manuscripts division of the University of Oklahoma. In the preparation of the manuscript itself, the typing and editorial suggestions of Mrs. Harriet Peterson improved my own rough efforts. Finally, for proofreading and indexing, not to mention extreme patience during my long preoccupation, I am inextricably indebted to my wife, Amy. All shortcomings of the total product are of course my own.

MAX L. MOORHEAD

Norman, Oklahoma
February 17, 1958

NEW MEXICO'S ROYAL ROAD

Trade and Travel on the Chihuahua Trail

1.

Blazing the Camino Real

THE MISSOURI PIONEERS who opened the so-called Santa Fé Trail in the early part of the nineteenth century not only established commercial contact between the frontier settlements of the United States and Mexico but also opened a road connecting with a major Mexican highway. Santa Fé was the terminus of a 1,600-mile road that passed through seven state capitals on its way to the metropolis. This was the *Camino Real,* a "king's highway," or, more properly, a public thoroughfare over which wagon and pack trains regularly passed. The real significance of the historic Santa Fé Trail was its connection with Mexico's longest Camino Real.

This "royal road" began to reach out to the north and west of Mexico City soon after the Spanish Conquest. The capture of the Aztec metropolis in 1521 was followed by a rapid occupation of the arid and broken northern plateau, where one silver mine after another was discovered. By 1580 the Spanish frontier extended to the twenty-seventh parallel, approximately 850 miles from Mexico City, the Ultima Thule being a cluster of settlements in and around the Valle de San Bartolomé, now Villa Allende, Chihuahua.

Between the capital and this outpost of civilization the savage land was precariously held by a scattering of mining camps, towns, ranches, and garrisons, all linked together by a network of wagon traces. Wild, nomadic Indian tribes, especially in the northern reaches, kept the Spanish conquerors ever on the defensive. Travelers found safety only in large caravans, and these often required military escort. The most frequently traveled road stretching to the north and northwest parallel to the Sierra Madre del Oeste served the richest mining centers, and this was the Camino Real which eventually reached Santa Fé. In 1580 it passed successively through the towns of San Juan del Río and Querétaro (both founded in 1531), Celaya (1570), Silao (1553), León (1576), San Juan de los Lagos (1563), Aguas Calientes (1575), Zacatecas (1546), Fresnillo (1554), Sombrerete (1555), Nombre de Dios (1563), Durango (1563), and finally Santa Bárbara (1563) in the district known as the Valle de San Bartolomé.[1] With only slight deviation, this and its subsequent extension to Chihuahua, El Paso, Albuquerque, and Santa Fé was to become the route of the Mexican Central Railroad (*Ferrocarril Nacional*) and the more recent Christopher Columbus Highway (Mexico's national Route 45).

For about twenty years the Spanish frontier paused at the Valle de San Bartolomé, for beyond, especially to the northeast, lay the dread Bolsón de Mapimí—five hundred miles of treacherous desert extending all the way to the Big Bend of the Río Grande. Even today this arid pocket embracing the

[1] The northward expansion of the mining frontier in this period is most fully discussed in John Lloyd Mecham, *Francisco de Ibarra and Nueva Vizcaya* and Philip Wayne Powell, *Soldiers, Indians, and Silver: The Northward Advance of New Spain, 1550–1600*.

[4]

eastern half of the state of Chihuahua and the western half of Coahuila is peopled only on the fringes. To the far north, on the upper reaches of the Río Grande, beyond the great *despoblado,* lay the Pueblo Indian civilization of New Mexico. The Pueblo land had been visited by Coronado in 1540–41, and it still beckoned to seekers of both souls and silver in 1580, but the road thither was both circuitous and precarious. Coronado had reached New Mexico from the west, traveling along the Pacific slope of the Sierra Madre del Oeste and through the valley of the Gila, a route far removed from the central Camino Real. Moreover, his large following had so antagonized the Indians along that route that they were still up in arms.

Forty years after Coronado, the Pueblos were visited again, this time by missionaries and traders from Santa Bárbara. With special permission from the crown Father Agustín Rodríguez, two other Franciscan laymen, a number of Indian servants, and a military escort under Captain Francisco Sánchez Chamuscado set out on horseback in 1581 to establish missions among the Pueblos, trade with them, and further explore their territory. Fearing the waterless wastelands immediately to the north, this party followed a continuous system of rivers which prevented not only their getting lost but also any undue suffering from lack of water. However, it added immensely to the distance of travel. The route lay northeastward of Santa Bárbara, down the Río de Parral to its confluence with the Río Florido, down the Florido to the Río Conchos, and down the Conchos to the Río Grande at what is now Ojinaga (opposite Presidio, Texas). From that point their course turned northwestward, up the Río Grande to the present city of Juárez (opposite El Paso, Texas), and then northward up the same river to the Pueblo towns which lined its banks.

It is not clear from the records whether they crossed over to the right bank at El Paso or whether they remained on the

[5]

western bank on their upstream route, but they seem not to have followed the route of the subsequent Camino Real across the Jornada del Muerto, which figuratively strings a westward bow in the Río Grande beginning about seventy miles north of El Paso. Thus, it is uncertain how much of the Camino Real in New Mexico they actually may have blazed. Beyond the Jornada del Muerto for the next 230 or 240 miles they visited most of the Pueblo villages on both sides of the river. They also re-explored what Coronado had discovered from the Zuñi towns in the west to the headwaters of the Canadian River in the east. Captain Chamuscado and the escort returned to Santa Bárbara, presumably by the same route, but all three missionaries were killed by their Pueblo hosts.[2]

A belated attempt to rescue the friars was made by Antonio de Espejo, a wealthy merchant, who set out from Santa Bárbara over the same river route late in 1582. He was accompanied by Friar Bernardino Beltrán, some Indian servants, and a military escort. Arriving too late to save the beleaguered missionaries, Espejo's party visited almost all of the Pueblo towns on the Río Grande and explored widely to the west and east. Its return route in 1583 was down the Pecos River to the Río Grande, far below El Paso, and thence by their former trail.[3]

Two other *entradas* into New Mexico occurred in 1590 and 1593, but neither seems to have found a shorter route from the terminus of the central Camino Real. The first was led by Gaspar Castaño de Sosa, who without royal authorization took a large part of his colony from what is now Monclova, Coahuila, into New Mexico by way of the Pecos River. He and

[2] These adventures are recorded in the Gallegos relation, which appears in George P. Hammond and Agapito Rey (eds.), "The Rodríguez Expedition into New Mexico, 1581–82," *New Mexico Historical Review,* Vol. II, Nos. 3, 4 (July, October, 1927), 239–68, 334–64.

[3] George P. Hammond and Agapito Rey (eds.), *The Expeditions into New Mexico Made by Antonio de Espejo, 1582–83.*

his followers were arrested in the same year, 1590, by a troop under Captain Juan Morlete, and forcibly returned by way of the Río Grande. Castaño de Sosa had transported his colony in wagons or carts, and these, on their ignominious return, were the first vehicles to pass over the New Mexican portion of the later Camino Real.[4] Little is known of the expedition of Francisco Leyva de Bonilla and Antonio Gutiérrez de Humaña, who left Santa Bárbara for New Mexico in 1593. Presumably they traveled the river route blazed by Father Rodríguez and Captain Chamuscado. After reaching what is now San Ildefonso on the upper Río Grande, they made an excursion to the buffalo plains in the east, where a falling out occurred. Humaña stabbed Leyva to death, but was in turn killed with almost all of his followers by hostile Indians. Their fate was not known until 1598, when the Oñate expedition arrived.[5]

The expedition of Don Juan de Oñate, a son of one of the wealthiest silver miners of Zacatecas, is most famous for succeeding in its prime objectives: the pacification of the Pueblos and colonization of New Mexico. A third major contribution, however, and one of utmost importance here, was the discovery of a new route which extended the Camino Real for another seven hundred miles. This became the Chihuahua Trail, the link between the mining frontier of Nueva Viscaya and the mission frontier of Nuevo México—the very life line of the missions, garrisons, ranches, and towns of the latter province during the two and one-half centuries of its occupation by Spain. During the succeeding quarter-century, when New Mexico belonged to the Republic of Mexico, it was the road

4 Dorothy Hull, "Castaño de Sosa's Expedition to New Mexico in 1590," *Old Santa Fé*, Vol. III, No. 12 (October, 1916), 307–32.

5 The account of this tragedy related by an Indian witness is summarized in Herbert E. Bolton (ed.), *Spanish Explorations in the Southwest, 1542–1706*, 201ff.

by which merchants from Missouri—the so-called Santa Fé traders—reached the interior markets of Mexico to trade their dry goods and hardware for bullion and mules. In 1846 it was the invasion route of the American army which added New Mexico to the United States, and in the twentieth century the route of a major railroad and a paved highway. Since Oñate's trail, and not that of Coronado, Rodríguez and Chamuscado, Espejo and Beltrán, Castaño de Sosa and Morlete, or Humaña and Leyva, was that which became the Camino Real, a more precise study of his itinerary is quite in order.

Oñate's expedition was authorized in 1595, but thereafter became enmeshed in official red tape for more than two years, passing its final inspection on the banks of the Río Conchos in February of 1598. The huge emigrant train consisted of 130 men, the wives and children of many of them; arms, implements, and provisions sufficient to satisfy royal requirements for a new colony; eighty-three wagons, carts, and carriages, and some seven thousand head of livestock—horses, mules, oxen, beef cattle, sheep, goats, and pigs. Marching over the desolate plain, it stretched out for a distance of almost three miles.[6]

From Zacatecas, where much of the caravan was outfitted, through Fresnillo, Sombrerete, Nombre de Dios, Durango, and the Valle de San Bartolomé to the banks of the Conchos the emigrants traversed fairly well-explored terrain. To the north, however, lay *tierra incógnita,* a great deserted plain broken by detached sierras, almost devoid of vegetation, and watered only by localized thunderstorms, occasional springs, and even less frequent rivers which carried surface moisture only during the rainy season. In order to reach the upper Río Grande at El Paso by the most direct route, Oñate meant to strike boldly through this forbidding *despoblado* with all its attendant

---

[6] Records of the final inspection, in George P. Hammond and Agapito Rey (eds.), *Don Juan de Oñate, Colonizer of New Mexico, 1595–1628,* I, 199–308.

risks to his people and animals. The Pueblo land lay due north, while the river route pursued by his predecessors veered far to the east.

On February 9, 1598, two days after leaving the banks of the Conchos, the caravan reached another river, the San Pedro, where another month of delay was occasioned. There they awaited the arrival from the south of a contingent of tardy friars and the return from the north of a party sent ahead to explore the shortest route to the Pass of the Río Grande. This latter group was led by Vicente Zaldívar, Oñate's sergeant major, who set out on February 14, and it is he rather than Oñate who deserves credit for blazing the new road to New Mexico. The official journal, a mere record of campsites and distances marched,[7] barely mentions the Zaldívar exploration, but a chronicle written by another member of the expedition, Captain Gaspar Pérez de Villagrá,[8] provides fuller detail. According to this authority, three Indian guides who pretended perfect acquaintance with the desolate wastes ahead became hopelessly lost, and only after wandering about for several days —three without any water at all—did Zaldívar's party find their bearings. This was accomplished when a small band of nomadic Indians crossed their trail and guided them safely to the Río Grande. By March 10, after an absence of two weeks, the scouting party was reunited with the main caravan on the banks of the Río San Pedro.[9]

7 "Discurso de las jornadas que hizo el campo de su Majestad desde la Nueva España a la provincia de la Nuevo México," *Colección de documentos inéditos relativos al descubrimiento, conquista y colonización de las posesiones españoles en América*, compiled by Joaquín Pacheco, Francisco de Cárdenas, and Luís Torres de Mendoza, XVI, 228–76. Except where otherwise noted, my version of Oñate's itinerary is based on this record. An English translation of the original manuscript appears in Hammond and Rey (eds.), *Don Juan de Oñate*, I, 309–28.

8 Gaspar Pérez de Villagrá, *History of New Mexico*, edited by Frederick Webb Hodge and Gilberto Espinosa. The original edition was published at Alcalá in 1610.

9 *Ibid.*, 108–109.

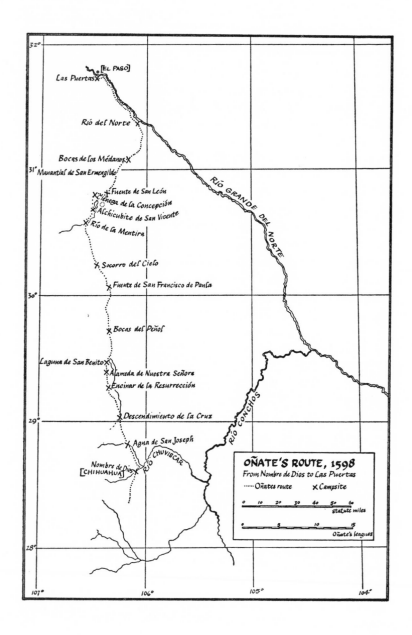

32°
[EL PASO]
Las Puertas ✗

Río del Norte ✗

Bocas de los Médanos ✗
31° Manantial de San Ermengildo
✗ Fuente de San León
✗ Ciénega de la Concepción
✗ Alchicubite de San Vicente
✗ Río de la Mentira

✗ Socorro del Cielo

✗ Fuente de San Francisco de Paula
30°

✗ Bocas del Peñol

Laguna de San Benito ✗
✗ Alameda de Nuestra Señora
✗ Encinar de la Resurrección

✗ Descendimiento de la Cruz
29°

✗ Agua de San Joseph

Nombre de Dios [CHIHUAHUA]

RÍO CHUVISCAR

RÍO GRANDE DEL NORTE

RÍO CONCHOS

28°

107°   106°   105°   104°

OÑATE'S ROUTE, 1598
From Nombre de Dios to Las Puertas
····· Oñate's route   ✗ Campsite

0   10   20   30   40   50   60
statute miles

0   5   10   15
Oñate's leagues

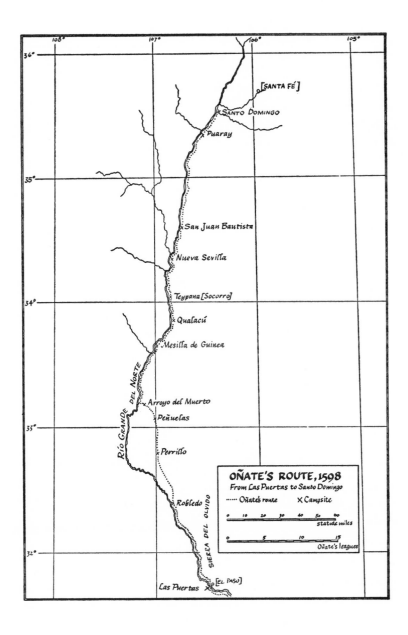

36°

107°

106°

105°

108°

[SANTA FÉ]

× Santo Domingo

× Puaray

35°

× San Juan Bautista

× Nueva Sevilla

34°

Teypana [Socorro]

× Qualacú

Mesilla de Guinea

Río Grande del Norte

× Arroyo del Muerto

Peñuelas

33°

× Perrillo

× Robledo

Sierra del Olvido

OÑATE'S ROUTE, 1598

From Las Puertas to Santo Domingo

······ Oñate's route   × Campsite

0   10   20   30   40   50   60
statute miles

0   5   10   15
Oñate's leagues

32°

Las Puertas × × [EL PASO]

By this time the friars had arrived from the south, and so camp was broken on March 10, and two days later, at what was calculated to be 29° 15' north latitude, the caravan reached another river, which they named the Nombre de Dios. Being the next large stream north of the San Pedro, this was undoubtedly the Río Chuviscar, and the campsite, notwithstanding a discrepancy in recorded latitude, was in the vicinity of the present city of Chihuahua (founded in 1709 at latitude 28° 38'). Both the setting and the landmarks beyond are unmistakable. Here the jagged mountains form a pocket with an opening to the east through which flows Chihuahua creek, a tributary of the Chuviscar. Another creek in this valley and also a mission (founded in 1697 and now a suburb of the city) still bear the name Nombre de Dios. The Camino Real which Oñate blazed from this point on was the Chihuahua Trail of later date.

In tracing the route of Oñate's caravan, a number of difficulties arise. The official journal errs understandably in recording both latitudes and distances of travel, for both of these were imperfectly estimated in the sixteenth century. The distances are given in Spanish leagues (normally from 2.6 to 3 miles in length) which are inconsistently and exaggeratedly reckoned in the journal at from 3 to almost 5 miles.[10] This makes identification of every campsite impossible, but by checking the distances traveled against the landmarks described and favoring the latter in instances of discrepancy, a number of the locations and thus the general route can be determined with reasonable accuracy.

10 From Chihuahua (the Nombre de Dios camp) to the pueblo of Santo Domingo on the upper Río Grande is approximately 600 miles by Oñate's road, but only 136 leagues in his record (an average of 4.42 miles per league). For the 260 miles from Chihuahua to El Paso the journal registers only 58 leagues (averaging 4.48 miles), while for the 340 miles from El Paso to Santo Domingo it records 78 (4.36 miles per league).

Thus, Oñate's "Sierrazuela de las Ogeras," a small spur of mountains which his road skirted to the east and where the train rested on March 18 three leagues beyond the "Nombre de Dios" camp, was very likely the present Sierra de Sacramento. Likewise the "Agua de San Joseph," a league farther north, where they camped the next day, was undoubtedly the Río Sacramento. Indeed, Oñate's friars gave the river its modern name in commemoration of Holy Thursday, the feast of the Blessed Sacrament.[11] Near the ford of the river a hundred years later the Hacienda de San José de Sacramento was established by Captain Pedro Núñez Falcón, in 1764 six families resided there,[12] and in 1847 it was a victorious battleground for the United States army invading Chihuahua. Oñate's caravan rested at the Sacramento over Good Friday, March 20, while a second reconnaissance of the terrain ahead was begun by Zaldívar's scouting party. The latter now remained a few days in advance of the emigrant train all of the way to the Río Grande, which they found after a captured Indian obligingly sketched out their course on the bare ground.[13]

Meanwhile, on March 21, the main caravan following the newly blazed trail left the Sacramento and traveled nine leagues in two days into a broad, longitudinal valley which they called the "Valle de San Martín," which was bordered on the east by the "Sierra de Levante," a range of hills, and on the west by the "Sierra de Oñate," a more formidable mountain chain. The campsite of March 22, Easter Sunday, was in a grove of live oaks which they appropriately christened the "Encinar de la Resurrección." Near by among some springs one of the horses stepped into a pool, and the travelers were

11 Villagrá, *History of New Mexico*, 110.
12 Francisco R. Almada, *Geografía del estado de Chihuahua*, 374; Pedro de Tamaron y Romeral, "Visita del Obispado de Durango, 1759–63" (transcript in The Bancroft Library at Berkeley, Calif.), 580–90.
13 Villagrá, *History of New Mexico*, 113–26.

startled by a jet of water which burst forth to the height of a man. The springs were thereupon named the "Ojos Milagrosos." In the valley through which they were traveling there are still several springs (although none particularly "miraculous"), and the *encinillas,* or live oaks, now supply the name of the valley itself, its lagoon, a village, and a railroad station. However, Oñate's campsite can be located only vaguely as being in the southern part of the valley of Encinillas. The caravan had passed the site of the Hacienda de los Sauces and was in the vicinity of the Hacienda of Encinillas, both of which were established almost a century later by Benito Pérez de Rivera. In 1684, Encinillas boasted six thousand head of cattle, and in 1764 forty-eight families were supported by the forced labor of 137 convicts and 12 Indian prisoners of war. Still another hacienda, El Peñol, was established on an arroyo of the same name in the valley during the nineteenth century.[14]

A march of two rather long leagues to a stand of cottonwoods, called the "Alameda de Nuestra Señora," and another of one league, on March 25, brought the caravan to some small springs and a large lagoon having the same taste and smell as the lake at Mexico City. This they called the "Laguna de San Benito," which could only have been the Laguna de Encinillas, a shallow body of brackish water in the valley bottom, stretching from ten to fifteen miles northward and having a width of from two to three miles, depending upon the rains. It is fed in part by a number of small springs to the west and constitutes the largest body of standing water on the entire Chihuahua Trail.

Four leagues farther north, on March 28, the caravan reached the "Bocas del Peñol de Vélez," where the ten- to fifteen-mile-wide valley of Encinillas through which they had

14 Almada, *Geografía del estado de Chihuahua,* 259; Tamaron, "Visita del Obispado de Durango," 580–90.

been traveling for the last thirty-five or forty miles is all but closed by the convergence of the bordering mountain ranges. In later times this narrow pass, the highest elevation (approximately 5,300 feet) on the road between Chihuahua and El Paso, was variously known as Las Bocas, La Puerta, and El Callejón. The journal places it at exactly 30° north latitude, but it is more nearly 29° 40′.

After a two-day rest at the pass the train proceeded five leagues in two marches to the "Fuente de San Francisco de Paula," which it reached on March 31. They had apparently missed the Ojo de Gallego, a spring in the mountains to the east of the road which sometimes sent a creek flowing across the trail twelve miles south of this camp, which was probably the Ojo de Chivato of later date. About twenty-five miles beyond the pass, this was the last spring encountered by Oñate's company for the next nine leagues. Fortunately, however, a cloudburst overtook the caravan in open country three leagues beyond the spring and halted it in the midst of several great pools of water sufficient to quench the thirst of the entire herd of livestock. This place, which they gratefully called "El Socorro del Cielo," cannot now be fixed on the map, but the Charquito de Jesús María, a small water hole in a gulch at the foot of a steep mountain about eighteen miles north of Chivato, is in this vicinity.

After remaining at the pools of rain water for two days, the train continued northward, making six short leagues in two marches, and arrived on April 4 at a river which they called the "Río de la Mentira," the green trees along its banks belying its dry bed. They did find water "two harquebus shots away," however, at a marsh extending to the east for three leagues, which was fed by some warm springs. This they called the "Baños de San Isidro" and located at 30° 30′ north latitude. The dry river could only have been the Río Carmen, which flows across the road from the western sierras. The marsh was probably a recent overflow of the Río Carmen, a frequent occurrence during the rainy season. There are several warm springs in this vicinity, the most celebrated of which is the Ojo Caliente near the ford of the Río Carmen. The Hacienda de Ojo Caliente de Santa Rosa was established there during the seventeenth century but did not long survive.[15] Of more importance was another estate, the Hacienda de San Fernando de Carrizal, about ten miles north of the Ojo Caliente and a few miles west of the main road. It was abandoned early in the eighteenth century because of attacks by the Apaches, but was resettled in 1758 as a garrison town, the Presidio de Carrizal.[16]

On April 7, after resting at the marsh for two days, Oñate's caravan reached "a well-known sierra and marsh with very good water" two leagues farther north, which they called the "Alchicubite de San Vicente." The only real sierra thereabouts is the Magdalena, which is more than ten miles east of the road, but the reference is probably to the Cerro de Noria, a prominent mound immediately to the east of the brackish Lago de Patos, which could have been mistaken for a marsh. The Río Carmen empties into this body of shallow water. About eight miles to the west of the road is a square, flat-topped mound only about twenty feet high, but with a hot spring on its summit which occasionally sends boiling water twenty feet and steam more than fifty feet into the air.[17]

The next campsite, three leagues farther north, was called the "Ciénega de la Concepción" and placed at the southern

15 Brigadier Pedro de Rivera to the Marqués de Casafuerte, El Paso del Norte, September 26, 1726, in Alfred Barnaby Thomas (ed.). *After Coronado: Spanish Exploration Northeast of New Mexico, 1696–1727*, 213–14.

16 *Ibid.*; Tamaron, "Visita del Obispado de Durango," 140–49; Vito Alessio Robles (ed.), in Nicolás de Lafora, *Relación del viaje que hizo a los presidios internos situados en la frontera de la América Septentrional*, 85–86n.

17 Adolph Wislizenus, *Memoir of a Tour to Northern Mexico, Connected with Col. Doniphan's Expedition, in 1846 and 1847*, 44–45.

margin of the "Médanos." There is no permanent marsh north of the Lago de Patos, but the Ojo de Lucero, a spring immediately to the west of the direct route to El Paso and at the southern extremity of the "Médanos" sometimes overflowed during the rainy season and emptied into a sink to the east of the road.[18] The "Médanos," on the other hand, are unmistakable. These great sand dunes sprawling over the entire country from the Ojo de Lucero to the Río Grande cover 770 square miles and once constituted a major impediment to travel, particularly between what are now the railroad stations of Candelaria and Samalayuca. With great difficulty pedestrians and pack animals could continue northward through the billowing sands to the Ojo de Samalayuca and eventually to the Pass of the Río Grande, but heavily laden wagons, such as those accompanying Oñate's train, were obliged to skirt the southeastern margin and reach the river twenty or more miles downstream. Even this detour had its share of deep sand and long waterless distances.

After resting at the southern margin of the Médanos an extra day, Oñate's company took the detour, traveling due east for a league and a half at what was reckoned as 31° north latitude until they reached a spring which they called the "Fuente de San León." Either this spring or the "Manantial de San Ermenegildo," the next day's camp three leagues beyond, could have been the Charcos de Grado of later date. There are few such small pools fed by poor springs on the so-called Jornada de Cantarrecio. A march of another three leagues brought the train to the "Bocas de los Médanos" on April 12, and this was undoubtedly the gap between the Sierra del Presidio and some detached mountains to the south. The wagons and most of the company were left at this pass for a week while the thirsty livestock were driven six leagues north

18 *Ibid.*, 44.

to the river. Then the draft animals returned for the wagons, which were taken through the deep sands with doubled teams in two trips, each requiring two days. The first division reached the long-sought "Río del Norte" on April 20 at a place eight and one-half leagues (about forty miles) below El Paso, probably near the present town of San Ignacio. The journal fixes the latitude at 31° 30', which is only approximate.

While the company rested on the banks of the Río Grande, the oxen were driven back to the "Bocas" for the remaining wagons, and a scouting party was sent upstream to locate the ford at El Paso. When all had reassembled on April 27, the caravan began a leisurely march up the right bank of the Río Grande making only three leagues in three days and resting on the fourth. The last, Ascension Day, April 30, was also a day of general rejoicing, for Governor Oñate went through the elaborate ceremony of taking official possession of the river and the province which it drained. Another three days of leisurely travel brought the caravan five and one-half leagues beyond, to the "Puertas," where the river veers southeastward from its southerly course and flows through the narrow gorge of El Paso. Here the mission of Nuestra Señora de Guadalupe was founded in 1659 and the Villa of El Paso del Norte (now Ciudad Juárez) in 1680.

At Oñate's camp in the "Puertas," about forty Mansos Indians arrived in friendly fashion. They showed the Spaniards the tracks made by the carts of Castaño de Sosa's company as it left New Mexico under arrest seven years before, gave them some description of the ill-fated colonists, and on May 4 helped Oñate's caravan, especially the sheep, in fording the Río Grande. Only on the left bank could the wagons, carts, and carriages proceed through the narrow river pass. And even there, to the west of what is now El Paso, Texas, the trail was broken and treacherous. Four days were spent negotiating only two and one-half leagues, and one of these days was spent resting the oxen and another in repairing the wagons, which were heavily damaged on the precipitous trail. Only seven leagues were made during the next four days, and on May 12 a small party was again sent out to reconnoiter. On the twentieth, after the main caravan had traveled only six more leagues, the scouts rejoined it. The course was now north-northwest, with the Río Grande on the left and the Organ Mountains on the right. The latter are called in the journal the "Sierra del Olvido," as the scouts who had passed it beforehand had now forgotten having seen it.

Little more than the distances between nondescript campsites appears in the journal until the entry for May 21. The road lay along the river and was undoubtedly that traveled by Castaño de Sosa and Morlete, if not by earlier expeditions. Nothing distinguished the desolate route for sixteen leagues from the ford at El Paso except a few campsites of later date, none of which can be correlated to those of Oñate's caravan. Two, however, are of later importance. The Paraje de Bracitos, about twenty-eight miles from El Paso, became a regular campsite on a little arm of the Río Grande encircling a sandy island, the mesquite and chaparral to the west being repeatedly burned off by traveling companies who rested there. A few miles north of this campsite the celebrated battle of Bracitos would be won by the invading American army on Christmas Day of 1846. The other regular campsite was the Paraje de Doña Ana, twenty-two miles above the Bracitos, at or near the present town of Doña Ana (founded sometime between 1838 and 1842).

About eleven miles above the Paraje de Doña Ana, Oñate's caravan stopped on May 20 and remained over the next day. The simple notation in the journal for May 21 that "we buried Pedro Robledo" identifies this as one of the most important campsites on the Chihuahua Trail. Robledo remained the name of the camping ground for the next three hundred years, and is still applied to the mountain on the opposite side of the river. The significance of the location was that here begins, or ends, the westward bow of the Río Grande, through a channel too narrow and precipitous for pack trains, much less wagons, to negotiate; and the most feasible road northward lay around the eastern side of the small Sierra de San Diego and across a level plateau separated from the river bend by the Caballo and Fray Cristóbal ranges. This was the dread Jornada del Muerto, a ninety-mile march over an almost waterless desert to the camp of Fray Cristóbal, where the river is met again and once more resumes its north-to-south course.

After burying Robledo on the twenty-first, Oñate took a picked force of men and set out across the Jornada for the pueblos beyond, hoping to procure provisions for the main caravan and to arrange for an amicable reception of the colony. The emigrant train lagged behind, and the journal now records the march of Oñate's advance party. The latter traveled only two leagues the first day, camping on the high plain without water, refreshing their horses and oxen by taking them across the intervening mountains to the river, a league distant. The stock seem to have been watered at what was later called the Paraje de San Diego, which could also be reached with some inconvenience by following the river about ten or twelve miles upstream from Robledo.

The next day, having returned to the desert road and pursued a northern course that took them ever farther from the river, the advance party made four leagues and camped at one of the rare water holes on the Jornada. The journal entry of May 23 explains that it was discovered as a result of finding a dog with muddy feet, and thus El Perrillo, a name which endured well into the nineteenth century, most probably refers to the little dog who found water for Oñate's party. About twenty-four miles north of Robledo, El Perrillo is situated between an isolated mountain and Granada station on the railroad, which now follows the Jornada del Muerto. The next march was of four leagues to a few small pools near some volcanic rocks which provided only enough water for the men, and so the animals were again taken through the mountains to the river, which was now more distant than before. From the distance traveled north of El Perrillo, the pools near the volcanic rocks would appear to be in the vicinity of the Cruz de Alemán, a seventeenth-century grave and later a regular campsite on the Jornada. Alemán station on the present railroad still marks the approximate location. Here Oñate's advance party abandoned what was later the Camino Real and struck out northwestward toward the river, passing between the northern end of the Caballo Mountains and the southern end of the Fray Cristóbal Range. This march, on May 25, reached a creek at two leagues which they called the "Arroyo de los Muertos" for reasons unrecorded but which may conceivably have been the origin of the name Jornada del Muerto. The creek probably emanated from the Ojo del Muerto, a spring in the mountains five miles off the main road to which draft animals were frequently driven for water. Oñate's men found the arroyo's water poor, and so continued for another league to the Río Grande, reaching it near present Elephant Butte Dam. The next day, abandoning their carts, which could not negotiate the precipitous river bank, they made only two leagues, but on the day following they traveled seven. This brought them on May 27 to a marsh at the foot of a black cliff which they called the "Mesilla de Guinea," probably the present Black Mesa to the south of and on the opposite side of the river from San Marcial.

As the wagon train, which was a few days behind, was unable

to follow Oñate's rugged trail through the mountains and down the steep river bank, it most probably continued northward over the desert plain for another forty-five miles, as did almost all later caravans, stopping at a sink known as the Laguna del Muerto, where there was water only after the rains, and reaching the Río Grande again at the northern base of the Fray Cristóbal Range, where a regular campsite was later established. According to tradition, Fray Cristóbal Mountain was named for an early friar whose hand and face the peak supposedly resembled.[19] This ended the ninety-mile Jornada del Muerto, which subsequent caravans usually negotiated in three forced marches, traveling mainly at night in order to avoid the desert heat.

From the "Mesilla de Guinea," Oñate's advance party rode four leagues over a winding road known later as the Paso del Contadero, on May 28 passing the Piro village, Trenequel, on the opposite side of the river, and the Cerro de San Pascual, on the east bank, where a Piro mission existed from 1632 to 1675 and a favorite campsite thereafter.[20] This march reached another Piro town, Qualacú,[21] where the inhabitants fled on the approach of the horsemen. Some of them were induced to return, and Oñate's men camped for a month outside the town, subsisting in large part on maize requisitioned from the pueblo, along with provisions brought ahead from the wagon train on June 12.

[19] The name was current at least as early as the Pueblo revolt of 1680 and may have originated in Oñate's time. His cousin, Friar Cristóbal de Salazar, accompanied the advance party across this route in 1598 and died on his way back to Mexico in the following year. Oñate to the Viceroy, March 2, 1599, and to the King, April 7, 1599, in Hammond and Rey (eds.), *Don Juan de Oñate*, I, 488, 492.

[20] Alonso de Benavides, *Fray Alonso de Benavides' Revised Memorial of 1634*, edited by Frederick Webb Hodge, George P. Hammond, and Agapito Rey, 247, n. 72.

[21] Hodge (ed.), in Villagrá, *History of New Mexico*, 145n.

From these first Piro villages on up the Río Grande, Oñate's route not only followed that of Father Rodríguez and succeeding expeditions but also that of a much earlier Spanish party. While Coronado was marching over the buffalo plains to the northeast in 1541, searching for Gran Quivira, one of his captains was exploring down the Río Grande. No known journal or detailed report of this venture has survived, but Coronado's chronicler informs us that a small party marched eighty leagues down the river from the headquarters at Tiguex (near present Bernalillo) and found four large native villages.[22] Notwithstanding the exaggerated distance, these could only have been the southern Piro towns now visited by Oñate, the ruins of which are still in evidence.

On June 14, Oñate resumed his march and passed three other favorite campsites of later date: the Paraje de Valverde, an oasis-like grove of cottonwoods, which was occupied briefly in the early nineteenth century; the Bosque del Apache, a similar woods well named for the frequent visits hostile Indians made to it; and the Paraje de Luís López, a seventeenth-century hacienda which was destroyed during the Pueblo Revolt and was situated at the southern terminus of a series of tortuous slopes and bends in the road, known as the Vueltas de Luís López.[23] Toward the northern extremity of this difficult trail Oñate's riders arrived on June 14 opposite the Piro town of Teypana, having traveled three leagues from Qualacú. For the first time the inhabitants remained in their village to receive

22 "The Relation of Pedro de Castañeda," in George P. Winship (ed.), *The Coronado Expeditions, 1540–1542*, 511.

23 The Hacienda de Luís López occupied land on both sides of the river, and a hamlet on the west side about five miles below Socorro still bears the proprietor's name. The owner may have been the Luís López who was a resident of Bernalillo in 1696. Governor Antonio de Otermín's table of marches, January 16, 1682, in Charles W. Hackett (ed.), *The Revolt of the Pueblo Indians and Otermín's Attempted Reconquest, 1680–82*, II, 364; Jessie B. Bailey, *Diego de Vargas and the Reconquest of New Mexico*, 62.

the Spaniards, and their abundant contributions of sorely needed provisions induced Oñate's men to christen it "Socorro," a name still borne by the New Mexican town near by.

A march of four leagues on June 15 brought them over another tortuous road to the hill of Acomilla, opposite the present town of the same name on the other side of the river. And on the next day, three leagues farther on, they reached another, smaller Piro town, in a picturesque situation of the river, which they nostalgically named "Nueva Sevilla." This was La Joya de Sevilleta of later date, from which emerged the present town of La Joya. There most of the party remained until June 21 while a few went to explore the village of Abó, in the mountains to the east.

When travel was resumed on the twenty-first, the journal became less specific in regard to the Indian villages passed. On that day they made four leagues to a pueblo which they occupied for four days and called "San Juan Bautista," but which was shortly abandoned. Having passed the future sites of La Joyita, a small hamlet, the Hacienda de Felipe Romero, and the Estancia de Barrancas (both abandoned during the Pueblo revolt of 1680)[24] and San Gabriel de las Nutrias, an eighteenth-century tent town situated in a green meadow,[25] Oñate's men probably found "San Juan Bautista" in the vicinity of another future campsite, the Casa Colorado, opposite the present town of Jarales on the west side of the river.

For the next six leagues on June 25 and five more on the following day, the journal mentions only passing many pueblos

24 Felipe Romero served in Governor Otermín's army during the Pueblo Revolt. Muster rolls, in Hackett (ed.), *Revolt of the Pueblo Indians*, II, 104, 198. For the Estancia de Barrancas, see the testimony of Sebastián de Herrera, *ibid.*, II, 171–72, and Bailey, *Diego de Vargas*, 5, 31–32.

25 San Gabriel de Nutrias had thirty families living in animal-skin tents shortly after the middle of the eighteenth century, but they were almost defenseless against the marauding Apaches. Lafora, *Relación del viaje que hizo a los presidios internos*, 95–96.

[24]

and planted fields on both sides of the Río Grande. The distance would have placed the last camp a few miles north of present Albuquerque. Along the way they passed the future site of the Hacienda de Thomé Domínguez de Mendoza, which was destroyed in the Pueblo revolt but was later reoccupied as Tomé, the southernmost regular town on the east side of the river during the Spanish period.[26] Beyond this was the Hacienda de Francisco Valencia, also destroyed during the revolt but reoccupied in 1740 as the Pueblo de Valencia, a town of Christian Indians redeemed from their Apache and Comanche captors.[27] A number of lesser establishments later dotted the river bank along the next thirty miles, but the most important site now passed by Oñate's party was that later occupied by Albuquerque. Here the Hacienda de Mejía, destroyed during the Pueblo revolt, was used as a supply base by Governor Diego de Vargas during the reconquest of the province in the 1690's.[28] The Villa de Albuquerque itself was founded in 1706 and shortly became the main Spanish settlement in the Río Abajo, or lower river district. In the 1770's it had seventy-five Spanish families protected by eighty well-armed citizen militia. The inhabitants were scattered along the river valley for several miles, but owing to a lack of oxen and especially to fear of hostile Indians, the abundant cropland was often idle. Moreover, wood was so scarce that the settlers depended upon dried horse manure for fuel. In 1779 the town

[26] The proprietor of the original hacienda, for whom the later town was named, was an officer in Governor Otermín's army. Fray Francisco de Ayeta to the Viceroy, El Paso del Norte, September 11, 1680, in Hackett (ed.), *Revolt of the Pueblo Indians*, I, 106; Bailey, *Diego de Vargas*, 32.

[27] Otermín's table of marches, August 28, 1680, in Hackett (ed.), *Revolt of the Pueblo Indians*, I, 27; Friar Juan Agustín Morfi, "Geographical Description of New Mexico, 1782," in Alfred B. Thomas (ed.), *Forgotten Frontiers: A Study of the Spanish Indian Policy of Don Juan Bautista de Anza, Governor of New Mexico, 1777–1787*, 102.

[28] Bailey, *Diego de Vargas*, 23–33, 72–75.

proper was reorganized so that the public buildings enclosed a regular square for better defense.[29]

On June 27, Oñate's party resumed its march from the camp north of present Albuquerque and made five leagues to the Tiwa pueblo of Puaray, near present Bernalillo, where Father Rodríguez and one of his fellow missionaries had been killed seventeen years before. Along the way they had passed the Tiwa pueblo of Alameda, on the west side of the river, and the Tewa town of Sandía, on the east side, which latter still exists. Oñate's party remained at Puaray for three days. The present town of Bernalillo in this vicinity predates the Pueblo revolt of 1680, during which Puaray was permanently abandoned.[30]

When the march was resumed on June 30, they passed what would later be the town of Algodones, entered the Keres pueblo of San Felipe (three leagues beyond Puaray), and rested almost four leagues farther on at that pueblo of the same nation which they christened Santo Domingo, where Galisteo Creek empties into the Río Grande.

The remainder of the journal recounts visits to other pueblos which are off the route of the Camino Real and is therefore of no concern here. Santo Domingo was the last town on the Río Grande over which the wagon road would pass, for here, after the founding of Santa Fé in either 1609 or 1610, it began a steep ascent toward the northeast for about twenty-six miles. It should be mentioned, however, that Oñate's wagon train reached Santo Domingo on July 27, 1598, four weeks after his own arrival with the advance party. Only sixty-one of the original eighty-three vehicles arrived with the train, the

---

[29] Lafora, *Relación del viaje que hizo a los presidios internos*, 76; Morfi, "Geographical Description of New Mexico," in Thomas (ed.), *Forgotten Frontiers*, 101.

[30] Hackett (ed.) in *Revolt of the Pueblo Indians*, I, 30; Hodge, Hammond, and Rey (eds.) in Benavides, *Revised Memorial of 1634*, n. 252, 257.

others having been left at the wayside to spare the wearied oxen from complete exhaustion. It had taken the train five months to travel the 750 miles from the banks of the Conchos River, where the *tierra incógnita* began. The same distance was covered in less than four months by seventy colonists with four wagons who arrived on December 24, 1600,[31] but their trail had already been blazed by the Governor's train.

Meanwhile, the province of New Mexico was divided up among the friars for the instruction and conversion of the Indians, while the immense land itself was explored in several directions by groups of Oñate's soldiers. The exploration to the east, of the broad buffalo range and the Wichita villages on the Arkansas River, and to the west, of the Acoma, Zuñi, and Hopi villages of the mesas and the Gulf of California, duplicated the achievements of Coronado, although the routes were not identical.[32] These discoveries, together with the dissensions and desertions of the colonists and finally the recall of Governor Oñate in 1606, are all important historically, but have no direct bearing on the development of the Camino Real. Oñate, although a failure as a governor, did succeed where all others had failed in three important objectives: in pacifying the Pueblo inhabitants, in planting an enduring Spanish colony in New Mexico, and in opening a direct road from the mining frontier that would keep the new province alive.

31 Muster roll and record of inspection, in Hammond and Rey (eds.), *Don Juan de Oñate*, I, 514–79.
32 The itineraries of the two major expeditions appear in *ibid.* II, 746–60, 1012–31.

2.

Colonial Caravan Trade

THE FAILURE of Juan de Oñate to discover wealth in New
Mexico and to provide the colony with a benevolent government disappointed both the Viceroy and the King. Had it not
been for the unrelenting appeals of the Franciscan friars, the
province would have been abandoned again, as after Coronado's *entrada*. But the missionaries prevailed, the King agreed
to subsidize their establishments, the colonists were induced
to stick it out, and a new governor established the provincial
capital at Santa Fé. During the seventeenth century the mission rather than the homestead was the mainstay of the province, and even the wagon trains which provisioned it from
the south were controlled by the friars. The Pueblo revolt of
1680 forced the abandonment of the province for several years,
but it was successfully reoccupied before 1700, and during the
eighteenth century civil and military considerations rose above
those of the religious. An annual caravan service provided by

the government kept New Mexico alive, but its economy became monopolized and subjected to the interests of the south. The new mining center of Chihuahua became the regional metropolis, and the merchants of that city exerted a commercial tyranny over the New Mexicans that was relieved only by the collapse of Spanish controls and the arrival from across the eastern plains of foreign merchandise.

The northern terminus of the Camino Real was established by Oñate's successor at the close of 1609 or early in the following year. La Villa Real de Santa Fé de San Francisco was established by Governor Pedro de Peralta on the northern side of the Santa Fé River about twenty-six miles from the Pueblo of Santo Domingo. The town was situated in a pleasant valley surrounded by brown hills studded with pines and cedars at the southwestern base of a high range of mountains.

During its first years the town sheltered the families of 250 Spaniards who, together with their servants, numbered almost 1,000 souls.[1] By 1766 the population had grown to 2,324 and included the families of 274 Spanish, Creole, and mixed-blood residents, of 80 soldiers of the garrison, and of 89 Indian householders.[2] The Governor's Palace, the barracks, a chapel, and a number of private buildings occupied the attractive public square, while the parish church and a convent were situated some distance to the east.[3] The town was still only three blocks wide in 1807, but stretched along the little river for about a mile. Seen from a distance, the miserable, flat-roofed adobe buildings—all of only one story except for two churches with imposing towers—looked like a fleet of river boats. The shed-like *portales* fronting the buildings on the square shaded brick sidewalks and gave the streets an appearance of excessive nar-

[1] Benavides, *Revised Memorial of 1634,* 68.
[2] Lafora, *Relación del viaje que hizo a los presidios internos,* 98.
[3] Morfi, "Geographical Description of New Mexico, 1782," in Thomas (ed.), *Forgotten Frontiers,* 91–92.

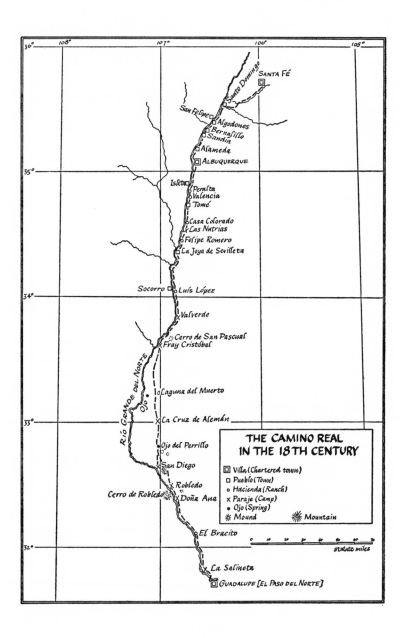

THE CAMINO REAL
IN THE 18TH CENTURY

▣	Villa (Chartered town)	
▢	Pueblo (Town)	
○	Hacienda (Ranch)	
×	Paraje (Camp)	
●	Ojo (Spring)	
✳	Mound	✳ Mountain

statute miles

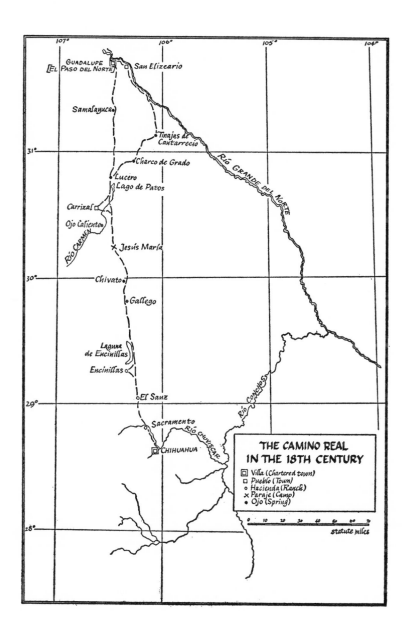

107°   106°   105°   104°

[El] GUADALUPE PASO DEL NORTE   San Elizeario

Samalayuca

31°

Tinajas de Cantarrecio

Río GRANDE DEL NORTE

Charco de Grado

Lucero
Lago de Patos

Carrizal

Ojo Caliente

Río CARMEN

Jesús María

30°   Chivato

Gallego

Laguna de Encinillas

Encinillas

El Sauz

Río CONCHOS

29°

Sacramento

Río CHUVISCAR

CHIHUAHUA

THE CAMINO REAL
IN THE 18TH CENTURY

⊡ Villa (Chartered town)
□ Pueblo (Town)
○ Hacienda (Ranch)
✕ Paraje (Camp)
● Ojo (Spring)

0   10   20   30   40   50   60   70

statute miles

28°

rowness.[4] Santa Fé was not an imposing city, but it was the best the far-flung province had to offer.

Shortly after its founding Santa Fé became a wagon-train terminal, the destination of a supply caravan which traversed the 1,500-mile Camino Real from Mexico City. This service, established shortly after 1609 and reorganized in 1631 and 1664, was designed to provide only for the missions of New Mexico, but it constituted almost the sole means of communication and supply for the entire province during the seventeenth century. Since heavy traffic over what became the Chihuahua Trail in the next century amounted almost exclusively to the comings and goings of this caravan, its organization and operation deserve more than casual consideration.[5]

According to its specifications, the caravan service was subsidized by the royal treasury and was required to make a trip to New Mexico every three years. It supposedly took about six months to reach Santa Fé, an equal time to distribute its cargo, and another six months for the return, one and one-half years being considered a normal period for the round trip. The scheduled departure from Mexico City, however, seems to have been somewhat irregular. For instance, although one caravan arrived in New Mexico in the fall of 1621 and returned the following year, the next train did not reach that province until at least the end of 1625. Friar Alonso de Benavides, who arrived with this train, remarked on the infrequency of caravan arrivals and the consequent suffering of the missionaries. Supplies which were supposed to last three years sometimes arrived only at six- or seven-year intervals.[6]

4 Zebulon Montgomery Pike, *The Expeditions of Zebulon Montgomery Pike,* ed. by Elliott Coues, II, 607–608.

5 The best extensive study of the mission caravans is that of France V. Scholes, "The Supply Service of the New Mexican Missions in the Seventeenth Century," *New Mexico Historical Review,* Vol. V, Nos. 1, 2, 4 (January, April, October, 1930), 93–115, 186–210, 386–404.

6 Benavides, *Revised Memorial of 1634,* 174–75.

In the absence of foreign travelers on the Camino Real who might have considered the mission caravan worthy of description, we must reconstruct its physical appearance from the prosaic specifications of the official contract. Normally, the entire train consisted of thirty-two wagons and was organized into two sections which were further subdivided into detachments of eight wagons. Each of the two sections was under the supervision of a *mayordomo,* or wagonmaster, and the lead wagon of each of its detachments flew the royal banner. The caravan was supposedly escorted by a company of from twelve to fourteen soldiers under a captain, and the train was further enlarged by a large herd of beef cattle and spare draft animals. The wagons themselves were not the primitive, two-wheeled ox-carts employed for the most part by Oñate and so familiar to the Spanish provinces throughout four centuries. Rather, they were heavy-service wagons with four iron-tired wheels, capable of carrying about 4,000 pounds each and, when fully laden, requiring a team of eight mules. Their arched hoods, not unlike those of the later-day "prairie schooners," required forty yards of coarse woolen fabric. Something of the rugged construction of the wagons and of the hazards of the road is suggested by an itemization of their supplies and tools. Each detachment of eight wagons was required to carry 16 spare axles, 150 extra spokes, 24 reserve iron tires (each weighing 27 pounds), 500 pounds of tallow for lubrication, 24 pounds of cord for repairing the wagon hood and cargo coverings, an assortment of nails, bolts, washers, harping pins, cleats, linchpins, and ribs, and—among other tools—hammers, saws, adzes, crowbars, and a twenty-seven-pound sledge. Each wagon was also supplied with an extra team of eight mules, and as replacements for the caravan at large, an extra drove of thirty-two.[7]

[7] Contract of April 30, 1631, in Scholes, "The Supply Service of the New Mexican Missions," *New Mexico Historical Review,* Vol. V, No. 1 (January, 1930), 105–109.

In theory the supply service was established and maintained for the exclusive use of the religious stations, but in practice some wagons were commandeered or chartered for purely secular purposes, first by the governors and later by the merchants of New Mexico. In the absence of other transportation facilities the triennial caravan became almost a public service. Northbound from Mexico City it carried not only friars and their mission supplies, but also settlers, newly appointed officials, baggage, royal decrees, mail, and even private merchandise. Southbound from Santa Fé it carried retiring officials and friars, traders, the produce of the province, and occasionally convicts and prisoners of war. Having discharged its legitimate cargo of mission supplies in New Mexico, the wagons could readily accommodate the exports of the province, much of which was sold in the mining communities to the south. Prior to 1688 there was some doubt about the legality of the mercantile cargo, but it seems not to have been prohibited in fact.[8]

Several Spanish governors of New Mexico augmented their salaries by engaging in commercial traffic on the side notwithstanding laws of the realm specifically forbidding this practice.[9] Nor did the governors attempt to conceal their business operations from the magistrates. In 1638, Governor Luís de Rosas sold to merchants in Parral a consignment consisting of seventeen boxes and ten bales of goods: about 2,000 yards of coarse woolen dress fabric, 46 drapes, 70 other hangings, 408 blankets, 24 cushions, 8 overskirts, 79 assorted doublets and jackets, 124 painted buffalo hides, 207 antelope skins, 900 candles, and about 57 bushels of pine nuts. He had the invoice of this transaction notarized at Santa Fé and the receipt likewise officially witnessed at Parral.[10]

8 Scholes, *ibid.*, No. 2 (April, 1930), 187–88.
9 *Recopilación de leyes de los reynos de las Indias, libro V, titulo 2, ley* xvii.

Nor were the caravan contractors themselves above profiteering from the mission supply service. In 1665, according to a complaint by the friars, the contractor for the wagons placed the entire three-year supply for the missions in one section of the train and sold space in the other to passengers and merchants shipping commercial freight. This not only grossly overloaded the sixteen wagons carrying the legitimate cargo, but also occasioned inordinate delays in taking on and discharging the unauthorized freight. The caravan of that year stopped at Zacatecas for a load of iron which was consigned to the mines of Parral and remained several days for the arrival of the contractor himself, who had loitered in Mexico City long after its departure. Sixteen days were thereafter lost at Parral in unloading the iron and taking on additional merchandise for New Mexico, and another delay occurred about 225 miles beyond (probably at the Laguna de Encinillas), where a redistribution of cargo was made to free ten wagons, which then took on a large amount of unrefined salt and carried it back to Parral. The remaining twenty-two wagons went on to the Río Grande, but they arrived just in time for the spring floods, and three months were consumed in waiting for the swollen river to subside and in traveling the remaining 250 miles to the New Mexican settlements. To make up for lost time and extra wear on the wagons, the contractor then unloaded the supplies for all of the missions at San Felipe instead of delivering them to the separate pueblos and convents as required by the contract. Finally, most of the wagons on the return trip were again employed in carrying salt to the mines of Parral.[11]

The complaints of the friars did not entirely ameliorate the inadequacies of the supply service, for the objectionable

10 "A Trade Invoice of 1638," *New Mexico Historical Review*, Vol. X, No. 3 (July, 1937), 242–46.
11 Scholes, "The Supply Service of the New Mexican Missions," *ibid.*, Vol. V, No. 4 (October, 1930), 395–96.

contract of 1664 was merely amended in 1668 so as to legalize some of the questionable practices of the past. However, after repeated revisions, the friars were permitted in 1674 to buy not only their own supplies but also the wagons and mules for their transportation, and thus they became their own contractors.[12] Even this arrangement, however, did not secure their control over the natives.

Friar Francisco de Ayeta, the commissary for the New Mexican missions, sensed the impending collapse of Christianity in the province, and on his return to Mexico City with the caravan of 1676 presented the Viceroy with a gloomy report. A drought of several years' duration had produced near-famine in the missions, the triennial caravan was unable to provide prompt and adequate provisions, and the missionaries therefore were unable to accommodate the many Indians on their relief rolls. As the material benefits of the new faith diminished, the spiritual convictions of the neophytes also depreciated, and the restlessness of the latter was further aggravated by harsher measures to restrain them from reverting to their ancient rites and by the continued secular exaction of burdensome tribute and personal service. In 1677 the mission caravan brought additional troops and horses to reinforce Spanish control, but these proved insufficient, and the blow fell three years later.

Aided by roving bands of Apaches who had yearly become bolder in their depredations, the Pueblo nations rose in unison in 1680 under the remarkable leadership of a disgruntled medicine man. Exploiting the element of surprise, they murdered 400 Spaniards—21 of them missionaries—and forced the 2,200 survivors to retreat, most of them on foot, down the Camino Real for 330 miles. Nor did the exodus from New Mexico end until all had crossed the Río Grande and encamped

[12] *Ibid.,* 398.

Mexican *arrieros* with an *atajo* of pack-mules

From Josiah Gregg's *Commerce of the Prairies*

From Josiah Gregg's *Commerce of the Prairies*

March of the caravan

at El Paso del Norte. The extreme distress of the refugees was relieved shortly before they reached this destination by the timely arrival from Mexico City of an emergency supply train.[13] This had been ordered especially for their relief by Father Ayeta.

Footsore, heartsick, hungry, and bereft of almost all their personal belongings, the refugees were camped at Fray Cristóbal Mountain, at the northern entrance of the Jornada del Muerto, when the supply train arrived at El Paso, 150 miles below. Unable to ford the river at the usual crossing because of high water, Father Ayeta and the twenty-four wagons had to continue upstream over flooded terrain for about ten miles, where another attempt to cross the swollen river was made on the morning of September 18, 1680. Six spans of mules were hitched to the first wagon, and the good friar himself, aided by several skilled Indian swimmers, drove them into the river. It was too deep, however, the water rising three feet over the wagon bed, and although the mules were able to struggle to a more shallow footing, they could not extricate the wagon, and Father Ayeta had to cut them loose. Fortunately, Governor Antonio de Otermín arrived from the north with an advance party just in time to rescue the friar from the turbulent waters, but it was not until evening that the wagon was hauled safely to the east bank. Seeing the impossibility of getting the other wagons across, Father Ayeta and the Governor decided to bring the supplies over on the backs of swimming horses, and the provisions were ultimately carried to the desperate refugees by pack-train instead of wagons.[14]

Relieved by the new provisions, the refugees finally reached

13 The fullest documentary study of the historic uprising and exodus is that of Hackett (ed.), *Revolt of the Pueblo Indians*.

14 Gov. Otermín, ordinance, La Salineta, September 18, 1680, and Fr. Francisco de Ayeta to the Commissary General, Real Chico, December 20, 1680, in *ibid.*, I, 130–31, 212–13.

[37]

El Paso, where they formed temporary settlements, and for seventeen years these constituted the northern limit of secure Spanish control. Beyond that barbarism reigned once more, but the flight from New Mexico had one blessing. A new and very strategic settlement was formed at El Paso.

Before the Pueblo revolt, there had been a mission and convent at the Pass, Nuestra Señora de Guadalupe del Paso del Norte, which was established in 1659 by Friar García de San Francisco and Father Francisco de Salazar. It was a congregation of several bands of Manso and Suma Indians located two miles below the lower ford of the Río Grande. During the next twenty years a number of Spanish families came in to farm along the river in this vicinity, and they organized a municipal government of sorts. The Villa of El Paso del Norte, however, properly dates from the arrival of Governor Otermín's New Mexican refugees in 1680. The latter were settled in several camps, and a presidio for their protection was established in 1683, about eighteen miles below the mission, being moved to the mission itself in the following year when a general uprising of the Indians to the south occurred. In addition to the mission, town, and presidio at Guadalupe, there was the Pueblo of San Lorenzo four miles downstream, which was the principal refugee camp. Below this at a distance of about one mile was the Pueblo of San Antonio Senecú, a relocation of Piro Indians from their New Mexican village of the same name; about two and one-half miles farther, the Pueblo de Corpus Christi de Isleta, a similarly relocated Tewa town; and at another five miles, the Pueblo of Socorro del Sur, also of Piro refugees.[15]

To reach these settlements from the north bank, the river

15 Anne E. Hughes, "The Beginning of Spanish Settlement in the El Paso District," *University of California Publications in History*, Vol. I, 308–11, 322–28, 367–99.

was easily forded most of the year at two places, two and six miles upstream from the plaza of the Villa. When the river was high, however, caravans had to unload and dismantle the wagons, pack the cargo and wagon sections, animals, and all personnel on rafts, to be towed across with ropes by Indians swimming the turbulent waters.[16] In the latter part of the eighteenth century the governor of New Mexico built and maintained a bridge across the Río Grande at the lower ford to avoid this inconvenience, but it was repeatedly washed out. It was over five hundred feet long and seventeen feet wide, a simple bed of pine logs supported by eight caissons. A supplementary structure spanned the irrigation ditch on the right bank of the river.[17]

A dam immediately below the *acequia madre* diverted a large volume of river water through a network of ditches for the irrigation of extensive fields, vineyards, and orchards, and the rural population of El Paso produced an abundance of fruit, wine, and brandy for sale in the southern towns. The population of El Paso del Norte was scattered along the right bank of the river for several miles. Including the presidio of fifty officers and men and the outlying communities, there were almost five thousand people in 1764.[18]

The reconquest of the rebellious Pueblos by Governor

16 Tamaron, "Visita del Obispado de Durango," 140; Lafora, *Relación del viaje que hizo a los presidios internos*, 90.

17 Gov. Fernando Chacón to Brigadier Pedro de Nava, El Paso del Norte, October 17, 1800, Museum of New Mexico, Governor's Palace at Santa Fé, Spanish Archives (hereinafter cited as M.N.M., Spanish Archives), archive 1512. See also archives 1503, 1604, and 2658; and Pike, *Expeditions*, II, 740.

18 At the villa there were 2,478 Spaniards and mixed bloods; at the mission of Guadalupe, 294 Indians; at San Lorenzo, 192 Spaniards and 58 Indians; at Senecú, 425 Indians and 148 Spaniards; at Isleta, 428 Indians and 131 Spaniards; and at Socorro, 182 Indians and 444 Spaniards. Tamaron, "Visita del Obispado de Durango," 123; Lafora, *Relación del viaje que hizo a los presidios internos*, 88–89; Morfi, "Geographical Description of New Mexico, 1782," in Thomas (ed.), *Forgotten Frontiers*, 108–10.

Diego de Vargas at the close of the seventeenth century was accompanied by the reoccupation of New Mexico. The first civilians returned in 1693, when more than eight hundred men, women, and children started back up the Río Grande from the El Paso district in twelve wagons. The brush which had overgrown portions of the road during the thirteen previous years was trampled down by nine hundred head of cattle driven in advance of the returning settlers. The next year Father Francisco Farfán left the Pass with another caravan, of seventy-six families which were recruited from the mining center of Parral.[19]

Meanwhile, another settlement of vital importance to the life line of New Mexico was being formed at Chihuahua, about 265 miles south of El Paso. First, in 1697, the mission of Nombre de Dios was founded by Friar Gerónimo Martínez to serve a congregation of Conchos Indians. It was not far from Oñate's campsite of the same name a hundred years earlier. Miners and farmers moved into the valley in 1705 and established a community which was recognized by the governor of Nueva Vizcaya in 1709 and officially named San Francisco de Cuéllar. By 1718 the population and mineral importance were such that the Viceroy raised it to the rank of a chartered city, and the name was changed to La Villa de San Felipe el Real de Chihuahua.[20] This was the city of Chihuahua, the wealthy silver-mining center on which the province of New Mexico became so dependent for the next century and a quarter.

Chihuahua was situated on the south bank of the little Río Chihuahua (or Chuviscar), a tributary of the Conchos, in an arid valley almost completely encircled by rugged but picturesque mountain peaks. In 1766 it had a population of four

19 Bailey, *Diego de Vargas*, 187–90.
20 Almada, *Geografía del estado de Chihuahua*, 373; Alessio Robles (ed.) in Lafora, *Relación del viaje que hizo a los presidios internos*, 69n.

hundred Spanish, *mestizo,* and *mulato* families, and these were suffering from the decline of the mines and from the continual depredations of the Apaches, who had murdered them in the very environs of the city and run off most of their livestock. Less than a mile upstream was the mission of Guadalupe, serving some thirty families of Yaqui Indians and a small Spanish population, and on the opposite side of the river the mission and pueblo of Nombre de Dios.[21] During the last quarter of the eighteenth century Chihuahua became the headquarters of the military command for the northern provinces of New Spain, and in 1807 its population was estimated at seven thousand. At that time it was described as a town built around an oblong square containing the principal church, the royal treasury, the municipal office, and the richest mercantile stores. At the southern end of town was another small but elegant church, and at the western end a military chapel, the barracks, the military academy, a Franciscan convent, and a superb hospital, formerly built and maintained by the Jesuits. About a mile to the south of town was a large aqueduct which conveyed water to the reservoir, from which it was piped to various parts of the city. There were fifteen mines in the vicinity of the city, thirteen producing principally silver, one gold, and one copper. The smelters were situated in the suburbs and produced huge piles of cinders which encircled the town.[22]

The merchants of Chihuahua did not gain control of the commerce of New Mexico until about the middle of the eighteenth century, for the mission caravans continued to supply that province with secular as well as religious supplies for several years after the Reconquest. Its functions in 1714 are revealed in the records of a lawsuit. On January 6 of that year, the caravan from Mexico City had reached the Río de las

21 Lafora, *ibid.,* 69–70.
22 Pike, *Expeditions,* II, 761, 764–66.

Nazas, between Durango and Parral, and was encamped there for the night. Although it was now the dry season, a flash flood inundated the wagons and ruined much of the cargo. Included in the damage was a consignment of merchandise (tobacco, chocolate, sugar, and imported fabrics) owned by Juan N. Vallejo, a merchant from Parral, who now brought suit against the custodian of the New Mexican missions, whom he held responsible. Also named as defendants in the case were Antonio Sánchez, the wagonmaster, who had been issued power of attorney by the friars, and Nicolás Bustrín, the actual owner of the wagons and mules. Vallejo hoped to attach the wagons and mules as security for his claim, but the result of his suit is not revealed in the mission records. The testimony does reveal three important facts: that the mission supplies were again being carried in wagons leased by the friars from private contractors, that merchants still availed themselves of this convenience, and that the Franciscans themselves assumed at least partial responsibility for the safe conduct of the merchandise.[23]

During these early years of the century, the caravans operating to and from Mexico City seem not to have followed a fixed schedule, even when carrying the regular mail. In 1712, for instance, the caravan left Santa Fé for the south in May, its departure being announced twelve days in advance by the town crier with drum and bugle accompaniment.[24] By the middle of the century, when the caravan had become an annual service, it left New Mexico in December,[25] but eventually the departure season was fixed as autumn, usually in the month of November. This allowed the New Mexican merchants an op-

[23] Testimony of Juan Hartus Vallejo, Juan González de Retana, Nicolás Bustrín and Antonio Sánchez, Parral and Mexico City, February 23–September 26, 1714, Biblioteca Nacional at Mexico City, Archivo Franciscano, Custodio de Nuevo México, Legajo 6, Expediente 5.

[24] Gov. Marqués de la Penuela, proclamation, Santa Fé, May 10, 1712, M.N.M., Spanish Archives, 17.

[25] Tamaron, "Visita del Obispado de Durango," 130–35.

portunity to attend the annual Taos fair, which was held in July or August, and there procure from the Comanches and other nomadic tribes trade goods that were marketable in the southern cities. So many New Mexican merchants attended the Taos fair in 1776 that the governor saw fit to delay publication of an important decree until they had returned to their home towns.[26] By this time two important changes seem to have been made in the caravan service. It was now operated directly by the royal government rather than the Franciscan Order, and the train was more largely made up of pack mules than of wagons. Moreover, although a regular caravan left Santa Fé in November of each year throughout the latter part of the eighteenth century and well into the nineteenth, other trains were made up from time to time for special purposes, particularly for carrying official dispatches or prisoners to the cities of Chihuahua and Mexico City.

One change in the scheduled departure of the regular caravan was occasioned by the granting of trade privileges for an annual fair at the Valle de San Bartolomé in 1806. Since the duty-free period of the fair was to be from December 18 to 23, the governor of New Mexico was instructed to set the train's departure date somewhat earlier than usual, so that the merchants could get to the fair in time for its opening. From ten to twelve days were estimated as the time needed for loaded mules to travel from Chihuahua to San Bartolomé, and the exact time of departure was to be announced by public proclamation.[27] Since it took forty days for the caravan to reach Chihuahua and ten or twelve more to get to San Bartolomé, it would have had to leave Santa Fé about October 28 in order to reach the fair by the opening date.

[26] Ralph Emerson Twitchell, *The Leading Facts of New Mexican History*, I, 453–54.

[27] Nemesio Salcedo to Gov. Joaquín Real de Alancaster, Chihuahua, March 5, 1806, M.N.M., Spanish Archives, 1972.

Owing mainly to the ever present danger of Indian attack, especially on the long, deserted stretches of the Camino Real, the caravans were usually supplied with ample military protection. In addition to the sizable towns of Santa Fé, Albuquerque, El Paso del Norte, and Chihuahua, which had garrisons of either regular troops or citizen militia, the caravans received protection on the road from two presidios. In 1758 the Presidio of Carrizal was established at the hacienda of that name near the ford of the Río Carmen, about one hundred miles south of El Paso del Norte. In 1766 it was manned only by a corporal and ten ragged soldiers, however, and they offered little protection to the wagon trains or even to the 161 inhabitants of the hacienda.[28] In 1773 another new fort was built on the Río Grande, about twenty miles below El Paso del Norte. This was the Presidio of San Elizeario, the spelling of which name varies in the records, as does the location of the fort itself. Originally it was situated on the right bank at or near the present town of San Elizario, Texas, which, thanks to the subsequent meanderings of the Río Grande in that vicinity, is now on the left bank. In 1785 it had a garrison of fifteen troops, but sometime before 1814 the garrison was moved to another site, leaving an undefended town.[29]

The caravans themselves were always accompanied by a body of armed men, usually including a nucleus of regular troops. Strength in numbers was a minimum requirement. A train accompanied by only two hundred men in 1760 was attacked about halfway between El Paso del Norte and Chihuahua by a small band of hostile Indians, who, although outnumbered by the armed escort, managed to capture a large

[28] Tamaron, "Visita del Obispado de Durango," 140–49; Lafora, *Relación del viaje que hizo a los presidios internos*, 85–86.

[29] Alessio Robles (ed.), in *ibid.*, 17–18; Alfred B. Thomas (ed.) in *Teodoro de Croix and the Northern Frontier of New Spain, 1776–1783*, 21; Hubert Howe Bancroft, *History of the North Mexican States and Texas*, I, 646–47.

number of horses in the confusion of the skirmish.[30] It was customary for the local militia and presidial troops to furnish protection for the caravans, escorting them in relays to and from designated points on or near their jurisdictional boundaries. The regular caravan leaving Santa Fé in November of 1780 was particularly well provided for, being accompanied as far as the Jornada del Muerto by sixty regulars, fifty-five militia, and thirty-six Indian auxiliaries under the governor himself, who was on his way to Sonora. From Fray Cristóbal camp onward for the next fifty-three miles of the deserted Jornada, the train was without military protection, but by previous arrangement it was met at El Perrillo spring by a captain and forty soldiers from the presidios of San Elizeario and Carrizal, who escorted it the rest of the way to the city of Chihuahua.[31] In August of 1800, when the governor left Santa Fé on official business with an escort of thirty-two soldiers, several ranchers and merchants took advantage of the protection to drive 18,784 sheep and 213 head of cattle and to transport an assortment of woolen goods and peltries to the south, preferring this convenience to that of the regular caravan which left three months later.[32] When about 15,000 sheep were driven to the southern provinces in the spring of 1807, they were accompanied by some three hundred civilians, mostly New Mexican ranchers, and an escort of from thirty-five to forty troops.[33] The inhabitants of El Paso del Norte also relied on special military escort when they drove sheep to the south each spring.[34]

30 Tamaron, "Visita del Obispado de Durango," 130–35.

31 Gov. Juan Bautista de Anza to Teodoro de Croix, Santa Fé, May 26, 1780; Croix to Anza, Arispe, July 29, 1780; Croix to Capt. Francisco Martínez, October 3, 1780; and Anza, diary for November 9–22, 1780, in Thomas (ed.), Forgotten Frontiers, 176–79, 187–89, 193–94, 197–99.

32 Gov. Chacón to Nava, El Paso del Norte, August 30, 1800, M.N.M., Spanish Archives, 1503.

33 Pike, Expeditions, II, 631–32.

34 Gov. José Manrrique to Salcedo, Santa Fé, April 1, 1809, M.N.M., Spanish Archives, 2218.

By 1810 a postal convoy seems to have operated separately from the regular autumn caravan. That of 1810 left Santa Fé in March. It was made up of two captains, a lieutenant, and ten troops, and was supposed to meet the mail from the south and exchange pouches at Fray Cristóbal camp. Twenty residents of the towns of Alameda and Albuquerque traveled with this escort, as did six prisoners, aliens who had entered the country illegally from Louisiana. From Fray Cristóbal to the Presidio of San Elizeario, the prisoners and mail had the escort from Chihuahua for protection, while the twenty New Mexican citizens returned to Santa Fé with the mail from the south.[35]

Experience had taught the merchants of New Mexico that ordinary precautions for the forty-day trip to Chihuahua were not enough. When all of the travelers had joined the caravan, there were usually five hundred or more. Then at La Joya de Sevilleta, which was the southernmost regular settlement of New Mexico on the Camino Real, an inspection was made of all their merchandise and provisions, and particularly of their firearms, powder and ball, bows and arrows, shields, and horses. The provisions, among other things, included bread prepared from almost five hundred bushels of wheat, the ground meat from one hundred beeves, and corn, beans, and chick-peas in similarly large quantities. Sheep were also driven along, not only for market but also for fresh mutton en route. Finally, abundant water was stored in several casks for use in traveling across the Jornada del Muerto.[36]

The lieutenant in charge of the military escort was provided with detailed instruction from the commandant of the

35 Manrrique to Salcedo, Santa Fé, March 31, 1810, M.N.M., Spanish Archives, 2311.
36 Pedro Bautista Pino, "Exposición sucincta y sencilla de la provincia de Nuevo México," translated in H. Bailey Carroll and J. Villasana Haggard (eds.), *Three New Mexican Chronicles*, 106–107.

garrison at Santa Fé and held responsible for enforcing many of the caravan controls. His instructions in 1816 were presumably typical.[37] He was to escort the caravan out of Santa Fé on November 22 with a troop of twenty soldiers and proceed in regular daily marches to La Joya de Sevilleta. On entering this town, which was little more than a garrison of seven regular troops and their families, the lieutenant was held responsible for the protection of these persons and their property until the departure of the train, as well as others of the province who were assembled there to accompany it to the south. When all had assembled, he was to make in duplicate a complete muster roll, listing all of the personnel, merchandise, livestock, arms, and ammunition, one copy of which was for the commandant of the Santa Fé garrison, the other for the commandant general at Chihuahua. A registry of persons accompanying the caravan seems also to have been sent to the authorities of their home towns and also to the governor of New Mexico.[38] The lieutenant was required to send home all men not properly armed for their own defense, and a special check of the horses was to be made before departure to make sure that all were properly branded. This precaution may well have been due to difficulties in the past occasioned by illegal recruitment of horses and mules in Chihuahua for the return trip, a practice which the authorities of both New Mexico and Nueva Vizcaya were trying to prevent.[39] On completing the review, the lieutenant was to align the caravan in such an order of march as to prevent the possibility of surprise attack and proceed to

[37] Lt. Col. Pedro María de Allande to Lt. José María de Arce, Santa Fé, November 20, 1816, M.N.M., Spanish Archives, 2681.

[38] Felipe Vijil to Gov. Mariano de la Peña, Valencia, November 30, 1812, M.N.M., Spanish Archives, 2469.

[39] Animals returning to New Mexico without brands were to be confiscated and returned to their proper owners in Chihuahua. Gov. José Rubio to Gov. Francisco Trebol Navarro, Chihuahua, January 20, 1778; Navarro, proclamation, Santa Fé, March 31, 1778, M.N.M., Spanish Archives, 711, 726.

the south in regular daily marches. Civilians were not to use the horses and mules of the military escort for either mounts or pack animals.

The escort officer was responsible for seeing that all men in the train fulfilled their assigned duties (that is, as drivers, herdsmen, guards, or scouts), and that none proceeded in advance of the caravan until reaching the ford of the Río Grande at El Paso del Norte. Meanwhile, should he receive news of the approach of hostile Indians while the caravan was encamped, he was to see that all horses belonging to both military and civilian personnel were in readiness for action. At El Paso del Norte he was to assemble and secure all horses and mules to prevent their straying, and was to leave all worn-out or injured animals of his command at the presidio of that city. The civilian company was to be given full liberty to buy and sell goods throughout the district, and all who wished to leave the convoy at this point were to be issued safe-conduct passes. A report of those leaving was to be made in duplicate and delivered to the commandant general at Chihuahua and, on the return of the caravan, to the governor of New Mexico. The departure from El Paso del Norte for Chihuahua was to be set so as to allow the merchants ample time to complete their business transactions.

From El Paso del Norte to Chihuahua the daily marches were to be more rapid than previously, and all military horses and mules in bad condition on reaching Carrizal were to be exchanged at that garrison. Again, the members of the caravan were to be restrained from going in advance of the escort, even on approaching Chihuahua, unless special permission was granted and advance notice made to the commandant at that city. At Chihuahua the lieutenant was to see that the arms and uniforms of his troops were kept presentable at all times, and that none of them become involved in difficulties with the people of that city, particularly in matters of debt. When they were ready to leave for the return trip after the merchants had completed their business, a new inspection and muster roll was to be made and reported to the commandant general. Such were the controls exercised for the protection of the caravans and of the towns through which they passed.

The merchandise sent to the south in the annual caravans was almost entirely the produce of the soil and a few crude manufactures. In addition to sheep, raw wool, hides (of buffalo, deer, and antelope), pine nuts, salt, and El Paso brandy, there were a few Indian blankets and, occasionally, some Indian captives of war destined to slavery in the Hacienda of Encinillas or in the mines of Chihuahua. In exchange for these goods the New Mexicans received ironware of all kinds—but especially tools and arms—domestic and imported fabrics, boots, shoes, and other articles of dress, and such delicacies as chocolate, sugar, tobacco, and liquors. Paper and ink were also among the imports, as were an all too small number of books.[40] As early as 1724 the New Mexicans were making annual trips to the government-controlled stores of Chihuahua, which furnished them with almost all their needs.[41]

Most of the trade from the south was monopolized within New Mexico by a few merchants from Chihuahua, to whom the local traders were almost continually in debt. Antonio Martín and Antonio Félix Sánchez, two New Mexican merchants, were sued in May of 1749 by Juan Joseph Aramburu of Chihuahua. Martín, it was charged, had purchased 300 pesos' worth of dry goods and silverware on credit at Aramburu's store eight years earlier and still had not paid, while Sánchez,

40 Gov. Chacón to the Consulado of Veracruz, Santa Fé, August 28, 1803, M.N.M., Spanish Archives, 1670 a.

41 Francisco Lorenzo de Cassados, declaration, Santa Fé, April 21, 1724, in Thomas (ed.), After Coronado, 246–47.

whose account was now ten years overdue, owed 328 pesos for similar purchases.[42]

The dire financial entanglement in which the New Mexicans became enmeshed was due in some part to their own ignorance, but mainly to a shortage of effective currency in the province and the unscrupulous policies of the merchants at Chihuahua. No more illuminating commentary on the latter exists in the records than the scorching indictment levied by Friar Juan Agustín Morfi in the 1770's.[43] In the relative absence of real money, Morfi explains, trade in New Mexico was reduced to mere barter, but this simple method of transaction was extremely complicated by a quadruple standard of values which was imposed by the merchants of Chihuahua for purposes of pure extortion.

The real monetary unit was the peso, but there were four concepts of its value in New Mexico during the eighteenth century. The official *peso de plata,* a silver coin which was practically nonexistent there, had a value of eight *reales* and was the standard later adopted by the United States for its silver dollar. As a substitution for it in New Mexico, there were three imaginary coins which were employed only in bookkeeping. The *peso a precios de proyecto* was worth only six *reales;* the *peso a precios antiguos,* only four *reales;* and the *peso de la tierra,* only two *reales.*

At these rates the lower classes of New Mexico, and even some of the merchants, became hopelessly confused in the transactions and victimized in a vicious circle of swindles. For

[42] Juan Joseph Aramburu, declaration, n. p., March 5, 1749, M.N.M., Spanish Archives, 506.

[43] Morfi, "Desórdenes que se advierten en Nuevo México y medios que se juzgan oportunos a repararlo para mejorar su constitución y hacer feliz aquel reyno" [Documentos para la historia de Nuevo México (transcript in The Bancroft Library at Berkeley, Calif.), I, 381–438]. Although generally attributed to Morfi, this treatise is unsigned, and some scholars question his authorship. Thomas (ed.), in *Teodoro de Croix,* 108n.

example, a merchant of Chihuahua could buy thirty-two yards of coarse woolen goods in the south for six *pesos de plata* and sell it in New Mexico at a *peso de la tierra* per yard, or a real value of eight *pesos de plata* in all. Since he was paid in local produce, he could accept remuneration in El Paso brandy, which was worth only one *peso de la tierra* per bottle when exchanged for manufactured goods, and thus acquire thirty-two bottles for the bolt of cloth. However, in reselling the brandy to other New Mexicans, the merchant could charge a *peso de plata* a bottle and thus eventually receive thirty-two *pesos de plata* for goods which had cost him only six. But again, since silver money did not circulate in the province, he must be paid in goods, and should the purchaser of the brandy wish to pay in corn from a future harvest, he was charged the prevailing *peso de precios antiguos* rate, four *reales* for each short bushel *(costal)* of grain, or fifty-one short bushels for the thirty-two bottles. After the harvest, when this was collected, he could sell it to the troops in the southern presidios for ten *reales* per short bushel, almost eighty-four *pesos de plata* in all, or more than ten times the original cost of his goods and freightage.

This sort of procedure, Morfi informs us, had been going on for a long time, and the merchants of New Mexico, being continually shortchanged, could never accumulate sufficient capital to own their own goods. They were obliged to buy on credit from Chihuahua, where they were paid low prices for their local produce and were charged exorbitant ones for their mercantile purchases, and thus were barely able to pay freight costs and still sustain themselves.

The situation seems not to have improved during the next quarter of a century, for the internal commerce of New Mexico was officially reported in 1803 as being managed by only twelve or fifteen local traders, and these were neither properly licensed nor even well versed in commercial matters. All but two or three of them operated on borrowed capital.[44]

Meanwhile, the merchants of Chihuahua during the last quarter of the eighteenth century extended their monopoly over supplies for the government's troops in the northern garrisons. Formerly these provisions were purchased and distributed by the military service itself, through the presidial quartermasters, but from about 1776 to 1786 (and again a few months later), the business reverted to private contractors. In February, 1787, a single merchant of Chihuahua, Francisco de Guizarnótegui, was awarded a five-year contract to supply all of the provisions purchased from the south by the seven presidial and four field companies of Nueva Vizcaya and the New Mexican garrison at Santa Fé.

According to this arrangement, the garrisons were to place their orders at the beginning of each year and provide Guizarnótegui with a voucher on the royal treasury at Chihuahua to cover the costs of his purchases, while he agreed to buy in Mexico City at certified wholesale prices and sell in the presidios at a profit of only 4 per cent. For goods purchased in Michoacán such as shoes, sugar, horses, and mules, he was allowed an additional 2.5 per cent. All duties and costs of transportation, including that of military escort on the Camino Real from the Presidio of Pasaje (about 123 miles south of Chihuahua) to the points of final destination were to be borne by the garrisons themselves. To defray the costs of freightage, Guizarnótegui was to receive two pesos for each twenty-five pounds carried from Mexico City to Chihuahua, which was half a peso less than the established rate, and an additional half-peso for each mule load (about three hundred pounds) brought from Chihuahua to the individual presidios. The gar-

[44] Gov. Chacón to the Consulado of Veracruz, Santa Fé, August 28, 1803, M.N.M., Spanish Archives, 1670 a.

From Josiah Gregg's *Commerce of the Prairies*

Arrival of the caravan at Santa Fé

From W. W. H. Davis's *El Gringo*

View of Santa Fé from the South

risons, however, had the option of making the latter delivery themselves.[45] The first treasury voucher issued to Guizarnótegui to cover his purchases was for 80,000 pesos,[46] but he was not to enjoy this huge volume of business for long. Complaints against him began to pile up shortly after he began to carry out the contract, the entire arrangement was soon under investigation by the government, and in 1790, with two years to go, the contract was cancelled.[47]

A new contract was then let, effective in the following year, this time to an association of twelve different merchants of Chihuahua. They undertook to purchase supplies from Spain, Mexico City, Puebla, and Querétaro which would be delivered to the presidios and be sold at a 6 per cent commission (at 8 per cent for goods bought in Michoacán). This was 2 per cent more than Guizarnótegui had obtained, but the new contractors also assumed the cost of packing, freighting, and storing, and the burden of duties, damages, and "the risks of the road." The garrisons, however, were again to furnish an armed escort from the Presidio of El Pasaje to Chihuahua, a stretch of road that was notoriously subject to ambushes by hostile Indians. Payment to the contractors again was to be made by treasury voucher in order to avoid the risk and expense of shipping coin, and it was specified, significantly enough, that the goods were to be paid for in "effective money,"[48] presumably the *pesos de plata* rate rather than the depreciated and imaginary values of New Mexico.

[45] Jacobo Ugarte y Loyola to the Audiencia of Mexico, Encinillas, March 2, 1787, Archivo General y Pública de la Nación at Mexico City (hereinafter cited as A.G.N.), Provincias Internas, Tomo XIII, Expediente 1.

[46] Ministro de la Real Hacienda, *pago de libranza*, Chihuahua, January 1, 1788, A.G.N., Provincias Internas, XIII, 3.

[47] The investigation yielded over three hundred folio sheets of testimony and reports, which are bound together in the above-cited Tomo XIII.

[48] Pedro Ramos de Verea, Antonio de Yribaren, Diego Ventura Márquez, Ventura de Porto, Sabino Diego de la Pedruesa, Francisco Manuel de Elguea,

Now draining even royal expenditures from the garrison of New Mexico, the monopolies and sharp practices of the merchants of Chihuahua continued to oppress the inhabitants of the frontier province for the remainder of the colonial period. The latter, however, endured the oppressive conditions only so long as there was no alternative. Early in the nineteenth century a new opportunity arose when merchants from far-off Missouri crossed the Great Plains and arrived in New Mexico with competitively priced merchandise, and this opening of the celebrated Santa Fé trade, together with the achieving of independence from all Spanish controls in the same year, inaugurated a new era for New Mexico.

Andrés Manuel Martínez, Pablo de Ochoa, Joseph Suárez, Pedro Yrigoyen, Mariano Barulto, and Joseph Mariano Solís, contract, Chihuahua, October 18, 1790 (certified copy), M.N.M., Spanish Archives, 1120.

3.

Merchant Caravans from Missouri

FOR MORE THAN two hundred years the Camino Real was the life line of New Mexico, and for almost half of that time the province was held by the merchants of Chihuahua in a state of economic dependence. During the eighteenth century, however, a few French traders filtered in from the Mississippi Valley, and early in the nineteenth century, Americans inaugurated an annual caravan trade from Missouri which not only undermined the Chihuahua monopoly over New Mexico, but also competed successfully with it and with that of European merchants for the markets of the Mexican interior.

French merchandise first appeared in New Mexico early in the eighteenth century in an indirect manner. Goods traded by the French in Louisiana to the Pawnee Indians were traded by them in turn to the Comanches, who brought them to the annual fair at Taos. Then, beginning in 1739, French merchants arrived in person, but they were officially unwelcome. The first party was allowed to remain for nine months and return home, but a second group, arriving in 1749, was interned in New Mexico. Still another, in 1750, was arrested and packed off to Sonora in the far west, and the last Frenchmen to arrive, in 1751, were sent under guard all the way south to Mexico City.[1] The Spanish monopoly of trade was scrupulously maintained. After 1762, when Louisiana was transferred to Spain, the advantages of such an overland commerce gradually dawned on the Spaniards themselves.

As the governor of New Mexico saw it, Louisiana's free trade with foreign possessions in the Caribbean and the navigability of the Mississippi and Red rivers could be exploited to the benefit of his own province. European manufactures could be imported at New Orleans, shipped to St. Louis or Natchitoches by river boat, and then packed by mule train to New Mexico at a saving of at least 40 per cent over the cost of transportation from Veracruz and Mexico City on the Camino Real.[2] With this economy in mind, he commissioned a veteran frontiersman to explore an overland trail between Santa Fé and St. Louis. This was done between 1792 and 1793, and the new road coincided very closely with the Santa Fé Trail of later years.[3] However, as so often occurred with Spanish discovery, official caution took precedence over bold enterprise, and the commercial advantages of the highway from St. Louis came to exist on paper only.

[1] Herbert Eugene Bolton, "French Intrusions into New Mexico, 1749–1752," in Henry Morse Stephens and H. E. Bolton (eds.), *The Pacific Ocean in History.*

[2] Gov. Fernando de la Concha to Jacobo Ugarte y Loyola, Santa Fé, June 15, 1789, M.N.M., Spanish Archives, 1049.

[3] Louis Houck (ed.), *The Spanish Regime in Missouri,* I, xxiv. The diary of the explorer Pedro de Vial appears in translation in *ibid.,* 350–58.

The province of Louisiana was returned to France in 1800 and sold to the United States in 1803. Shortly thereafter traders from the latter country began to feel their way across the plains. First came Jean Batiste Laland, a French-American, who was commissioned by William Morrison of Kaskaskia to extend his sphere of trade from the Pawnee villages on the Platte River to the Spanish towns of New Mexico. Laland reached Santa Fé in 1804, where he was immediately arrested and sent to Chihuahua. He was allowed to return to Santa Fé in 1805, but not to the United States.[4] Meanwhile, one James Purcell, of Kentucky, who had been living with the Indians on the western plains for about three years, arrived in Santa Fé in 1805 with a pack of goods to sell. He, too, was apparently interned, for he did not return to the United States until 1824.[5] A few other Americans, mostly of French extraction, filtered into New Mexico in this period, but they were similarly dealt with, and there was no incentive for large-scale American enterprise in that direction until the publication of Zebulon Montgomery Pike's revealing journal in 1810.[6]

Lieutenant Pike's southwestern expedition in 1806 and 1807 was at the time, and is even yet, cloaked in mystery. Officially, he was dispatched to establish friendly relations with the western Indians, collect scientific data, and explore the

[4] With Laland was another French-American from Illinois, Laurenz Durocher. Their permission to return to Santa Fé was communicated to the New Mexican governor, who acknowledged their arrival two months later. Nemesio Salcedo to Gov. Joaquín Real Alancaster, Chihuahua, September 9, and Alancaster to Salcedo, Santa Fé, November 20, 1805, M.N.M., Spanish Archives, 1889, 1925. See also Hubert Howe Bancroft, *History of New Mexico and Arizona*, 291.

[5] Pike, *Expeditions*, III, appendix, 16-17. Pike, who saw him at Santa Fé in 1807, calls him Jacob Pursley, but an item in the *Missouri Intelligencer* of April 10, 1824, announcing his return from New Mexico, refers to him as James Purcell. Hiram Martin Chittenden, *The American Fur-Trade of the Far West*, II, 493.

[6] Zebulon Montgomery Pike, *An Account of Expeditions to the Sources of the Mississippi and Through the Western Parts of Louisiana* (Philadelphia, 1810). The most fully annotated edition is that edited by Elliott Coues, which I have used in preparing this volume.

[57]

Arkansas and Red rivers. But he and his troops became con-
veniently lost, and, trespassing on Spanish territory, they sur-
rendered without resistance to a New Mexican patrol. They
were interned first at Santa Fé and then at Chihuahua, where
they underwent interrogation as suspected spies, but they
were shortly released and escorted back to the United States.
Nevertheless, while on the road to Chihuahua under heavy
guard, Pike managed to talk freely with members of the clergy
and the government, ascertaining the extent of their sympa-
thies toward the mother country, and to record surreptitiously
the information received. He not only kept a day-to-day record
of his itinerary on the Camino Real, but also acquired one or
more official reports on the economy of the Spanish frontier
provinces. Whether that was his official purpose or not, Pike,
when released, had the wherewithal for a comprehensive espionage report. One cannot read his journal without marveling
at the strategic information he was able to acquire.[7]

Of particular interest in the United States to commercial-
minded frontiersmen were Pike's notes on the economic situation in northern New Spain, for these revealed to the American public for the first time the significant imbalance of New
Mexico's trade: the cheapness of her own produce and the
dearness of her purchases from the south. A hundred pounds
of New Mexican flour brought only two dollars (or its Spanish
equivalent of two pesos); a load of salt, five dollars; and a
barrel of El Paso wine, fifteen. Locally raised sheep brought
only one dollar a head; beef cattle, five dollars; horses, eleven;
and mules, thirty. But for their purchases from the south the
people of the province had to pay twenty dollars a yard for
extra-fine cloth, four dollars a yard for linen, and in like pro-

[7] Suspicion that Pike's expedition was for the purpose of espionage as well
as exploration is cast by Isaac Joslin Cox in his *The Early Exploration of Louisiana*, while the implication is discounted by W. Eugene Hollon, in *The Lost
Pathfinder: Zebulon Montgomery Pike*.

portion for other textiles.[8] As these latter prices were far above those current in the United States, this engaging news set off a new series of American excursions to Santa Fé.

In the same year that this information was made public, a party of seven men crossed the plains from the upper Louisiana Territory, only to discover that Spanish policy had not changed. Their goods were confiscated, and they were sent to the Presidio of San Elizeario for a two-year confinement.[9] A larger party tried its fortune in 1812, but suffered the same fate,[10] and three years later a still larger group, twenty-six traders and trappers, were relieved of their goods, confined for a time, and sent back to the United States.[11] It was not until four years later, when a revolution overthrew Spanish authority in Mexico, that American traders and their merchandise were well received at Santa Fé.

The launching of this first successful trade, in 1821, coincided not only with the independence of Mexico but also with the admission of Missouri as an American state. Like New Mexico, Missouri was an agricultural and frontier state typically short of hard money and in real need of commercial development. Hard-bitten Missouri farmers had to supplement their meager income from hunting, trapping, or trading with the Indians to make ends meet. And it was with these pursuits in

8 Pike, *Expeditions*, II, 739–40.

9 The traders were Capt. Reuben Smith, Joseph McLanahan, James Patterson, Manuel Blanco (a Mexican), and three slaves. Gov. José Manrrique to Salcedo, Santa Fé, March 31, and Salcedo to Manrrique, Chihuahua, May 31, 1810, M.N.M., Spanish Archives, 2311, 2320.

10 This party included Robert McKnight, Benjamin Shrive, James Baird, Alfred Allen, Michael McDonough, William Mines, Samuel Chambers, Peter Baum, Thomas Cook, Carlos Miers (an interpreter), and possibly others. They were imprisoned at Chihuahua for nine years. *American State Papers*, XII, 435–52; Chittenden, *American Fur-Trade*, II, 508–10; Robert Glass Cleland, *This Reckless Breed of Men: The Trappers and Fur Traders of the Southwest*, 122–23.

11 The principals in this company were Auguste P. Chouteau, Julius De Mun, and Joseph Philbert. Chittenden, *American Fur-Trade*, II, 497–500.

mind that a company of frontiersmen under Captain William Becknell[12] took to the plains in the late summer of 1821. Becknell and his twenty or thirty followers meant only to hunt, trap, capture wild horses, and barter with the Comanches, and consequently they packed on their horses only a small amount of trade goods. Leaving the Missouri River at Arrow Rock Ferry on the first of September and traveling on the plains for ten weeks, they happened upon a detachment of troops from New Mexico. Neither group was conversant in the other's language, but Becknell's party was struck by the hospitable disposition of the soldiers and accompanied them to Santa Fé. They arrived on November 16, and through a French resident who served as their interpreter they learned of the new state of affairs. Just two months previous to their arrival, New Mexico had taken its oath of allegiance to the new national government of Mexico, and the monopolistic Spanish control was at an end. Governor Facundo Melgares personally invited Becknell's men to sell their stock of goods in New Mexico, and, of more significance, expressed a desire for regular trade with Missouri.[13]

12 William Becknell was an Indian fighter and veteran of the War of 1812. After his famous journey of 1821, he made several others into the West for trading and trapping and carried mail in 1825 for the Santa Fé road-survey party. He established a ferry across the Missouri River about 1828, commanded a militia company in 1832 during the Black Hawk War, and served for a time in the Missouri legislature. The journal of his trips to Santa Fé were kept by his brother, Thomas Becknell. F. F. Stephens, "Missouri and the Santa Fé Trade," *Missouri Historical Review*, Vol. XI, No. 4 (July, 1917), 291–94.

13 "The Journals of Captain Thomas Becknell from Boone's Lick to Santa Fé and from Santa Cruz to Green River," *Missouri Historical Review*, Vol. IV, No. 2 (January, 1910), 65–84. Two other parties of Americans reached Santa Fé in 1821. According to his journal, Becknell left all but one of his company in New Mexico and started back on December 13 "in company with two other men who had arrived there a few days before, by a different route." *Ibid.*, 78. The other party was a group of trappers which reached Santa Fé by way of the Rocky Mountains at the end of 1821 or early in 1822, led by Hugh Glenn of Cincinnati from his trading post near the mouth of the Verdigris River in what

The handsome profits realized by Becknell's party from their paltry trade goods, the announcement of Governor Melgares that further commercial ventures would be welcome, and the release in the same year of the American traders who had been interned at Chihuahua in 1812 were so encouraging that three caravans set out for Santa Fé in the following year. One of these was again led by Becknell, and although his was not the first to arrive nor the most valuable in cargo, it was the most important. It made two significant discoveries. In the first place, Becknell took three wagons with him to test their feasibility on the plains,[14] and these made out so well that succeeding caravans followed suit, so that eventually the caravans of the Santa Fé trade became almost exclusively wagon trains. The other discovery was of a shorter route to Santa Fé, one which avoided the more distant and difficult Raton Pass by leaving the Arkansas River near the 100th meridian and striking out southwestward across an arid desert.[15] This, the so-called Cimarron Cut-off, became a favorite with future traders, for it shortened the road to Santa Fé by more than one hundred miles.

There is no question that the opening of the Santa Fé trade was due primarily to the enterprise of William Becknell, but to this day the merchant who first pushed on down the Camino Real and sold American goods in the richer markets of Chihuahua remains an unknown pioneer. Nor is the date of this achievement definitely established. Some of the traders who came to Santa Fé in 1822 are credited with it by Josiah Gregg,

is now Oklahoma. A diary was kept by Glenn's partner: Jacob Fowler, *The Journal of Jacob Fowler*, edited by Elliott Coues (New York, 1898).

14 "The Journals of Captain Thomas Becknell," *Missouri Historical Review*, Vol. IV, No. 2 (January, 1910), 79–80. The Glenn-Fowler company, returning from New Mexico, followed the trace left by Becknell's wagons for at least two days. Entry for July 1, 1822, in Fowler, *Journal*, 167.

15 Josiah Gregg, *Commerce of the Prairies*, ed. by Max L. Moorhead, 14–15.

an unusually reliable contemporary authority, but Gregg was not associated with the overland trade until 1831, and his personal narrative, although the classic description of its development, was not written until the following decade.[16] The only record for the opening of the Chihuahua trade in 1822 is Gregg's table of the annual volume and value of the Santa Fé trade from 1822 to 1843, in which he estimates that of the $15,000 worth of merchandise the American traders brought to Santa Fé that year, $9,000 worth was taken on south to Chihuahua.[17]

In 1824, when eighty merchants from Missouri brought $35,000 worth of goods to Santa Fé, it was more than the New Mexican market could absorb. One of the traders found such a shortage of money in Santa Fé that year that he had difficulty

[16] Josiah Gregg was born in Tennessee in 1806 and came to Missouri in 1812, where he taught school and studied law for a short time. He joined a Santa Fé caravan in 1831 and remained in the inland trade with Mexico until 1840, traveling almost annually to Santa Fé, sometimes to Chihuahua, and once to Durango, Zacatecas, and Aguascalientes. His brother, Jacob Gregg, had accompanied a train to Santa Fé in 1824, was with the road survey of 1825, and went on to Chihuahua in the same year. Josiah Gregg pioneered a shorter route to Santa Fé from Van Buren, Arkansas, in 1839, drove mules to Texas in 1841, became a storekeeper in Van Buren, and in 1843 went east to prepare his travel notes for publication. The result was his *Commerce of the Prairies* (2 vols., New York, 1844), which went into several editions, including some in German, and is generally recognized still as the best authority on the Santa Fé trade.

In 1845, Gregg studied medicine for a year at the University of Louisville, quit to re-enter the Santa Fé trade, but instead joined the Arkansas Volunteers when war broke out with Mexico. He marched with General John Wool's army to Saltillo, accompanied a dispatch escort to Chihuahua, and mustered out of the service in 1847. He returned to New York to buy goods for a new trade venture, but when this fell through, he went back to Saltillo, practiced medicine there during the winter of 1847-48, and then joined a botanical expedition to Mexico City, the Mexican west coast, and California. In California he visited mining camps on the Trinity River in 1849 and led a party in search of a land route to Trinidad Bay, discovered Humboldt Bay instead, and died while returning in 1850. Paul Horgan's introduction to *Diary and Letters of Josiah Gregg*, ed. by Maurice G. Fulton, I, 3-40; II, 3-30; Moorhead (ed.), in Gregg, *Commerce of the Prairies*, xvii-xxxviii.

[17] The accompanying statistical table appears with explanatory notes in *ibid.*, 331-33n.

in disposing of his wares.[18] Another reported that about half of the merchants, failing to realize a profit and seeking a better market, moved on south into Nueva Vizcaya.[19] In the following year, when ninety merchants introduced $65,000 worth of goods, reports reaching Washington declared that the Santa Fé trade had been "completely overdone," that the New Mexican villages were filled with American goods, and that there was no money in circulation with which to purchase more. Even mules could not be taken in exchange with any prospect of profit.[20] In that year, according to Gregg's table, $5,000 worth of goods were sold in Chihuahua.

Thus, it had early become apparent that the little city of Santa Fé, with its population of only 5,000, and even the entire province of New Mexico, with its 43,000 inhabitants, could not absorb the ever increasing store of goods brought in by the merchants of Missouri. With its scant population, primitive economy, and unfavorable balance of trade with the interior, New Mexico was without the wherewithal to buy.

GREGG'S TABLE OF THE VALUE AND VOLUME
OF THE SANTA FÉ TRADE

Year	Value of Merchandise	Number of Wagons	Total Number of Men	Number of Proprietors	Value of Goods to Chihuahua
1822	$ 15,000		70	60	$ 9,000
1823	12,000		50	30	3,000
1824	35,000	26	100	80	3,000
1825	65,000	37	130	90	5,000
1826	90,000	60	100	70	7,000

18 "The Santa Fé Trail: M. M. Marmaduke Journal," ed. by F. A. Sampson, *Missouri Historical Review*, Vol. VI, No. 1 (October, 1911), 8.

19 Augustus Storrs to Sen. Thomas Hart Benton, Franklin, Mo., November, 1824, in *Niles' Weekly Register*, Vol. XXVII (January 15, 1825), 312–16.

20 *Niles' Weekly Register*, Vol. XXIX (December 24, 1825), 263.

Year	Value of Merchandise	Number of Wagons	Total Number of Men	Number of Proprietors	Value of Goods to Chihuahua
1827	85,000	55	90	50	8,000
1828	150,000	100	200	80	20,000
1829	60,000	30	50	20	5,000
1830	120,000	70	140	60	20,000
1831	250,000	130	320	80	80,000
1832	140,000	70	150	40	50,000
1833	180,000	105	185	60	80,000
1834	150,000	80	160	50	70,000
1835	140,000	75	140	40	70,000
1836	130,000	70	135	35	50,000
1837	150,000	80	160	35	60,000
1838	90,000	50	100	20	80,000
1839	250,000	130	250	40	100,000
1840	50,000	30	60	5	10,000
1841	150,000	60	100	12	80,000
1842	160,000	70	120	15	90,000
1843	450,000	230	350	30	300,000

During the last years of Spanish control its inhabitants had purchased 112,000 pesos' worth of goods a year from the south and sold only 60,000 pesos' worth in return. Even the government pay roll, which brought in about 38,000 pesos, failed to offset the imbalance, and the annual deficit of about 14,000 pesos not only drained the province of hard money but kept its inhabitants indebted as well.[21] On the other hand, the city of Chihuahua had a population almost twice that of Santa Fé. It profited from rich mining operations that supported approx-

---

[21] Pino, "Exposición," in Carroll and Haggard (eds.), *Three New Mexican Chronicles*, 36. The population of Santa Fé and its environs in 1827 was only 5,160 and that of New Mexico only 43,433 according to Governor Antonio Narbona's census. *Ibid.*, 88n.

imately thirty smelters and a mint that stamped out more than 500,000 pesos' worth of coin a year.[22] It was no wonder that Chihuahua rather than Santa Fé eventually became the principal emporium of the overland trade.

Although the more enterprising merchants from Missouri forsook New Mexico for the more lucrative markets of the south, the impact of their invasion of New Mexico had begun to revolutionize its economy. As early as 1824, the New Mexicans were buying larger amounts of manufactured goods from Missouri than from Chihuahua, for those of American make were of both better quality and lower price. The monopoly of the southern merchants was broken, and the unfavorable balance of New Mexico's trade was partially reversed. Now the New Mexicans were demanding hard money in the south for their own produce in order to buy their needs from the Americans. They even purchased beyond their own requirements and resold the surplus at handsome profits in Chihuahua and other southern markets where formerly they had gone into debt. Even the New Mexican treasury was enriched, for customs duties were collected on the importations from Missouri, and those on dry goods ranged up to 25 per cent ad valorem.[23]

Meanwhile, the national government of Mexico took notice of the new threat to its internal trade. Asked for an opinion on the subject, the governor of Chihuahua attributed the success of the American merchants to the long-standing neglect of New Mexico by Spain, the multiplicity of internal duties still imposed on goods sent there from the interior, and the great

[22] *Memoria de la Hacienda Nacional de la República de México, 1845,* Doc. 4. See also "Inland Trade with Mexico," in James Ohio Pattie, *The Personal Narrative of James O. Pattie of Kentucky,* ed. by Timothy Flint, 255–300. This appendix was written by a Dr. Willard, who is identified only as a member of a caravan which went from St. Charles, Missouri, to Santa Fé and Chihuahua in 1824 and 1826.

[23] Storrs to Benton, Franklin, November, 1824, *Niles' Weekly Register,* Vol. XXVII, 312–16.

distance of New Mexico from the main commercial centers of the nation. The American caravans, he reported, were now offering equivalent merchandise in New Mexico for one-third the customary price, but their additional freighting costs would prevent the Americans from competing successfully with Mexican merchants in the interior.[24] In this latter supposition he proved to be quite mistaken.

The governor of New Mexico, on the other hand, could see nothing but benefit from the enlargement of the new overland trade, and to encourage it, in 1825 he commissioned a special envoy to negotiate with American authorities for its protection from the Indians of the intermediate plains. This envoy was Manuel Simón Escudero, a member of the Chihuahua legislature. Accompanying a Missouri caravan returning from Santa Fé, Escudero obtained a favorable recommendation from the United States Indian agent at St. Louis and laid the New Mexican proposals before the Mexican minister at Washington. Of more than passing interest in regard to this mission is the fact that Escudero was accompanied by two Mexican merchants, one from Chihuahua and another from Sonora, and a pack train of five hundred horses and mules.[25] These were the first-known Mexican merchants to trade with the United States by way of the Santa Fé Trail, but they were by no means the last.

By the time Escudero reached Washington, a bill for additional encouragement and protection of the new commerce had already been introduced in the Senate by Thomas Hart Ben-

24 Gov. José de Urquidi to the Ministro de Relaciones, Chihuahua, May 13, 1825, Archivo de la Secretaría de Relaciones Exteriores at Mexico City (hereinafter cited as A.S.R.E.), L-E-1055, Tomo I, 129–36.

25 Gov. Antonio Narbona to the Ministro de Relaciones, Santa Fé, March 4, 1826, A.S.R.E., L-E-1055, I, 160–61; *Niles' Weekly Register*, Vol. XXIX (October 8, 1825), 85; José Agustín Escudero, annotations, in Carroll and Haggard (eds.), *Three New Mexican Chronicles*, 113–15.

ton, of Missouri. Up to that time the federal government had offered but scant support, merely permitting the caravans to pass through Indian Territory and accepting Mexican pesos in place of dollars at the federal land office in Missouri.[26] In 1825, as the result of Senator Benton's efforts and of the growing national interest in the overland trade, American consuls were appointed to reside at Santa Fé and Chihuahua, a peace pact was made with the Osage Indians, and a new road to Santa Fé was marked out from Missouri by a federal survey party. Military protection of the caravans, however, was not forthcoming for some years.

The consul appointed for Santa Fé was Augustus Storrs,[27] who arrived at his post in the summer of 1825. Joshua Pilcher, a prominent fur trader, was appointed to the post at Chihuahua but did not accept,[28] and the position remained vacant for several years.

Senator Benton's bill, which was passed by Congress on March 2, 1825, and approved by the President the next day, provided only for spending as much as $20,000 to obtain the consent of the Indians for free and unmolested passage of the caravans through their range and $10,000 for the survey and

26 Storrs to Benton, Franklin, November, 1824, *Niles' Weekly Register*, Vol. XXVII (January 15, 1825), 312–16.

27 Augustus Storrs, a native of New Hampshire, accompanied the caravan under Becknell and Marmaduke which left Missouri in May, 1824, and on his return gave Senator Benton a detailed report entitled *Answers of Augustus Storrs, of Missouri, to Certain Queries upon the Origin, present State, and future Prospects, of Trade and Intercourse between Missouri and the Internal Provinces of Mexico, propounded by the Hon. Mr. Benton, Jan. 5, 1825,* 18 Cong., 1 sess., *Senate Doc. No. 7.* This frequently quoted report was submitted in support of Benton's bill for the authorization of a government-sponsored survey and marking of the Santa Fé road. Storrs was captain of the Santa Fé caravan of 1825. Moorhead (ed.), in Gregg, *Commerce of the Prairies,* 17n.

28 Storrs to Gov. Narbona, Santa Fé, September 23, 1825, A.S.R.E., L-E-1055, I, 149–50; Joshua Pilcher to Secretary of State Henry Clay, St. Louis, Mo., August 18, 1826, United States National Archives at Washington (hereinafter cited as U.S.N.A.), Consular Letters, Chihuahua, Vol. I.

marking of a road over which they would pass. Under the direction of Benjamin H. Reeves and George C. Sibley, of Missouri, and Pierre Menard, of Illinois, the road commission began its survey at Fort Osage (near Franklin, Missouri) on July 17, concluded an arrangement with the Osage and Kansas tribes at Council Grove for the passage of the caravans on August 10, and completed marking of the route to the international border, on the upper Arkansas River, on September 11, 1825. In the summer of 1826, after successful negotiations with the Mexican government, the survey was concluded, extending the trail beyond the Arkansas to Taos, New Mexico, a total distance of 743 miles.[29] It proved to be a thankless task, however, for the mounds they erected to mark the road and the distances between them which they measured so precisely were little heeded by the merchant caravans. Trains from Missouri soon took their departure from Independence rather than Franklin, struck out on their own across the prairies, forded the Arkansas River at several different places, and made Santa Fé rather than Taos their destination.[30]

The treaty which the commissioners concluded with the Osage and Kansas tribes succeeded in eliminating further trouble from that quarter, but farther west the Pawnees and Comanches, and to a lesser extent the Cheyennes, Arapahoes, and Kiowas, remained a constant menace to the caravans. The first casualties from Indian attack were suffered by a train returning in 1828: two men killed and several hundred horses and mules run off.[31] In February, 1829, Senator Benton introduced a bill authorizing the use of federal troops for the protection of the traders. The bill passed the Senate, and although

[29] For the journals and diaries of the survey, see Kate L. Gregg (ed.), *The Road to Santa Fé: The Journal and Diaries of George Champlin Sibley and Others Pertaining to the Surveying and Marking of a Road from the Missouri Frontier to the Settlements of New Mexico, 1825–1827.*

[30] Gregg, *Commerce of the Prairies,* 30 et passim.

[31] *Ibid.,* 18.

it was not voted upon by the House, four companies of infantry under Major Bennet Riley were sent to escort the merchants of that year to and from the Arkansas crossing. These proved to be ineffective. Although they beat off an Indian attack on the wagon train a short distance beyond the Arkansas crossing, they were attacked themselves while awaiting its return from Santa Fé, and lost four soldiers and seventy-five horses and oxen in the encounter.[32] In 1832, President Andrew Jackson sent troops to meet the returning train at the Arkansas crossing, but they arrived after the wagons were well beyond that point of danger, and were consequently of little value. Thereafter the merchants provided their own protection, carrying rifles, pistols, and sometimes small cannon, and traveling in large organized caravans rather than in small individual trains. In 1834 an escort of sixty dragoons, or mounted infantry, under Captain Clifton Wharton and in 1843 a larger force of two hundred dragoons under Captain Philip St. George Cooke accompanied the caravans,[33] but except for these few instances, no military protection was provided by the United States government until the outbreak of the war with Mexico in 1846.

Meanwhile, the traders sought their government's protection from another peril. According to their complaints, the New Mexican authorities had been charging purely arbitrary duties on their merchandise, levying illegal taxes on their wagons and trading establishments, and otherwise subjecting them to unusual abuse.[34] These grievances were theoretically

32 Stephens, "Missouri and the Santa Fé Trade," *Missouri Historical Review*, Vol. X, No. 4 (July, 1916), 246–54. Details of Major Riley's escort appear in Otis E. Young, *The First Military Escort on the Santa Fé Trail, 1829.*

33 Gregg, *Commerce of the Prairies*, 21; Fred S. Perrine, "Military Escort on the Santa Fé Trail," *New Mexico Historical Review*, Vol. II, Nos. 2, 3 (April, July, 1927), 175–93, 269–304; Vol. III, No. 3 (July, 1928), 265–300.

34 Storrs to Narbona, Santa Fé, September 23, 1825, A.S.R.E., L-E-1055, I, 149–50; Alfonso Wetmore to Secretary of War Lewis Cass, Franklin, Mo., October 11, 1831, *Missouri Historical Review*, Vol. VIII, No. 4 (July, 1914), 179–84.

eliminated by the conclusion in 1831 of a treaty of amity and commerce between the United States and Mexico. Containing a "most-favored-nation" clause, this granted Americans in Mexico the same privileges and immunities as the more respected English merchants and residents.[35] However, judging from the continuation of complaints, the agreement was not strictly enforced.

Relations between the American merchants and the authorities in both Santa Fé and Chihuahua became especially strained during and immediately after the Texas Revolution. This rebellion, resulting in the *de facto* independence from Mexico of the Texas Republic in 1836, was looked upon by many Mexicans as an American-incited revolt. Although President Antonio López de Santa Anna was captured by the Texans and forced to sign a treaty granting Texas its independence, the Mexican Congress rejected the capitulation, and for the next ten years there existed between the two republics a "cold war," toward which the United States and its citizens had difficulty in remaining aloof. The recognition of the Texas Republic by the United States in 1837 was followed by a persistent movement for its annexation, and this further strained relations between the United States and Mexico. New Mexico and the Santa Fé traders became directly involved as a result of Texas' territorial claims, which extended to all lands east of the Río Grande, and thus encompassed most of the principal towns of New Mexico, including Santa Fé itself. Eventually, in 1841, the government of Texas sent a mission to Santa Fé, avowedly to promote trade, but actually to invite the New Mexican citizenry to forsake their Mexican allegiance and share in the blessings of Texas freedom. Whether or not the

35 William Ray Manning, *Early Diplomatic Relations Between the United States and Mexico*, 169–70; Stephens, "Missouri and the Santa Fe Trade," *Missouri Historical Review*, Vol. X, No. 4 (July, 1916), 259.

intent was peaceful and legal, the so-called Texan Santa Fé Expedition was looked upon by the government of New Mexico as an armed invasion by a hostile state. The expedition was made up of about 270 volunteer soldiers under General Hugh McLeod and some fifty civilians, some acting as official commissioners, others as merchants, and a few as mere tourists. In the latter category was George Kendall, of the New Orleans *Picayune,* whose account of the adventure became a classic in Western American literature.[36]

Setting out from Texas in the spring of 1841 and enduring considerable hardships on the high plains, the expedition arrived at the frontier settlements of New Mexico only to find the inhabitants up in arms. Most of the party were captured, disarmed, and led on a harrowing "death march" from Santa Fé to Chihuahua. Kendall supplies the lurid details. They were imprisoned for a time at Chihuahua and again at Mexico City before being released. Meanwhile, the American merchants in New Mexico, being suspected of collusion with the Texans, suffered gross indignities, and as a result of new and more militant forays from Texas, the reprisals were prolonged for two more years.

During the winter of 1842–43 and the following summer, three bands of marauders under leaders commissioned by Texas were operating on the frontier for the purpose of harrying New Mexico's caravan commerce with Missouri. One party, under Colonel Charles A. Warfield, attacked the frontier village of Mora, killing about five inhabitants and running off a number of horses. Another, under Captain John McDaniel, fell upon a lone merchant train on the Arkansas River, killed the proprietor, and looted his baggage, which contained about

---

36 George Wilkins Kendall, *Narrative of the Texan Santa Fé Expedition* (2 vols., New York, 1844). A recently published account is Noel M. Loomis, *The Texan–Santa Fé Pioneers* (Norman, 1958).

ten or twelve thousand dollars in specie, bullion, and furs. This outrage was particularly resented since the proprietor, Antonio José Chávez, was a member of one of the most prominent families of New Mexico.[37] Still another party, under Colonel Jacob Snively, attacked an advance guard of about one hundred New Mexican militiamen on the Cimarron Cutoff, killing twenty-three, wounding several others, and capturing all the survivors except two. When the spring caravan made up of both Mexican and American merchants arrived at the Arkansas crossing from the United States, Colonel Snively and part of his company crossed to the American side of the river, but were arrested and disarmed by the military escort under Captain Philip St. George Cooke. Although Colonel Warfield and the remainder of the marauders followed the caravan for some distance beyond the Arkansas, they did not attack it, and this concluded the border hostilities. In order to avoid further outbreaks, President Santa Anna suspended the caravan trade altogether in September of 1843. The danger having ceased, however, he permitted its resumption in April of 1844, in plenty of time for the departure of the next regular caravan.[38]

While laboring under these difficulties, the overland traders faced others imposed by the customs laws of their own country. By 1831 the value of the merchandise they took to Santa Fé was approximately $250,000, and $80,000 worth of this was being sent to Chihuahua and other interior markets.[39] There,

[37] Antonio José Chávez was the son of Francisco Javier Chávez, acting governor of New Mexico in 1832, and the brother of Mariano Chávez, acting governor in 1835 and a prominent *hacendado* and merchant who owned property on both sides of the Río Grande near Padillas. Antonio José Chávez had left Santa Fé in February, 1843, with fifty-five mules, two wagons, and five servants, but before encountering McDaniel and his party in April, he had lost fifty mules from cold and exposure and was forced to abandon one of his wagons. Gregg, *Commerce of the Prairies*, 337–38n.; 340–41n.

[38] *Ibid.*, 337–45.

[39] See Gregg's table above.

however, they found difficulty in competing with both foreign and American merchants who imported their goods through the Mexican seaports. The difficulty arose from the fact that the chief demand in the interior markets was for expensive European and Asian dry goods, and that these, imported by their competitors directly from Europe and Asia, paid only the Mexican tariff. The overland traders, on the other hand, were importing the same merchandise through the eastern ports of the United States, where they paid the American customs duties, and then carrying them into Mexico, where they were charged a second import duty. Complaining of this double taxation in 1831, one Missouri merchant proposed the enactment of a rebate on the American duties for all goods re-exported in this manner. This, he declared, would place the overland traders on an equal footing with foreign competitors who imported through the Mexican ports only, and would allow the Americans to reach markets as far south as Durango and probably increase their inland trade with Mexico by as much as one million dollars a year.[40]

For the next ten years repeated applications to Congress were made by the inland traders without result. In 1842 the acting consul at Santa Fé added his recommendations to those of other traders. The Americans, he said, were unable to compete in the interior markets with merchants importing directly from Europe. The experience of the last several years had demonstrated that overland traders carrying only coarse, American-made goods to the interior courted inevitable loss because of the bulk of the cargo and the heavy duties charged by Mexico. With the advantage of a rebate, or debenture, on American duties, however, they could handle the more expensive and more profitable foreign goods, and, owing to the

40 Wetmore to Cass, Franklin, October 11, 1831, *Missouri Historical Review*, Vol. VIII, No. 4 (July, 1914), 179–84.

natural roads across the plains and through northern Mexico, they could drive out the foreign merchants and establish an American monopoly over the markets of Chihuahua, and even capture much of the trade of Durango and Sonora. This would benefit not only the merchants of Missouri but the importers of the eastern United States as well. The increased trade would further cement friendly relations with Mexico, and the increased traffic across the plains would impress the western Indians and instill in them a greater respect for the federal government.[41] Pursuing the argument further in the following year, he recommended the encouragement of the inland over the maritime trade with Mexico. A drawback, or rebate, bill had twice passed the Senate, but had failed both times in the House. Its final passage would, he thought, increase the inland trade by about two million dollars a year.[42]

The desired Drawback Act was finally passed and became law on March 3, 1845. It provided that foreign merchandise imported into the United States with full payment of duties and proper notification of intentions could be re-exported in their original packages to Santa Fé or Chihuahua by way of Van Buren or Fulton, Arkansas, or Independence, Missouri, if accompanied by certified invoices. The goods thus re-exported were subject to inspection by American agents at both the specified frontier towns and the points of destination, and the exporter was further required to give bond in three times the amount of the United States duties, his reimbursement being for all but 2.5 per cent.[43]

The new legislation stimulated a tremendous increase in the inland trade. In 1844 the amount of goods carried to Santa

[41] Manuel Alvarez, Memorial to Congress, Washington, February, 1842 (copy), M.N.M., Read Collection, Folder A.
[42] Alvarez to Secretary of State James Buchanan, Independence, Mo., July 1, 1843, U.S.N.A., Consular Despatches, Santa Fé, Vol. I.
[43] 30 Cong., 1 sess., *House Report No. 458*, pp. 59–61.

Fé had been valued at $200,000. After passage of the Drawback Act, the value rose to $342,000 in 1845 and an estimated $1,-000,000 in 1846, when a record 363 wagons crossed the plains, 315 of them passing on through Santa Fé to the interior markets.[44] In the quarter-century between the opening of international trade with Santa Fé and its conclusion by the American military invasion and annexation of New Mexico, a remarkable development had taken place. In 1822 seventy men with pack animals and only three wagons had carried $15,000 worth of goods, mainly of American manufacture, to Santa Fé, and had taken about $9,000 of it on to Chihuahua. In 1846 caravans engaging 750 men and 363 wagons had taken approximately $1,000,000 worth of goods, a large portion of it foreign, to Santa Fé, and had sold all but a very small amount of it in Chihuahua and other interior cities. The methods by which this business was so enterprisingly expanded is worth special consideration.

[44] Gregg, *Commerce of the Prairies*, 344n.; Ralph P. Bieber (ed.), in James Josiah Webb, *Adventures in the Santa Fe Trade, 1844–47*, 108n., 186n.; Col. Alexander W. Doniphan to Adj. Gen. Roger Jones, Chihuahua, March 4, 1847, 30 Cong., 1 sess., *Senate Exec. Doc. No. 1*, Vol. I, 498–502.

4.

Techniques of the
Overland Trade

THE MOST STRIKING characteristic of the overland trade with
Mexico was its ever increasing capitalization. A simple venture
when begun by Becknell's hunters and trappers, it rapidly
developed into a very complex business—one involving not
only an accumulating investment but also an increasing reliance on hired help, on buying and selling in gross lots, on
importing from abroad, on exporting more deeply into the
interior of Mexico, on extending long-term credit, and on
freighting by specially adapted conveyances.

The "Santa Fé trade" was actually a misnomer. After the
first two decades most of the merchandise was actually sold
in the interior of the country—in El Paso del Norte, Chihuahua, Durango, Zacatecas, Aguascalientes, and eventually even
Mexico City. Santa Fé became a mere port of entry, and most

of the wagons passed through it without even breaking their loads. Between 1822 and 1832, according to Josiah Gregg's estimates,[1] the average annual Santa Fé caravan took one-fifth of its cargo ($19,000 worth of goods) to Chihuahua or beyond; and during the next eleven years more than one-half of the average cargo (or $90,000 worth of goods) was sent to the interior. Nor was the so-called Santa Fé trade primarily with Missouri. Before many years had passed, the more enterprising traders went to New York and Philadelphia to buy their goods at wholesale; others even ordered directly from Liverpool and Hamburg; and a few eventually crossed the sea in person to make their own purchases in Europe. Some eastern United States wholesale houses entered the Mexican trade directly, importing from Europe and sending consignments with the overland caravans under care of their own agents. By 1846 the Santa Fé trade was indeed a far-flung business.

By relying on the original articles of incorporation for Becknell's company of 1821[2] and on Gregg's contemporary estimates for operations from 1822 to 1843, some significant developments may be deduced. The pioneer venture involved 20 or 30 proprietors, no employees, and (at ten dollars per man) only from $200 to $300 worth of trade goods. During the next eleven years, from 1822 through 1832, the annual average was 60 proprietors, 60 employees, and $93,000 worth of merchandise; and from 1833 through 1843, 31 proprietors, 127 employees, and $173,000 in goods. This demonstrates a remarkably capitalistic development: fewer merchants employing more help and investing a greater amount of money in merchandise were coming to dominate the trade.

The growth of the overland trade was a natural one, each

1 See Gregg's table above.
2 Stephens, "Missouri and the Santa Fé Trade," *Missouri Historical Review*, Vol. XI, No. 3 (April, 1917), 291–93.

step being an attempt to expand operations, cut expenses, and gain more profit from the initial investment. For the first few years, when the caravans were formed at Franklin, Missouri, the traders purchased their goods at such local stores as that of James Harrison and Company. Some traders bought in St. Louis, where a few firms ordered assortments from Philadelphia and New York expressly made up for the Mexican trade.[3] The costs of such goods in Missouri stores was usually about 20 to 30 per cent above wholesale prices in the East, but profits of from 40 to 100 per cent could be expected on sales at Santa Fé.[4]

As the volume of business increased and the market price in New Mexico declined, the caravan traders began to eliminate the middlemen in Missouri by buying directly from the eastern wholesalers. According to the records of the American consul at Santa Fé, there were at least thirty-two different wholesale houses in the East with whom the traders did business. Twenty-one of these were in New York, seven in Philadelphia, and four others not identified by locality. The Mexican merchants who traded directly with the United States did much of their business with the Spanish firm of Peter Harmony, Nephews and Company at New York. Most of the consul's own business was with Francis B. Rhodes and Company, New York importers of English, French, German, and Venetian goods. This firm customarily allowed a 5 per cent discount on purchases paid for in cash.[5] Some Missouri storekeepers, losing their old customers to the eastern houses, offset their

3 Lewis E. Atherton, "Business Techniques in the Santa Fé Trade," *ibid.*, Vol. XXXIV, No. 3 (April, 1940), 366.

4 Hattie M. Anderson, "Frontier Economic Problems in Missouri," *ibid.*, Vol. XXXIV, No. 2 (January, 1940), 184.

5 Invoices and Account Book of Manuel Alvarez, M.N.M., Alvarez Papers, 1839–45, and Read Collection, Folder A.

losses by going into the Santa Fé trade themselves. Among these was James Aull, of Lexington.[6]

Almost every year Aull left his store in January, traveled by horseback or wagon to St. Louis, and by stage to Philadelphia, where he made his purchases for the Mexican trade. Making the rounds of the many wholesale houses in Philadelphia, he bought mainly from Siter, Price and Company and also relied on this firm as his eastern representative. It collected and crated all of his purchases and shipped them back to Missouri, the heavier goods by steamer to New Orleans and by river boat to St. Louis and Independence, where the caravan merchants outfitted their wagons after 1831. Aull himself usually returned from Philadelphia in March or April in order to prepare for the departure of the annual caravans in May.[7] In dealing directly with the eastern firms, the overland merchants encountered some difficulty in meeting their bills, since those houses seldom extended credit for more than twelve months at a time and the returns from Santa Fé and Chihuahua were usually slow in coming in. In the fall of 1831, Aull complained to his creditors that he had received only $1,200 from the $10,000 worth of goods he had sent to Santa Fé the previous spring and that the remainder was not due for another twelve months. Other traders were so short of cash as a result of such delays, he explained, that several had

[6] James Aull was born in Delaware in 1805, came to Missouri in 1825, established stores at Lexington, Independence, Richmond, and, in partnership with his brother Robert from about 1831 to 1836, at Liberty. In 1846 he formed a partnership with Samuel Owens, followed the American army to Santa Fé and Chihuahua, remained in the latter city after the occupation ended, and was killed in a robbery of his store there in 1847. "Letters of James and Robert Aull," ed. by Ralph P. Bieber, *Missouri Historical Society Collection*, Vol. V, 296n.; Lewis E. Atherton, "James and Robert Aull—a Frontier Missouri Mercantile Firm," *Missouri Historical Review*, Vol. XXX, No. 1 (October, 1935), 3–27.

[7] *Ibid.*, 5–9.

decided not to go back east for more goods in January, as was their custom, but to wait until April or May.[8]

In addition to their obligations to the eastern wholesalers, the overland traders in Missouri had to meet the expenses of transporting their purchases. From the eastern seaboard to Independence the nominal freight rate was twelve dollars per hundred pounds, and this usually amounted to from 10 to 25 per cent of the cost of the merchandise itself. This expense, however, could be cut considerably by quantity shipment, of a single cargo involving the consignments of several merchants.[9] From Independence to Santa Fé, freightage for those relying on other than their own wagons or pack mules amounted to from ten to twelve dollars a hundredweight, and from Santa Fé to Chihuahua, the rate was six to eight dollars.[10]

Buying for the Mexican trade required more imagination than care. Except for certain staples that competed with Mexican production and were therefore on the prohibited list, almost anything could be included in a "Santa Fé assortment." Gregg recommended that about half of each merchant's purchases should be domestic cottons, with bleached and unbleached cloth in equal proportions, and half fine European fabrics.[11] Cloth, purchased by the bolt and sold by the yard, constituted the bulk of each assortment, but the invoices from eastern wholesalers and the manifests for the Santa Fé customs house list a bewildering variety of merchandise. In addition

8 Aull to Siter, Price & Co., Lexington, Mo., October 31, 1831, in "Letters of James and Robert Aull," *Missouri Historical Society Collection*, Vol. V, 277.

9 Siter, Price & Co. to Samuel C. Owens, Philadelphia, March 26, 1846, *ibid.*, 277.

10 Gregg, *Commerce of the Prairies*, 332n. In 1845 the consul at Santa Fé reported that freightage could be obtained from the Atlantic Seaboard all the way to Santa Fé for about twelve dollars a hundredweight. Alvarez to Secretary of the Treasury Robert J. Walker, Independence, June 18, 1845, M.N.M., Read Collection, Alvarez Letter Book.

11 Gregg, *Commerce of the Prairies*, 80.

to such dry goods as muslin, broadcloth, drills, prints, flannels, linen, calico, nankeen, pongee, taffeta, velveteen, cashmere, alpaca, merino, and silk, there were also the following items: clothing of all kinds; rings, necklaces, bracelets, earrings, crucifixes, beads, buttons, buckles, hairpins, ribbons, and handkerchieves; brushes, combs, razors, razor strops, mirrors, and cologne; clocks and watches; thread, needles, thimbles, scissors, and knitting pins; curtain hooks, wallpaper, window glass, and white lead; pots, pans, coffee mills, dishes, corks, and bottles; wrapping paper, writing paper, pen points, pencils, slates, and books; candlewick, matches, percussion caps, gunflints, gunpowder, rifles, and traps; knives, axes, shovels, hoes, and other tools; claret, sherry, and champagne.[12] Bottled goods were especially profitable. When Indians from the pueblos along the Río Grande in New Mexico came down to the caravan camps to sell fresh fruits and vegetables, some traders found that they preferred bottles to money in return for their produce and would pay up to half a dollar apiece for them. Thus, the thirsty trader could buy a dozen bottles of liquor for three or four dollars in Missouri, drink the contents during the long trip across the plains, and then trade the empty bottles for produce worth six dollars.[13]

During the early years most of the traders left Missouri with their goods in the spring, sold out in New Mexico during the summer, and returned in the fall, thus confining their operations to a few months of the year. But as the New Mexican market was easily glutted, some disposed of their goods at great sacrifice in order to leave in August with the returning caravan. One company of traders sustained a loss of from

[12] Various invoices and manifests, M.N.M., Alvarez Papers, Read Collection, and Twitchell Collection.

[13] Susan Shelby Magoffin, *Down the Santa Fé Trail and into Mexico, the Diary of Susan Shelby Magoffin, 1846–1847*, edited by Stella M. Drumm, 153.

$30,000 to $40,000 for this reason in 1830.[14] What kept such seasonal traders in business was the arrival of Mexican merchants from the interior who met the caravans at Santa Fé and bought from them in wholesale lots. This practice continued long after the Americans themselves began to seek the more lucrative interior markets. In one month alone, August of 1844, eight Mexican merchants took from Santa Fé more than $90,-000 worth of American imports to sell in Chihuahua, Durango, and Aguascalientes.[15]

When American merchants reached Chihuahua, it was their custom to rent space for a store, usually on the main plaza, and to offer their goods at both wholesale and retail. Some maintained stores for an entire season or more, selling most profitably to the lesser Mexican traders from surrounding villages, but most of them preferred to sell their entire stock at wholesale as soon as a fair bargain could be closed, and then return to the United States for another consignment. The usual method of wholesaling in Chihuahua had little regard for the quality of the merchandise involved. Almost all cotton goods were priced at from two to three *reales* per *vara* (about twenty-seven to forty cents a yard) regardless of their original cost, and "general assortments" went for from 60 to 100 per cent above their first cost. Cloth and almost all other measurable goods except ribbons were often sold by the *vara*, which was estimated by adding 8 per cent to the yardage. One of the main reasons some merchants preferred to dispose of their goods at wholesale was to avoid the accumulation of copper coins, which constituted almost the only currency in petty buying and selling. The retailers sometimes amassed thou-

---

[14] Gregg, *Commerce of the Prairies*, 213; Antonio Barreiro, "Ojeada sobre Nuevo México," translated in Carroll and Haggard (eds.), *Three New Mexico Chronicles*, 109.

[15] Guías, Nos. 19–20, 22–27, Aduana de Nuevo México, M.N.M., Twitchell Collection, archives 7771, 7775, 7778.

sands of dollars' worth of these coins, and as those of one state were not legal tender in another, where they seldom brought over 10 per cent of their face value, the inconvenience to the traveling merchant was more than he could profitably bear.[16] Although in competition with Mexican merchants, the Americans usually maintained a cordial relationship with them. Frequently the traders lent money to each other regardless of nationality or place of residence, and they were not at all reluctant to call upon one another to cash letters of credit, collect debts, liquidate stock, or carry personal letters and money across the international line. Their account books and correspondence demonstrate a surprising amount of mutual trust and also of a willingness to obligate one another. Typical of this inclination was a transaction made in 1846 by Juan Otero, a New Mexican merchant from Peralta. As one of his countrymen, Manuel Yrizzari, was going to New York on his own account, Otero prevailed upon him to order $12,000 worth of merchandise from Peter Harmony, Nephews and Company, buy a number of wagons in the East, and bring the purchases to Independence, Missouri. He then sent the $12,000 payment in cash to Samuel Owens, a merchant of that town,[17] entrusting for its delivery James Wiley Magoffin, a prominent Chihuahua trader.[18] Owens was asked to receive the consignment

16 Gregg, *Commerce of the Prairies*, 297–99.

17 Samuel Combs Owens was born in Kentucky in 1800, came to Missouri about 1818, served in the state legislature, and was one of the founders of the town of Independence. He was a store manager there for James Aull from 1827 to 1836, when he formed a business of his own which lasted until 1844. He outfitted many traders, often on credit, and was captain of a caravan in 1844. In 1846 he formed a partnership with James Aull, took a train to Santa Fé and Chihuahua behind the American army, was elected major of the trader battalion which Colonel Doniphan formed near El Paso, died in the battle of Sacramento in 1847, and was buried at Chihuahua. Bieber (ed.), in Webb, *Adventures in the Santa Fe Trade*, 42n.; Col. Doniphan to Adj. Gen. Jones, Chihuahua, March 4, 1847, 30 Cong., 1 sess., *Senate Exec. Doc. No. 1*, Vol. I, 498–502.

18 James Wiley Magoffin was born in Kentucky in 1799, entered the Mexican

from Yrizarri, send the money to Peter Harmony, Nephews and Company, sell the wagons if he could get a good price, hire oxen and men (and also wagons if he could dispose of those purchased by Yrizarri), and then ship the goods to Otero at Peralta.[19]

An almost equally involved transaction was made by Edwin Norris, a New York merchant then in partnership with the wealthy German trader, Albert Speyer.[20] Norris and Speyer

trade sometime before 1825, when he was appointed American consul at Saltillo, and was a resident of Chihuahua by 1830, when he was married to María Gertrudis Valdés de Beremende. His wife and sons brought food and comfort to the Texan Santa Fé Expedition members imprisoned there in 1841. Known in Mexico as Don Santiago, James Magoffin was thought by many to have been a naturalized Mexican citizen, but the evidence indicates the contrary, and at times he served as commercial agent for the United States. From 1830 to 1846, he made almost annual trips to the United States for merchandise, and at least one trip, in 1836, to Mexico City. Sometime before 1841 he was joined in business by a younger brother, Samuel, and in 1844 moved his family to a farm near Independence, Missouri. He continued in the overland trade, however, served the American army as a secret agent in Santa Fé and Chihuahua in 1846, was captured by the Mexicans, and was held until after the war. He then established a handsome estate opposite El Paso del Norte which became the town of Magoffinville and was subsequently incorporated into El Paso, Texas. During the Civil War he sold supplies to the Confederacy, and in 1869 he died at San Antonio. Drumm (ed.), in Susan Magoffin, *Down the Santa Fé Trail*, ix–xix; Joseph Magoffin to William E. Connelley (ed.), El Paso, n. d., *Doniphan's Expedition and the Conquest of New Mexico and California*, 196–97n.; Ralph P. Bieber (ed.), in George Rutledge Gibson, *Journey of a Soldier under Kearny and Doniphan, 1846–1847*, 55n.; Kendall, *Narrative of the Texan Santa Fé Expedition*, II, 79, 84.

19 Otero to Owenes, Peralta, March 15, 1846, in "Letters of James and Robert Aull," *Missouri Historical Society Collection*, Vol. V, 291.

20 Albert Speyer was born in Prussia, migrated to the United States, made his home in New York City, engaged in the inland trade with Mexico at least as early as 1843, and continued in it until about 1848. A German Jew, he carried both British and Prussian passports and had great influence with the Mexican authorities. He was tried by an American military court at Chihuahua for carrying arms to Mexico during the war and abandoning his American teamsters in hostile territory, but was acquitted. In the spring of 1848 he went to Europe to purchase goods for the Mexican trade, and after leaving this business became a broker in New York City, where he was ruined in the "Black Friday" crash of 1869 while purchasing gold for Jay Gould. He committed suicide as a result. Bieber (ed.), in Webb, *Adventures in the Santa Fé Trade*, 54n.; Drumm (ed.),

brought a consignment of goods to Santa Fé in the latter part of 1844. As the market had already been glutted by the caravans of the previous spring, Norris, whom Speyer had left at Santa Fé while he took another train of goods to the interior, was unable to sell the entire stock. Before leaving for New York in the following April, Norris placed his unfinished business in the hands of the American consul. The latter was instructed to hold one copy of the inventory for Speyer, sell what merchandise he could, and collect more than $2,500 in debts owed Speyer and Company by two other American traders in New Mexico. The consul was not only unable to collect these debts or to dispose of more than $267 worth of the merchandise, but was also forced to forfeit to Speyer's own creditors at Santa Fé a bale of dry goods worth $175 and a wagon and some mules valued at $300. In order to leave for the United States on business of his own, the consul deposited the remainder of the goods with still another trader to hold for Speyer, and when he reached Independence, still other creditors attached three wagons. Additional seizures were also threatened there, but the consul managed to avert them and make his accounting to Norris at New York in July of the same year.[21]

Although the returns from the overland trade with Mexico were mainly in specie, which was sorely needed on the western frontier of the United States, another valuable commodity was the mule, especially in the early years of the trade. In 1823 the returning caravan brought in four hundred jacks, jennets, and mules; in 1825, over six hundred; and 1832, over thirteen hundred.[22] Some of these Mexican animals were sold in Mis-

in Susan Magoffin, *Down the Santa Fé Trail*, 246–47n.; James Hobbs, *Wild Life in the Far West; Personal Adventures of a Border Mountain Man*, 61–95.

21 Edwin Norris to Albert Speyer, New York, July 24, 1845, M.N.M., Alvarez Papers, 1839–45.

22 Stephens, "Missouri and the Santa Fé Trade," *Missouri Historical Review*, Vol. XI, No. 4 (July, 1917), 304.

souri for breeding purposes, others were employed in the caravan trade, and still others were sold in the southern states for plantation work. The latter market seems to have been early saturated, however, for in 1840 David Waldo[23] suffered a severe loss on the 113 New Mexican mules which he tried to sell in Arkansas, Louisiana, and Texas.[24] For the overland trade itself, nonetheless, the mule was indispensable.

Although Becknell's 1821 venture relied on pack horses, and oxen were employed for the first time by Major Riley when he escorted the caravan of 1829, the mule was the principal beast of burden and draft animal on the Santa Fé Trail and Camino Real. There was much to recommend him. Packing by mule in northern Mexico was cheaper than freighting by wagons, for a train of from fifty to two hundred mules could travel together for weeks and even months on the hard surface of the arid plateau without any protection for their hooves. They could carry loads up to four hundred pounds apiece and make from twelve to fifteen miles a day. They were especially advantageous in rough country, for they could clamber along the most craggy and precipitous trail with a sure-footedness than no horse could equal. Even after wagons became common on the roads to Santa Fé and Chihuahua, the mule train, or *atajo,* as it was called, was never completely abandoned.[25]

23 Dr. David Waldo was born in Virginia in 1802, came to Missouri in 1820, studied medicine at Transylvania University, and was a practicing physician after 1827. In 1830 or before, he entered the Santa Fé trade and remained associated with it for over thirty years, amassing a considerable fortune. Although he became a Mexican citizen in 1831, he retained his allegiance to the United States, served as a captain in the American army during the invasion of New Mexico, was an official translator there during the occupation, and returned to Independence thereafter, where he married and later engaged in trade with and freighting to Utah and the Platte River country. He died in 1878. Drumm (ed.), in Susan Magoffin, *Down the Santa Fé Trail,* 64–65n.; Connelley (ed.), in *Doniphan's Expedition,* 133–34n.; Record of naturalization of David Waldo, Taos, June 17, 1831 (copy), M.N.M., Read Collection, Folder A.

24 Waldo to Manuel Alvarez, Independence, April 20, 1841, M.N.M., Alvarez Papers 1839–45.

The *atajo* was a model of efficiency when managed by experienced Mexican labor. Six *arrieros*, or muleteers, could handle up to fifty mules at a time, and the cheapness of the *atajo* was due in large part to the low wages for which they worked. They expected only from two to five dollars a month, plus the simplest food and shelter. Their skill in roping, riding, loading, and caring for the mules impressed even the most veteran foreign traders and travelers and was therefore attentively described in their diaries and memoirs.[26] From these and from the specifications in American military pack manuals of later date,[27] it is clear that the transport division of the United States Army adopted not only the Mexican mule but also the *arriero's* techniques and even his Spanish terminology for the elaborate equipment of the *atajo*.

In preparation for a *jornada*, or day's journey, the *atajo* was first assembled by the *arrieros*, who either drove the grazing mules to their line of packs or, more often, enticed them there by leading the *mulera*, or bell mare, the others devotedly following. Well-broken mules instinctively found their own packs and patiently stood by them. Others were secured with a deftly thrown *riata*, or noose; blindfolded with the *tapajos*, a piece of embroidered leather, so as not to become frightened. All were then saddled with a succession of paraphernalia: the *salea*, a soft piece of raw sheepskin, the *xerga*, a woolen blanket, the *aparejo*, or packsaddle, which was a large leather pouch stuffed with straw to prevent chafing, the *carga*, or load itself, and finally the *petate*, or mat, to protect the latter from the rain. The *aparejo* was fastened around the mule's waist with a broad hempen belt drawn corset-tight and around its rump with a wide crupper to keep it from slipping forward. The

---

25 Gregg, *Commerce of the Prairies*, 24–25, 127–29.

26 *Ibid.*, 127–31; Kendall, *Narrative of the Texan Santa Fé Expedition*, II, 169–72; George Frederick Augustus Ruxton, *Life in the Far West*, 180–81.

27 H. W. Daly, *Manual of Pack Transportation*, 164–65 *et passim*.

carga, although weighing more than the *arriero* himself, was pitched on the mule's back with a single heave and adjusted so as to balance evenly. Usually two cases or crates coupled together and straddling the *aparejo* constituted the load, and these were bound to the packsaddle with an intricate network of knotted ropes. Then the blindfold was removed, and the mule was ready to travel. Although painfully tight at the outset, the girths and ropes gradually loosened during the jostling march as the weight of the load settled the *aparejo,* and from time to time the skillful *arrieros* cinched them up again one after another without slowing the progress of the train as a whole. The mules did not have to be driven along the road but merely led by the *mulera,* which they followed in perfect alignment.

Although wagons soon began to replace pack trains in the outbound caravans, the *atajo* was frequently employed for the return trip. Once the bulky bales of dry goods were sold, the traders were encumbered by little more than a compact cargo of coin, silver bars, and gold dust. Many of the wagons were therefore sold in Mexico, where they were worth more than in Missouri (especially after the added wear and tear of a return trip), and were replaced with newly purchased Mexican mules which were worth more in Missouri than in Mexico. With this double saving, the traders then packed their specie in sacks made of fresh rawhide, which shrank on drying and, pressing the contents tightly, eliminated all friction. A pair of these packages, containing between $1,000 and $2,000, constituted a normal load for a single mule.[28]

In the outbound caravans, composed mainly of wagons, the mule was much preferred over the horse, but about half of the traders favored oxen instead. Oxen in equal numbers could pull heavier loads than mules, particularly through muddy

[28] Gregg, *Commerce of the Prairies,* 213, 293–94.

[88]

or sandy stretches, but they more frequently fell off in strength as the prairie grass became drier and shorter, and they often arrived at Santa Fé in a sorry plight. Mules cost more than oxen, but they lasted longer, traveled faster, and seldom had to be shod.[29] Their major weakness was that they were more easily stampeded, especially during Indian attacks. One early trader asserted that it was common for mule teams, even after traveling four or five hundred miles, to take fright suddenly from their own shadows and break out into a full gallop over the plains.[30]

Ordinarily mule teams pulled laden wagons across the plains to Santa Fé and then down the Camino Real to Chihuahua with little damage to themselves, but when traveling during the winter months—out of the regular season—hundreds sometimes perished. One notable example should illustrate. When Speyer and Norris came to Santa Fé in 1844, they left Independence in September, four months after the regular caravan had departed. They had over $33,000 worth of merchandise in twenty-five wagons, drawn by about two hundred mules. On reaching the Cimarron River and encamping near Willow Bar (268 miles short of Santa Fé), they were overtaken and marooned by a severe snow and sleet storm. As the ground became covered, the mules were reduced to feeding on the bark of willow trees and eventually chewing on each other's tails. Most of them died from cold and hunger, and when the storm abated, Speyer had to drive into Santa Fé and recruit replacements. There several American traders and teamsters volunteered to help bring in the wagons, and one, Samuel Owens, who had arrived earlier and was about to push on to Chihuahua with eight wagons and about sixty-four mules, sold

29 *Ibid.*, 25, 285–86.
30 "Major Alphonso Wetmore's Diary of a Journey to Santa Fé, 1828," ed. by F. F. Stephens, *Missouri Historical Review*, Vol. VIII, No. 4 (July, 1914), 188.

Speyer his entire stock—merchandise, wagons, and mules. Two other traders, Edward J. Glasgow[31] and Henry Connelly,[32] who reached Santa Fé shortly after Speyer, reported that they had suffered almost equal losses in the same storm.[33]

More frequently mules were lost to marauding Indians. After acquiring Owens' mules, retrieving his marooned wagons, clearing the customs house, and enlisting additional teamsters, Speyer left Norris in Santa Fé to dispose of a few bales of goods and started on the road to Chihuahua. About 150 miles south of Santa Fé, he was attacked by a small band

[31] Edward J. Glasgow was born in Illinois in 1820, studied at St. Louis University and St. Charles College in Missouri, and entered the Mexican trade in 1840 at Mazatlán, Hermosillo, Guaymas, and Durango. In 1842 he came to Chihuahua, opened a store in partnership with Dr. Henry Connelly, and thereafter made almost annual trips to the United States for merchandise. He followed the American army to Santa Fé and Chihuahua, was elected captain of a company in the special trader battalion, and remained in Chihuahua until 1848. Returning to Missouri, he engaged in business at St. Louis until 1878, and died there in 1908. Edward J. Glasgow, "Narrative of Some Events in the Life of Edward James Glasgow (ca. 1900)," manuscript in possession of his son, General William J. Glasgow, at El Paso, Texas.

[32] Dr. Henry Connelly was born in Kentucky in 1800 and graduated in medicine at Transylvania University in 1828. In the same year he opened a practice at Liberty, Missouri., but left for Chihuahua. There he became a clerk in Ludwell Powell's store, bought it out, and established another at the mining town of Jesús María, where he married a Mexican lady. He became a naturalized Mexican citizen about 1832, a partner of Edward Glasgow at Chihuahua in 1843, and a resident of that city until after the Mexican war. He was captured by the Mexican army and held for a time on espionage charges, and some time after his release settled at Peralta, New Mexico, where he was married for the second time—to Dolores Perea, widow of José Chávez—and established a store. Expanding operations to Albuquerque, Santa Fé, and Las Vegas, he became head of the largest mercantile business in New Mexico. He was elected to the legislative council of New Mexico and was appointed territorial governor in 1861 and again in 1864. He died at Santa Fé in 1866. Bieber (ed.), in Webb, *Adventures in the Santa Fé Trade*, 102n.; Drumm (ed.), in Susan Magoffin, *Down the Santa Fé Trail*, 104–105n.; Connelley (ed.), in *Doniphan's Expedition*, 276–82n.; Henry Connelly to John Black, Chihuahua, March 18, 1844, U.S.N.A., Consulate General, Mexico, Correspondence, 1842–44.

[33] Webb, *Adventures in the Santa Fe Trade*, 107; Wislizenus, *Memoir of a Tour to Northern Mexico*, 13–14; Hobbs, *Wild Life in the Far West*, 59–60.

of Navajos. These were driven off without loss to the train, but a hundred miles farther on, on the Jornada del Muerto, nine Apaches swooped down upon the caravan unexpectedly and drove off all the mules, leaving the huge train of heavily laden wagons stranded on the desert. In this predicament Speyer sent some of his men on what must have seemed a hopeless pursuit of the raiders and turned back toward Santa Fé himself to buy a third set of teams. After a chase lasting two weeks, however, his men recovered his mules, a few animals which the Apaches had previously stolen from other traders, and nine Apache scalps, which latter brought a handsome bounty in Chihuahua. The men also managed to overtake Speyer before he reached Santa Fé and made a needless and expensive purchase of more mules.[34]

The wagons in the overland trade were of several makes, but the favorite was the so-called Conestoga. It was then manufactured in Pennsylvania, at Pittsburgh, but was still patterned after the historic covered wagons of Lancaster County. The distinctive features of the Conestoga, Pittsburgh wagon, or Prairie Schooner (as it was variously called) were the long, sagging bed and outward-sloping sideboards and tail gate (which combined to settle the jostling cargo toward the center), the high, graceful arches supporting the hood which tilted fore and aft at the ends, and the great canvas cover itself, drawn tight at the front and back to keep out the sun and rain. Traditionally, the wagon framing and spokes were made of white oak, the hubs of gum, the arches, axletrees, and singletrees of hickory, and the boards of poplar. As the wooden parts were of light construction, they were reinforced at every point of friction and strain by heavy ironwork. The bodies were conventionally painted red and blue, a bright contrast to the black ironwork

[34] *Ibid.*, 66–71.

and the billowing white cover.[35] Seen from a distance, a train of these "schooners" presented an imposing sight. The mule teams were always harnessed with the smallest animals in the lead, with those following increasing in size. Astride the left rear mule sat the driver, a long whip in one hand and a single rein in the other.[36] At least an equal number of spare mules was taken on each long trip to replace those which tired.

The Conestogas stood up well on the prairies, but on reaching the high, arid plains of New Mexico, the wooden wheels shrank noticeably, and it was frequently necessary to cut or wedge the loose iron tires to take up the slack. Spare axles were always carried, and those in use were lubricated with resin and tallow. In spite of their sturdy construction, the wagons usually returned from the Mexican trip bleached, warped, and shrunken, the spokes and iron-shod rims bound with rawhide to keep them from falling apart.[37] Frequently, before the next trip out, they had to be replaced at Independence, where new wagons cost from $100 to $200 apiece, depending upon their size.[38]

On the outbound trips, the cargo also suffered. Veteran traders took every precaution to stow their packages in such a manner that no jolting on the road could disturb their arrangement. To shelter them from rain, it was recommended that at least two stout Osnaburg sheets be spread over each wagon, one of them wide enough to reach the bottom of the body on each side. A pair of mackinaw blankets could be spread

35 John Omwake and others, *The Conestoga Six-Horse Bell Teams of Eastern Pennsylvania*, 17, 62–72, 74–75.

36 Frank S. Edwards, *A Campaign in New Mexico with Colonel Doniphan*, 79–80.

37 Gregg, *Commerce of the Prairies*, 73; "Report of Lt. J. W. Abert on His Examination of New Mexico in the Years 1846–47," 30 Cong., 1 sess., *House Exec. Doc. No. 31*, p. 446.

38 Webb, *Adventures in the Santa Fé Trade*, 45; David Waldo, as quoted in Thomas Jefferson Farnham, *Mexico: Its Geography, People and Institutions*, 33; John Russell Bartlett, *Personal Narrative of Explorations and Incidents in Texas, New Mexico, California, Sonora, and Chihuahua*, II, 436.

between the two sheets to add further insulation and also to escape confiscation at the customs house as contraband, for the blankets could be sold surreptitiously in New Mexico for a handsome profit.[39] The best protection against water damage to the cargo was a wrapping of painted burlap for each package of merchandise.[40]

When the Drawback Act of 1845 was passed, allowing the merchants a rebate of duties paid on imported European goods taken to Mexico in their original packages, a special ruling on cargo coverings worked an undue hardship on the traders. The Secretary of the Treasury had instructed the customs collectors to require that goods eligible for the debenture be encased in "wooden boxes or coverings."[41] This was construed by the inspectors to mean that the original packages had to be encased in wooden boxes, and to this the traders strongly objected. Their complaint was that such boxes weighed half again as much as the originally packaged merchandise. As the wagons leaving Independence carried on the average only 4,500 pounds, and the freight charge from the Atlantic ports to Santa Fé was then about $12 a hundredweight, the additional wooden boxes, amounting to one-third of the cargo, would cost an additional $180 per wagon. Furthermore, as the duty in New Mexico was then levied at a flat rate of $600 per wagonload, without respect to the value of the cargo, the extra boxes amounted to about $200 per wagon in duties. The added transportation and duty cost was nearly equal to the difference between the "long" and "short" price in the American seaports and was thus excessively burdensome.[42]

39 Gregg, *Commerce of the Prairies*, 27.

40 Alvarez to Walker, Independence, June 18, 1845, M.N.M., Read Collection, Alvarez Letter Book.

41 Robert J. Walker, circular instruction, Washington, April 10, 1845, in 30 Cong., 1 sess., *House Report No. 458*, pp. 52–53.

42 Alvarez to Walker, Independence, June 18, 1845, M.N.M., Read Collection, Alvarez Letter Book.

Apparently the Treasury Department's ruling was shortly modified, or at least its enforcement was bearable, for these complaints soon ceased, and, as has already been indicated, a record million-dollar cargo was exported from Independence in 1846. And however burdensome the regulations emanating from Washington may have appeared to the traders, they paled into insignificance when compared to those imposed by the Mexican authorities or to the ordinary hardships of the road.

5.

The Roads to Chihuahua

As an important center of trade in northern Mexico, Chihuahua was linked by roads and trails with a number of other cities: Saltillo and Monterrey in the east, Mazatlán and Guaymas in the west, Durango and Zacatecas in the south, and El Paso del Norte and Santa Fé in the north, to mention only a few. For the merchants of Missouri the most common route to Chihuahua was a most circuitous one, northwestward to the great bend of the Arkansas River, southwestward to Santa Fé, and then almost due southward along the Camino Real. A much more direct route, passing through Texas, was pioneered in 1839, but it was seldom followed until after the Mexican War. Meanwhile, the Camino Real from Santa Fé to Chihuahua had undergone but slight change since the days of the colonial caravans, and the trail across the plains from Independence remained entirely without improvement.

The main road to Chihuahua from the frontier settlements

of Missouri as far as the New Mexican port of entry was the so-called Santa Fé Trail. It was no trail at all, however, notwithstanding the present existence of numerous historical markers or even the vestiges of deep wagon ruts at scattered points on the prairie. In the first place, the point of departure of the caravans from the Missouri River shifted with the years —from Arrow Rock Ferry to Franklin, to Independence, and eventually to Westport, where Kansas City now stands. In the second place, from the great bend of the Arkansas onward, there were two radically different routes, not to mention a number of minor variations. And finally, no one course was consistently enough followed by individual wagon trains to become a single road.

The route laid out by the federal surveyors in 1825 and 1826, although exceptionally well marked, was one of the least used by the trader wagons. Each caravan captain was an explorer in his own right, and the great expanse of prairie and plain tended to disperse rather than channel the overland traffic. One train of wagons would detour a mile or more from the trace of its immediate predecessor in order to meet with fresh grass for its own livestock, and an individual wagon would shun the track of the one just ahead to avoid miring in its ruts. The tendency was to follow river bottoms and draws in dry weather and higher ground in wet weather. In open country, where the wagons traveled two and even four abreast, the trail of a single caravan was frequently as much as fifty yards wide. One need only compare the various records of travel to discover that the Santa Fé Trail was not a road, nor even a trace, but a series of tracks meandering over the plains in only the most general single course. Several campsites on the trail were common to most of the caravans, but even between these points varying distances recorded by different travelers demonstrate the individuality of their respective routes.[1] The following table, which compares the route surveyed by the federal road commission with that favored by the veteran trader Josiah Gregg and that of Albert Speyer's train in 1846, as recorded by Adolph Wislizenus, illustrates the discrepancies:[2]

Campsites and Towns	Federal Survey Miles	Aggr. Miles	Gregg Miles	Aggr. Miles	Wislizenus Miles	Aggr. Miles
Independence						
Big Blue R. ford	15	15	—	—	17	17
Round Grove	—	—	35	35	18	35
The Narrows	48	63	30	65	29	64
110-Mile Creek	37	100	30	95	25	89
Bridge Creek	—	—	8	103	8	97
Council Grove	49	149	42	145	46	143
Diamond Spring	16	165	15	160	15	159
Cottonwood Creek	30	195	27	187	27	185
Little Arkansas R.	42	237	42	229	38	223
Cow Creek	—	—	20	249	20	243
Arkansas R.	19	256	16	265	16	259
Walnut Creek (up Arkansas R.)	27	283	8	273	8	267
Ash Creek (up Arkansas R.)	—	—	19	292	19	286
Pawnee Fork (up Arkansas R.)	37	320	6	298	6	292

[1] Compare especially Gregg, *Commerce of the Prairies;* K. L. Gregg (ed.), *The Road to Santa Fé;* Susan Magoffin, *Down the Santa Fé Trail;* Wislizenus, *Memoir of a Tour to Northern Mexico;* Webb, *Adventures in the Santa Fé Trade;* Kenyon Riddle, *Records and Maps of the Old Santa Fé Trail;* "Santa Fé Trail: M. M. Marmaduke Journal," *Missouri Historical Review,* Vol. VI, No. 1 (October, 1911), 1–10; "Major Alphonso Wetmore's Diary," *ibid.,* Vol. VIII, No. 4 (July, 1914), 177–97; "The Journals of Capt. Thomas Becknell," *ibid.,* Vol. IV, No. 2 (January, 1910), 65–84.

[2] K. L. Gregg (ed.), *The Road to Santa Fé,* map on front and back sheets; Gregg, *Commerce of the Prairies,* 217n.; Wislizenus, *Memoir of a Tour to Northern Mexico,* 118–23.

Campsites and Towns	Federal Survey		Gregg		Wislizenus	
	Miles	Aggr. Miles	Miles	Aggr. Miles	Miles	Aggr. Miles
The Caches (up Arkansas R.)	85	405	69	367	61	353
Arkansas R. ford	44	449	20	387	20	373
Chouteau Is. (up Arkansas R.)	15	464	—	—	—	—
Sand Creek (on Cimarron Cut-Off)	—	—	50	437	50	423
Lower Cimarron Spring	34	498	8	445	8	431
Middle Cimarron Spring	37	535	36	481	34	465
Upper Cimarron Spring	38	573	44	525	—	—
Cold Spring	—	—	5	530	46	511
McNee's Creek	28	601	25	555	26	537
Rabbit Ears Creek	11	612	20	575	24	561
Round Mound	16	628	8	583	—	—
Rock Creek	—	—	8	591	20	581
Point of Rocks	31	659	19	610	20	601
Río Colorado ford (Canadian R.)	17	676	20	630	20	621
Ocate Creek	6	682	6	636	6	627
Santa Clara Spring	—	—	21	657	24	651
Río Mora	—	—	22	679	—	—
Taos (on pack trail)	48	730	—	—	—	—
Gallinas Creek	—	—	20	699	39	690
San Miguel del Vado (Pecos R. ford)	—	—	23	722	23	713
Pecos pueblo	—	—	23	745	24	737
Santa Fé	—	—	25	770	28	765

Small Santa Fé-bound trains were fitted out at the Missouri River towns and usually traveled alone to the banks of the

Neosho River, convening at Council Grove, now a Kansas town, in order to organize a single caravan.[3] When all of the wagons had assembled, a captain was elected by the traders, regulations were adopted, and all was put in readiness for the great march over the plains. From Council Grove onward for the next 143 miles to Pawnee Rock, it became customary for the caravans to proceed in two parallel columns. This formation shortened the long line of wagons and permitted a more rapid maneuver into a defensive square in the event of an Indian attack. Such a corral was also formed by the wagons at each night camp.

About three days out of Council Grove the caravans entered the range of the American buffalo, where the exhilaration of the chase now broke the monotony of wagon travel and where tongue and "hump meat" supplemented the prosaic fare of regular provisions. Westward, the prairie grass became thinner and shorter, the soil sandier, and the air drier. The Arkansas River was reached at various places along its great bend, but a crossing was seldom made until it had been followed upstream to the 100th meridian. At Pawnee Rock, near the present Kansas town of the same name, the line of wagons was further shortened by the formation of four columns, for this was the land of the marauding Pawnee, and soon they would enter the range of the dread Comanche. Pawnee Rock was a prominent sandstone monument which, until recently defaced, bore the inscriptions of scores of Santa Fé-bound travelers. The Arkansas was forded wherever convenient, but there were four favorite crossings for those taking the popular Cimarron Cutoff: one near present Ford, Kansas, about 75 miles beyond Pawnee Rock, where the river bends far to the south; another in the vicinity of present Dodge City, about 30 miles farther;

3 For this and the following description of caravan travel on the Santa Fé Trail, reliance has been made mainly on Gregg, *Commerce of the Prairies*, 22–77.

a third near the present town of Cimarron, about 19 miles beyond that; and a fourth at Chouteau's Island, about 40 miles still farther up the river. Caravans preferring the longer trail by way of Raton Pass continued up the Arkansas almost another 200 miles to Bent's Fort, near what is now La Junta, Colorado, before striking off to the south. Travel over Raton Pass was slow and precarious, seldom exceeding a mile or two a day on the steep incline, and all hands had to man the wheels to prevent a catastrophe on the down grade.[4] Beyond the pass, the mountain trail continued southward from present Raton, New Mexico, along the foothills of the Rockies to the hamlet of Las Vegas, where it merged with the shorter Cimarron Cutoff and continued on to Santa Fé.

The latter route, although saving more than 100 miles of travel, was a dreary, sometimes waterless *jornada* measuring 58 miles from the Arkansas River to the Cimarron. Having crossed the Arkansas beyond the 100th meridian, the caravans were now in Mexican territory, and sometimes they were met at the border by a military escort from New Mexico. This protection, however, was no more regular than that offered within American territory by troops of the United States. Along the desolate Cimarron Cut-off the caravans frequently met with large parties of Comanches or other wandering tribes. These openly attacked small wagon trains but merely visited large ones in order to beg or steal what they could.

The end of the arid *jornada* was the Lower Cimarron Spring, from which point the trail followed the valley of the Cimarron River, crossing and recrossing its sandy and almost waterless bed several times. Beyond the Middle Spring the trail passed through the southeastern corner of what is now Colorado and into the tip of the Oklahoma panhandle where Wil-

[4] Entry for August 7, 1846, in Abert, "Report," 30 Cong., 1 sess., *House Exec. Doc. No. 31.*

low Bar and the Upper Cimarron Spring were regular camp-sites. At Willow Bar after 1844 a favorite pastime among the teamsters was arranging the bleached bones of Speyer's mules into interesting patterns designed to amuse the next caravan passing through.[5] Shortly after leaving the Upper Spring, the trail left the Cimarron in order to maintain its southwesterly course and entered the present limits of New Mexico.

The next landmark of note was the picturesque Rabbit Ears, an imposing pair of towering rocks, to the northwest of modern Clayton, New Mexico. Then came Round Mound, which the travelers sometimes climbed to get a magnificent view of the surrounding plains and distant mountains, and after it the Point of Rocks, where Mexican troops often met the wagons and placed them in a "protective custody" until they reached the customs house at Santa Fé. Beyond the Point of Rocks, the trail crossed the Canadian River, or Río Colorado (as it was then known), and in this vicinity a branch of the road struck off westward through the mountains to Taos, some seventy or eighty miles distant. This trail was impassable for wagons.

Forty miles beyond the rocky ford of the Canadian was the small collection of mud huts known as Mora, situated on a small river of the same name. It was the first settlement of any kind the caravans had met since leaving Independence, Missouri, about 680 miles to the rear. Twenty miles beyond this, on the Río Gallinas, was another hamlet, Las Vegas, where the mountain branch of the Santa Fé Trail joined the Cimarron Cut-off.

The first regular town met on the trail was San Miguel del Vado, about 23 miles beyond Las Vegas, where the Pecos River

5 Wislizenus, *Memoir of a Tour to Northern Mexico*, 13–14; "William H. Richardson's Journal of Doniphan's Expedition," *Missouri Historical Review*, Vol. XII, No. 2 (January, 1928), 223; Bieber (ed.), in Webb, *Adventures in the Santa Fé Trade*, 107n.

was forded, and here still another Santa Fé Trail merged with the main road. In 1839, Josiah Gregg brought a wagon train from Van Buren, Arkansas, to Santa Fé, following the Canadian River rather than the Arkansas.[6] Although even shorter than the Cimarron Cut-off, this trail was seldom used until the years of the California gold rush. From San Miguel the main road skirted southwesterly around a spur of the mountains, much as do the present highway and railroad, and then, bending to the north and passing the abandoned pueblo of Pecos, entered Santa Fé from the southeast. From Independence the total distance to Santa Fé was variously estimated at from 770 to 800 miles by way of the Cimarron Cut-off and upward of 900 miles by way of Raton Pass. The entire trip by the former route usually took about eight or nine weeks.

Santa Fé was a strange and somewhat disappointing town at first view.[7] Although beautifully situated in a valley surrounded by mountains clad with cedar and pine, a clear stream irrigating its fields, gardens, and orchards, the town was irregularly laid out. Its narrow, crooked streets were little more than country roads. Seen from a distance, Santa Fé reminded the Americans of a prairie dog town, a fleet of flatboats, or, more frequently, a huge brickyard. Every structure in town was made of adobes, sun-dried bricks of mud and straw. The houses were all flat-roofed, of one story, and of a uniform drab color—lining the streets in such a manner as to present a nearly continuous wall. Each home had a large folding door and one or two windows with projecting frames, turned wooden bars,

[6] Gregg, *Commerce of the Prairies*, 225–62; *Diary and Letters of Josiah Gregg*, I, 43–69.

[7] The following description is drawn from Pike, *Expeditions*, II, 607–608; Gregg, *Commerce of the Prairies*, 77–78; Farnham, *Mexico*, 48; Gibson, *Journey of a Soldier*, 205–11; Philip St. George Cooke, *The Conquest of New Mexico and California*, 43–44; George Frederick Augustus Ruxton, *Adventures in Mexico and the Rocky Mountains*, 189; John Taylor Hughes, diary, in Connelley (ed.), *Doniphan's Expedition*, 214–15.

and strong shutters opening to the inside. The interiors were handsomely whitewashed, and in the better homes the dirt floor was covered with carpets.

The great plaza in the center of town was level and un-paved, but graced by rows of small cottonwoods which were watered by ditches on each side of the square. The buildings on three sides were adorned with *portales*—extensions of the flat roofs supported by rough pine columns—which shaded the sidewalks and markets from the blazing sun. Around the plaza were the traditional public buildings: the Governor's Palace occupying the better part of the north side, the customs house, the barracks and adjoining jail, the municipal building, and the military chapel. Facing the square also were several private residences and the shops of the American merchants. Santa Fé supported six churches but not a single public school.

The timeless and peaceful aspect of the town was at once changed by the arrival of the caravan. It was the signal for long-awaited excitement and rejoicing, like the arrival of the annual fleet at Veracruz in colonial times. A shout went up on all sides heralding the arrival of *los americanos* and *los carros,* and crowds of women and boys flocked around to see what the bearded Missourians had brought in their great hooded wag-ons. Nor were the townspeople alone in their anticipation. Others from miles around were on hand to enjoy the bargains and general festivities. Even the American teamsters entered into the spirit. Before reaching town, they had scrubbed the dust of the road from their faces, slicked down their hair, and donned their Sunday best to parade before the first feminine eyes they had met in weeks. There would be *fandangos* for nights on end, as long as the sales continued. For the merchants, however, there was also the tedious task of haggling with the customs house officials, not only for the entry of their goods, but also for clearance to Chihuahua and other destinations.

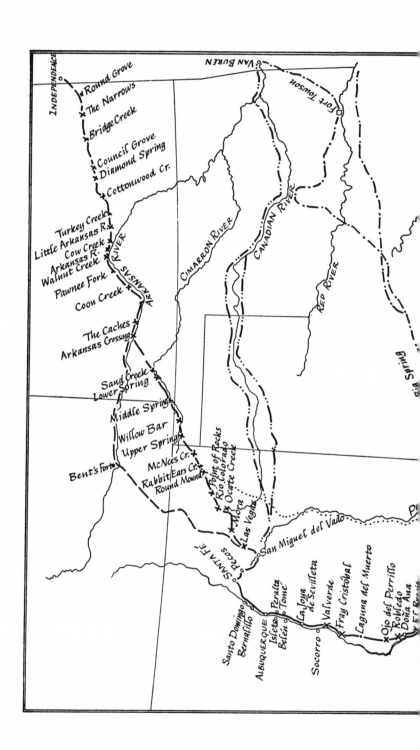

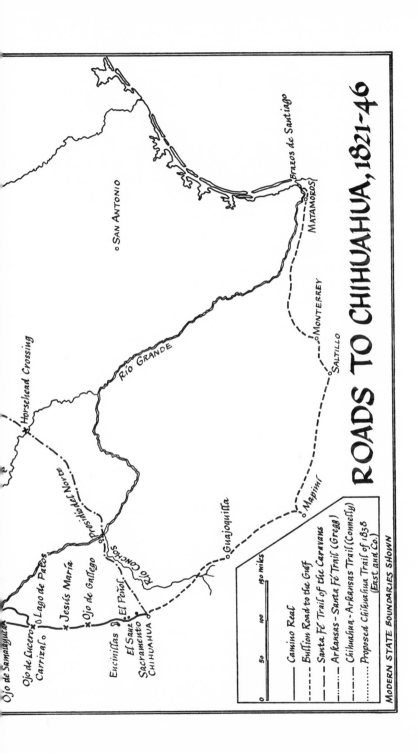

ROADS TO CHIHUAHUA, 1821-46

Ojo de Samalayuca
Ojo de Lucero
Carrizal
Lago de Patos
Jesús María
Ojo de Gallego
Encinillas
El Sauz
El Peñol
Sacramento
CHIHUAHUA
Guajoquilla
Horsehead Crossing
Presidio del Norte
Río Conchos
RÍO GRANDE
SAN ANTONIO
Brazos de Santiago
MATAMOROS
MONTERREY
SALTILLO
Mapimí

MODERN STATE BOUNDARIES SHOWN

		50	100	150 miles

——————— Camino Real
— — — — Bullion Road to the Gulf
– – – – – Santa Fé Trail of the Caravans
–·–·–·– Arkansas - Santa Fé Trail (Gregg)
–··–··– Chihuahua - Arkansas Trail (Connelly)
············· Proposed Chihuahua Trail of 1838
(East and Co.)

The road from Santa Fé to Chihuahua was essentially the Camino Real as opened by Oñate in 1598 and traversed almost annually by Spanish caravans during the next two centuries. But like the Santa Fé Trail it was a road in name only. None of it was surfaced or improved in any way except for the packing of the soil by the wheels of the wagons and the hooves of the mules. Nor was it a uniform route, for a number of alternate roads could be taken between several points along the way.

Although the main road from Santa Fé reached the valley of the Río Grande at the pueblo of Santo Domingo, another split off at La Bajada and met it a few miles upstream, at Peña Blanca. From Santo Domingo, the Camino Real lay on the east bank of the Río Grande for the next 150 miles to the camp of Fray Cristóbal, but another road crossed at San Felipe and followed the west bank, sometimes as far southward as Socorro. From Fray Cristóbal there was only a minor variation in the course over the Jornada del Muerto and then down the river again to El Paso del Norte, but from thence to the Ojo de Lucero there were two major alternatives: the Jornada del Cantarrecio, which continued along the river for another 40 miles and skirted the great sand hills; and the shorter but more difficult Jornada de Los Médanos, which passed through the dunes on an almost due-south course. From the junction of these two roads, near the Ojo de Lucero, onward to Chihuahua there were only minor deviations.

The Camino Real was fairly well confined to one general road bed only along the upper Río Grande, where bordering mountains and the river itself channelized traffic, but even there the trace hugged the river bed only during the dry season, keeping well above it during the rains. On the Jornada del Muerto and also beyond El Paso the broad plain permitted considerable deviation of one track from another, and this perhaps accounts for the discrepancies in the distances recorded between common campsites. A comparison of several travel journals with modern road maps, and with each other, shows a fairly uniform estimate of distance between the towns of New Mexico, especially between Santa Fé and Socorro, but thereafter, along the deserted and desolate stretches of the road, there is little agreement, and some of the distances are grossly exaggerated. The following table compares the mileage as given by Manuel Alvarez, the American consul at Santa Fé, by Wislizenus, who traveled with Speyer's train,[8] and by modern highway maps:

Campsites and Towns	Alvarez Miles	Aggr. Miles	Wislizenus Miles	Aggr. Miles	Highway Map Miles	Aggr. Miles
Villa de Santa Fé						
Opp. Pueblo de San Felipe	33	33	—	——	35	35
Pueblo de Algodones	3	36	—	——	3	38
Pueblo de Bernalillo	6	42	—	——	7	45
Pueblo de Sandía	4	46	—	——	3	48
Pueblo de Alameda	6	52	—	——	10	58
Villa de Albuquerque	12	64	63	63	7	62
Hacienda de Peralta	19	83	18	81	18	80
Pueblo de Tomé	9	92	8	89	9	89
Hacienda de Casa Colorado	9	101	10	99	—	——
Pueblo de la Joya de Sevilleta	15	116	19	118	28	117
Rancho de la Parida	20	136	18	136	—	——
Hacienda de Luís López	6	142	12	148	26	143
Ruins of Valverde	15	157	—	——	—	——
Fray Cristóbal	20	177	39	187	—	——

[8] "Distancias de Santa Fé a Chihuahua," M.N.M., Alvarez Papers, 1839–45, Note Book; Wislizenus, *Memoir of a Tour to Northern Mexico*, 29–49, 123–27.

Campsites and Towns	Alvarez		Wislizenus		Highway Map	
	Miles	Aggr. Miles	Miles	Aggr. Miles	Miles	Aggr. Miles
Laguna del Muerto	—	—	26	213	—	—
Alemán	—	—	16	229	—	—
Ojo del Perrillo	—	—	16	245	—	—
San Diego	78	255	—	—	—	—
Robledo	15	270	31	276	—	—
Pueblo de Doña Ana	16	286	10	286	138	281
Rancho del Bracito	18	304	25	311	—	—
Villa del Paso del Norte	33	337	34	345	50	331
Ojo de Samalayuca	36	373	34	379	34	365
Ojo de Lucero	39	412	—	—	35	400
Laguna de Patos	12	424	—	—	—	—
Presidio de Carrizal	18	442	64	443	—	—
Ojo Caliente	12	454	10	453	31	431
Jesús María	21	475	—	—	—	—
Ojo de Chivato	36	511	25	478	—	—
Ojo de Gallego	12	523	—	—	43	474
Laguna de Encinillas	27	550	28	516	—	—
Hacienda del Peñol	30	580	28	544	—	—
Hacienda del Sauz	—	—	—	—	71	545
Hacienda de Sacramento	33	613	22	566	15	560
Ciudad de Chihuahua	18	631	19	585	20	580

After clearing their goods through the customs house at Santa Fé, obtaining the necessary permits, and purchasing fresh mules or oxen, the traders bound for Chihuahua still found it advisable to travel in strength, awaiting the departure of other trains, if their own was insufficiently armed, before starting out on the Camino Real.[9] Although there was little to fear from

[9] The following description of travel on the Camino Real is drawn from Gregg, *Commerce of the Prairies*, 268–78; Kendall, *Narrative of the Texan Santa Fé Expedition*, I, 375–405; II, 11–62; Ruxton, *Adventures in Mexico and the*

hostile Indians near the towns of New Mexico, beyond Socorro the Navajos and Apaches were a constant menace. The eventual establishment of Doña Ana, another hamlet 167 miles farther south, offered no protection at all, and even the environs of El Paso del Norte were insecure. Nor did the towns along the road offer shelter for the men and mules, none having inns or other accommodations for large parties. At night they slept under the stars. Thus, travel on the Camino Real was much like that on the Santa Fé Trail. Camps were made near water and grass when possible, and the defensive corral of wagons was always formed at overnight stops.

From Santa Fé the road descended rapidly for about 30 miles in a southwesterly direction, passing through barren hills and rocky canyons, to the sandy valley of the Río Grande with its verdant fringes of cottonwood. Then, for the next 150 miles, the road lay southward down the valley, passing through a series of towns and ranches whose green irrigated fields and orchards contrasted sharply with the drab intervening stretches of desert. To the right lay the river; to the left sandy hillocks and mountains.

After passing the Keres pueblo of Santo Domingo, situated among the sand hills where Galisteo Creek joins the Río Grande, the road passed the hamlet of Algodones with its orchards enclosed by cactus-crested mud walls, that of Bernalillo, distinguished as being the residence of Julián Perea, one of the wealthiest merchants and ranchers in New Mexico, the drab Tewa pueblo of Sandía, and the little village of Alameda. Then came a string of ranches which merged with the city of Albuquerque to form an almost continuous settlement of seven

Rocky Mountains, 160–89; Wislizenus, *Memoir of a Tour to Northern Mexico*, 29–49; Cooke, *Conquest of New Mexico and California*, 54–79; F. S. Edwards, *A Campaign in New Mexico*, 181–82; Bartlett, *Personal Narrative of Explorations*, II, 402–21.

or eight miles along the river. Albuquerque itself, about sixty-two miles from Santa Fé, was the second most important town in the province, not only because of its size but also because it was the residence of the powerful governor, Manuel Armijo, who together with his brothers and nephews invested heavily in the trade with Missouri and the interior of Mexico.[10]

A few miles below the city were the haciendas of Sandoval and Varelas, and beyond a difficult chain of sand hills those of Chávez and Peralta and the town of Valencia. The Chávez estate was the largest met thus far, embracing corn fields, extensive pasture, cottonwood groves, the comfortable house of the owner, and the huts of his Indian servants, all enclosed by adobe walls and an irrigation ditch. Mariano Chávez, the proprietor, also owned the Hacienda de Padillas on the other side of the river and was the brother of the merchant Antonio José

[10] Manuel Armijo was born in the vicinity of Albuquerque, spent his boyhood as a shepherd, and according to legend stole sheep and resold them to their original owners, taught himself to read and write, and by 1822 was a person of some prominence locally. He became governor of New Mexico three times (1827–29, 1837–44, and 1845–46), and from gambling, embezzlement, and profiteering amassed a considerable fortune. He purchased trade goods in the United States at least as early as 1841 and until 1846. According to the American consul, he made every effort to squeeze out the Americans and gain a monopoly of the Santa Fé trade for his own family.

His reputation for dishonesty was general, but after the outbreak of the war with the United States, he sent $6,000 in cash and gold dust by American merchants to his creditors in New York to discharge a debt. His purchasing agent there was his nephew, Cristóbal Armijo, who was sometimes assisted by the latter's cousin, Juan Armijo. Another Juan Armijo, the Governor's brother, escorted a train of goods for him to Santa Fé just ahead of the invading American army. Other relatives engaging in the business were Ambrosio Armijo and his son José and a Rafael Armijo, who had a store at Albuquerque. Governor Armijo was charged with treason for abandoning his state to the Americans in 1846, but was acquitted at a trial at Mexico City and returned to New Mexico, where he died on December 9, 1853. Kendall, *Narrative of the Texan Santa Fé Expedition,* I, 346–61; Webb, *Adventures in the Santa Fé Trade,* 87–88, 179–86; William Watts Hardy Davis, *El Gringo, or New Mexico and Her People,* 362–63; P. Harmony, Nephews & Co. to Alvarez, New York City, February 10, 1847, M.N.M., Alvarez Papers, 1856; Guías and Facturas of August, 1844, and September, 1845, Aduana de Nuevo México, M.N.M., Twitchell Collection, 7771, 7823, 8244, 8256.

Chávez. Peralta was the seat of another family of *ricos*, the Oteros, at least three members of which (Juan, Antonio José, and Manuel Antonio) were also merchants. Both families also maintained residences at near-by Valencia.

The next town was Tomé, lying two or three miles beyond a conspicuous butte and stretching along the river for more than a mile. Then, after passing the Hacienda de Casa Colorado, which lay considerably above the river bed, the road passed through the hamlet of La Joyita near which black basaltic bluffs reached down almost to the river. A short distance farther was La Joya de Sevilleta, formerly a garrison town, where long, steep hills of sand closed in on the river, making the road extremely difficult for several miles. Then came the Rancho de Sabino and the Rancho de la Parida, where a steep, sandy hill had to be negotiated by doubling the teams and pulling the wagons over in relays. Even then they were frequently upset on the treacherous slope. Finally, shortly beyond Socorro, which was on the opposite bank, was the Hacienda de Luís López, a small settlement on both sides of the river, beyond which there was no habitation of any kind for the next 135 miles. Along this lonely stretch of road was a grove of cottonwoods near the ruins of the hacienda of Valverde, a favorite campsite after the abandonment of that estate because of Indian raids in the 1820's.

Beyond Valverde, at the end of the Paso del Contadero, a winding, precipitous road where the mountains again approach the Río Grande, was the last camp on the river for the next 90 miles. Fray Cristóbal camp, roughly 180 miles from Santa Fé, was sometimes pitched on the river bank and sometimes well up on the plateau behind Fray Cristóbal Mountain. In order to rest their animals, prepare food, and store fresh water for the forced marches ahead over the Jornada del Muerto, large wagon trains usually remained at this camp one or two days.

[111]

From Fray Cristóbal, the road, passing due south over the arid and elevated plain now separated from the river by a precipitous mountain range, was virtually without water except during or immediately after a rain, and the only fuel for campfires was dried yucca and mesquite. It was the custom of caravans to set out from Fray Cristóbal in the afternoon or early evening in order to avoid the wearisome heat and reach the Laguna del Muerto early the next morning after a 25-mile march. If there was no water in this sink, some could usually be found in the mountains about 5 miles to the west, at the Ojo del Muerto, but this was a hard drive for the animals and, being a favorite haunt of the Apaches, a dangerous one as well. Other water was sometimes found at Alemán camp, 18 miles south of the Laguna del Muerto, and at the Ojo del Perrillo, another 18 miles along the road. The river was reached again by passing from Perrillo on either side of the Sierra de San Diego, one trail reaching it at San Diego camp near present Rincon, New Mexico, after 16 miles, and the other after 31 miles at Robledo camp, near present Radium Springs.

Beyond the Jornada, the road again continued along the Río Grande, passing only Doña Ana (founded in 1838 or 1842), a settlement of ten or fifteen families in log houses atop a tabular bluff overlooking the river, and the Rancho del Bracito, then accepted as the boundary between New Mexico and the state of Chihuahua, before entering the pass or gap in the mountains where the river breaks through to the southeast and enters its Big Bend. To reach El Paso del Norte, the river could be forded at two places, one six and the other two miles above the town. The lower ford was just below a dam of stones and brush which raised the level of the water and turned it into a *madre acequia,* from which several smaller ditches led the water into the fields around the town. Both crossings were dangerous, on account of quicksand and the swiftness of the current even when the water was low. As in former times, the merchants sometimes had to unload the wagons and ferry the cargo across in dugout canoes, and sometimes even the wagons had to be dismantled and carried in the same manner. Frequently, soaked cargoes had to be unpacked and spread out to dry on the banks of the river.

The settlement of El Paso del Norte included not only the town but also a number of ranches and pueblos, a total population of about 4,000 people, scattered over the right bank of the river for ten or twelve miles. There were several good houses with gardens enclosed by walls; vineyards were still extensively cultivated as in the past; the inhabitants still carried on a large trade with Chihuahua in brandy, wine, and dried fruits; and livestock was still scarce, thanks to the continuing incursions of the Apaches. As this was the first town reached by the traders in the state of Chihuahua, there were the formalities of cargo inspection after a customs house was established in 1835. There was no public inn, but some traders found quarters in the homes of wealthy Mexican merchants or officials, while others camped out with the teamsters. All, however, enjoyed the *fandangos* which were held on the occasion of their arrival.

On leaving El Paso del Norte, the caravans were frequently joined by trains of pack mules laden with local produce and bound for Chihuahua. Although these often had escorts of their own—horsemen in wild costume and painted faces, armed with bows and arrows, much like their dreaded adversaries—the Mexican traders were eager to have the added protection of the larger American companies.

Mule trains and lightly loaded wagons usually took the direct road to Chihuahua, passing south to the Ojo de Samalayuca and then over the billowing Médanos to the next water hole. Some merchants purchased mules at El Paso del Norte, transferred their cargoes to them, and passed over the great ledge of sand dunes with empty wagons. Laden carts could also be pulled through the Médanos, but only with doubled teams and extreme effort on the part of both men and mules. For ten miles the huge piles of shifting sand supported not a blade of grass, and the trail itself was obliterated by the winds and marked only by the bleached, half-buried skeletons of mules which had perished in the past. At every step, horses and mules sank below their fetlocks, and it took all day to reach the gap at the southern edge of the dunes. This was the Puerta de la Piedra, so called for a large stone weighing some two hundred pounds which had found its way there in a most peculiar manner. According to legend, the stone had been found near the Ojo de Samalayuca many years before by Mexican *arrieros,* who, to demonstrate their strength, took turns raising and heaving it over their heads. Each successive muleteer felt called upon in passing to duplicate the feat, and although only a few were equal to the task, the stone was supposedly advanced in this manner from the desert spring all of the way across the dunes, a distance of from 12 to 14 miles![11] Beyond the Puerta de la Piedra it was still 27 miles to water, at the Ojo de Lucero.

Heavily loaded wagons seldom ventured over the Médanos, but on leaving El Paso del Norte continued down a southeasterly road along the right bank of the Río Grande for 40 or 50 miles, passing along the way the Presidio de San Elizeario, and then doubling back to the southwest over the Jornada del Cantarrecio. This traversed only a margin of the dunes. Fifteen miles from the river there was a water hole, Las Tinajas del Cantarrecio, and 25 miles farther, beyond a gap in the mountains, another, Los Charcos del Grado, which was still 15 miles from the Ojo de Lucero. This route was some 30 miles longer and consumed two more days of travel than

11 Kendall, *Narrative of the Texan Santa Fé Expedition,* II, 49–50.

that through the heart of the Médanos, but it was much preferred by the wagoners.

From the Ojo de Lucero the road continued southward, passing the stagnant Lago de Patos to the east and the Presidio de Carrizal on the west, where a branch of the road entered the town. Beyond this, about a mile west of the road, was the Ojo Caliente, which except for the usually dry Río Carmen, a mile beyond the warm spring, was the last water for almost 45 miles.

One night's camp had to be pitched on the Jornada de Jesús María, an arid and desolate stretch which, however, offered a level and hard-surfaced road for the wagons. Water could sometimes be found at the Ojo de Chivato at the foot of the Sierra de los Arados, but the next camp was usually at or near the Ojo de Gallegos, almost 45 miles from Ojo Caliente and about 150 from El Paso del Norte. Here the mountains on both sides, having remained in the distance since leaving the Médanos, now closed in on the road, and the latter had gained 1,600 feet in elevation since leaving El Paso del Norte. Beyond the Ojo de Gallegos and a smaller spring, the Ojo de Callecito, was the Puerto de los Arados, where the mountains separate again to form the broad, green valley of Encinillas.

In the bottom of this valley lay the brackish Laguna de Encinillas and the haciendas of Encinillas, El Peñol, and El Sauz, all owned at one time by General Angel Trías,[12] whose

12 Angel Trías, who inherited these estates from his father, was politically prominent at Chihuahua. After completing his formal education, he traveled in the United States and Europe, learned English, French, and German, and was noted for his wealth, cultural accomplishments, patriotic sentiments, and anti-American prejudices. At Chihuahua he rose from captain to general of the militia and served as a *regidor* and an *alcalde* on the city council, *prefecto politico* of the district, supreme court justice and governor (for five short terms between 1845 and 1846) of the state, and congressman of the republic. During his governorship he brought an end to the state-supported bounty on Apache scalps, led the resistance movement to the American invasion, and fought at the battle of Sacramento. He died in 1867. Webb, *Adventures in the Santa Fé Trade*, 225; Gregg, *Commerce of the Prairies*, 306–10, 312; Bartlett, *Personal*

immense herds of cattle were often surreptitiously drawn upon by passing travelers in need of fresh beef. And within the walls of the haciendas the inhabitants were confined as virtual prisoners by their fear of hostile Apaches. Beyond El Sauz, the southernmost of these estates, the road left the valley and traversed a hilly region to another inhabited place, the Rancho de Sacramento, and about 20 miles beyond the ford of the Sacramento River in this vicinity was the city of Chihuahua.

The chief emporium for most of the merchant trains from Missouri, Chihuahua was approximately 250 miles from El Paso del Norte, 580 from Santa Fé, and 1,350 from Independence. Laden wagon trains from Santa Fé took approximately forty days to reach it by the Camino Real; mule trains, twenty days; and post riders, fifteen.[13] Some of the more prosperous and enterprising merchants continued down the Camino Real to Durango, which was 400 miles beyond Chihuahua, to Zacatecas, 570 miles, or to Aguascalientes, 635 miles.

The twin spires of Chihuahua's cathedral first came into view from ten miles out, and later the picturesque setting of the city itself, situated among the cottonwoods lining the banks of the Río Chuviscar and almost completely surrounded by detached, brown mountain peaks. The road from the north swung around a spur of the mountains and entered the city from the east, passing several large haciendas deeply buried in luxuriant trees. The immediate approach along the little river was unpleasant, however, for the mean houses of the suburbs alternated with ugly piles of scoria and dross, the refuse of Chihuahua's smelters.

Narrative of Explorations, II, 426–27; Enrique González Flores, Chihuahua de la independencia a la revolución, 71–146 passim.

[13] Gregg, Commerce of the Prairies, 277–78; Hobbs, Wild Life in the Far West, 138; Pedro García Conde, "Ensayo estadístico sobre el estado de Chihuahua," Boletín de la Sociedad Mexicana de Geografía, Vol. V, 293–95.

Plaza of Albuquerque

From W. W. H. Davis's *El Gringo*

From William E. Connelley's *Doniphan's Expedition*

The American Army crossing the Jornada del Muerto

The city proper had a population of from 12,000 to 15,000 and was more regularly laid out than Santa Fé, its straight streets running at right angles in the cardinal directions. In the center of the spacious main plaza was an imposing fountain, and around it paved walks and streets. Facing the square were the principal public buildings: the ornate cathedral on the south, the mint and treasury on the west, the legislature's hall and public granary on the north, and the governor's palace on the east. A short distance to the west of the plaza was the unfinished church of San Francisco and the old Jesuit hospital, now converted into a military establishment with chapel, academy, and barracks. On the south side of town, running its full length, was the beautiful Alameda, a public walk almost completely shaded by rows of cottonwoods, and at the end of it the Plaza de Toros, or bull ring, which the traders sometimes used as a wagon yard. In a lesser plaza was a monument to the heroes of Mexico's independence who had been imprisoned and shot at Chihuahua in 1811. The city was well watered by the Río Chuviscar on the north side and by an imposing stone aqueduct on the south.

The houses of the city were mainly of one story, but many were handsome and well built of stone and whitewashed adobe. Conforming to the traditional Spanish pattern, the rooms of each were built with high ceilings around a patio and with thick walls having few windows, all of which provided a cool interior. Several American traders had permanent stores in town, and two, Benjamin Riddells[14] and a man named Steven-

14 Benjamin Riddells, born about 1808, was a resident merchant of Chihuahua at least as early as 1840. He acted in the capacity of American consul or commercial agent there from time to time, married a Mexican lady, and was still at Chihuahua in 1851. *Carta de Seguridad,* January 1, 1841, U.S.N.A., Consulate General, Mexico, Miscellaneous Record Books, Vol. I, 343; Hobbs, *Wild Life in the Far West,* 94; Bartlett, *Personal Narrative of Explorations,* II, 425; Wislizenus, *Memoir of a Tour to Northern Mexico,* 48.

son,[15] operated a hotel of sorts for the convenience of transient merchants.[16]

Several American traders were aware that the 1,350 miles from Independence to Chihuahua by way of Santa Fé was an unduly long haul, and that a more direct route from Missouri or even from Arkansas might result in a cheaper and quicker passage for their goods. Plans for the blazing of such a short cut were seriously considered by four American merchants in Chihuahua at least as early as 1838. In October of that year, George East,[17] John Patton, Lucian Thurston, and Riley Jackson petitioned the government for permission to open at their own expense a new road between Round Mound, a point on the Santa Fé Trail which was still 187 miles from the New Mex-

[15] *Stevenson* or *Stephenson*. This name occurs several times in the consulate records and travel journals. A man by the name of Stephenson led a caravan from Missouri to Chihuahua in 1828; another, or perhaps the same, named Stevenson was living with his Mexican wife at El Paso del Norte in 1841; an Archibald Stevenson was a merchant at Chihuahua from at least 1839 to 1847; and his brother Hugh was there from at least 1840 to 1846. William D. Jones to Stephen Curcier, Mexico City, August 28, 1839, Alfonso Anderson to John Black, Chihuahua, January 19, 1847, *Carta de Seguridad* for Archibald Stevenson, January 1, 1841, and January 19, 1846, U.S.N.A., Consulate General, Mexico, Letter Book, II, 91–92; Correspondence, 1845–48; Misc. Rec. Books, I, 342; II, 187; Kendall, *Narrative of the Texan Santa Fé Expedition*, II, 40; Connelley (ed.), in *Doniphan's Expedition*, 280n.

[16] Gregg, *Commerce of the Prairies*, 299–304; Ruxton, *Adventures in Mexico and the Rocky Mountains*, 151–52; Wislizenus, *Memoir of a Tour to Northern Mexico*, 48, 60; Hughes, diary, in Connelley (ed.), *Doniphan's Expedition*, 446–48; Bartlett, *Personal Narrative of Explorations*, II, 421–22, 431–35; F. S. Edwards, *A Campaign in New Mexico*, 121–25.

[17] Dr. George East was born in either 1803 or 1805, was a merchant at Chihuahua at least as early as 1838, was interned at Cusihuriachic with other resident Americans for four months during the Mexican War, and returned to the United States with Doniphan's troops. A son of the same name was with him in Chihuahua in 1843. George East to W. G. Jones, Chihuahua, February 20, 1838; East to J. Black, Chihuahua, October 2, 1843; Alfonso Anderson to Black, Chihuahua, January 19, 1847; *Carta de Seguridad*, January 1, 1841, and October 20, 1843, U.S.N.A., Consulate General, Mexico, Corresp., 1829–41, 1842–44, 1845–48; Misc. Rec. Books, I, 340; II, 251; Wislizenus, *Memoir of a Tour to Northern Mexico*, 50–54; *Diary and Letters of Josiah Gregg*, II, 107, 156, 158.

ican capital, and El Paso del Norte. Saving perhaps 120 miles and by-passing almost all of the New Mexican towns, this short cut, they asserted, would increase the volume of trade from the United States and thus also the revenues of the Mexican government.[18]

Their proposal was approved by the legislature of Chihuahua and submitted to the central government,[19] but before the latter acted, East and his associates informed the governor that further examination now indicated that the $4,000 which they had available for investment was insufficient, that the opening of the road might cost twice that much. As compensation for this additional expense, they asked for a refund of all duties which they should pay on the first merchandise introduced over their new road.[20] The Consejo de Gobierno at Mexico City found such a concession to be unconstitutional, however, for the road would be opened at private rather than public expense and by aliens rather than citizens. A special agreement with the United States would probably be required.[21] Nonetheless, the authorities of Chihuahua and New Mexico were ordered to report their views to the central government on the manner in which trade would be carried over such a short cut, the advantages and inconveniences which it might entail, and the precautions which might be necessary to assure the collection of proper duties.[22]

18 Secretario del Interior to Secretario de la Junta del Estado, Chihuahua, November 8, 1838, (certified copy), A.G.N., Fomento-Caminos, Tomo XI, Expediente 225. The correspondence cited in notes 19–25 is from this same file.

19 Gov. Bernardo Revilla to Ministro de Gobernación, Chihuahua, November 20, 1838.

20 East, Patton, Thurston, and Jackson to the Governor, Chihuahua, January 4, 1839.

21 Lucas Alamán to Ministro de Gobernación, Mexico City, February 19, 1839; Ministro de Relaciones Exteriores to Ministro de Gobernación, Mexico City, April 2, 1839.

22 Ministro de Relaciones Exteriores to Ministro de Gobernación, Mexico City, April 16, 1839.

In New Mexico, Governor Manuel Armijo was, of course, critical of the entire project. Such a road, he declared, could never be successfully used because of the scarcity of water on the immense intervening plain. Buffalo hunters and Comanche traders had assured him that the only feasible route through this region was along the Pecos River to its mouth and then up the Río Grande to El Paso del Norte, and this would bring the traders in contact with frontier settlements in New Mexico which could not be guarded adequately against smuggling. If the road should be authorized, it would mean the ruin of New Mexico, as its only revenue was the duties from the Missouri trade now collected at Santa Fé. The principal aim of East and his associates, Armijo concluded, was to facilitate smuggling, not to improve a road or quicken a legitimate traffic.[23] The treasurer of the state endorsed the Governor's sentiments.[24] The Commandant General of Chihuahua did not report his views until May of 1840, and by that time, as he stated, a caravan of Mexican traders had already blazed a shorter trail from Chihuahua to the American border, and so there was no further need to consider the initial proposal.[25]

In March of 1839, only five months after East and his associates had submitted their proposal, a Mexican caravan consisting of over one hundred men, including about fifty merchants and an escort of fifty dragoons, seven wagons, and about seven hundred mules set out from Chihuahua with $200,000 or $300,000 in specie and bullion to purchase goods in the United States. They followed the Chuviscar and the Conchos to the Río Grande and then crossed the plains of Texas and the Red River, reaching Fort Towson in the Indian Territory

[23] Gov. Armijo to Ministro de Gobernación, Santa Fé, September 26, 1839.

[24] José Antonio Chávez to Ministro de Gobernación, Santa Fé, October 11, 1839.

[25] Commandante General de Chihuahua, Informe, Chihuahua, May 4, 1840, quoted in Ministro de Guerra y Marina to Ministro de Relaciones Exteriores, Mexico City, May 21, 1840.

of the United States after three months of travel. Among the Chihuahua merchants in this party was at least one American, Dr. Henry Connelly, from whom Josiah Gregg obtained a detailed description of the venture.[26] The company had an agreement with the governor of Chihuahua for a military escort and, on the return, a reduction of tariff duties on their merchandise from the United States. In addition to the protection of the fifty dragoons, they carried a fieldpiece, a mortar, and two swivel guns, but as it turned out, they were not molested by hostile Indians.

Except for getting lost after crossing the Red River, which they mistook for the Brazos, and continuing north to the Canadian, which they thought was the Red, they met with no particular adventures. Some friendly Delawares guided them to Fort Towson, which Connelly reached several days in advance of the caravan, on June 21, in order to secure permission for it to enter the United States. After some negotiation with the authorities at the fort, permission was granted, and the caravan continued on to the western border of Arkansas, where they made their purchases. Altogether they loaded between sixty and seventy wagons, which they also purchased, and the return company was swelled to about 225 men, including the military escort.

It had been the intention of the merchants of Chihuahua to return that fall, but owing to various accidents and delays, they were not ready to leave until the season was too far advanced and did not actually get under way until the following spring. They took the Red River settlement of Texas on their route, passing that border in April, but for several days they were unable to find their former track, which had been partially obliterated by the winter rains. After wandering about beyond it, however, they finally discovered it again at a branch

26 Gregg, *Commerce of the Prairies*, 334–35n.

of the Colorado River of Texas and followed it to the Pecos. The Pecos was too deep to ford, and so they buoyed their wagon beds on emptied water kegs and ferried across. When they reached the Presidio del Norte, at the junction of the Conchos and the Río Grande, they learned that a new governor had taken office in Chihuahua who wanted to charge them the full duties. Forty-five days were spent at the presidio in negotiating a compromise, and finally, almost five months after leaving the United States and seventeen since their original departure from Chihuahua, they reached the city on August 27, 1840. The excessive time consumed by this caravan and especially the difficulty it encountered in making its way through the Cross Timbers and the bogs along the Red River ate up the profits of the company and discouraged others from following this trail.[27] Therefore, until after the Mexican War, the usual road to Chihuahua was by way of the Santa Fé Trail and the Camino Real.

Traders returning from Chihuahua with little more than specie as cargo sometimes took a much shorter route home, especially when their sales were completed after the departure for the United States of the regular caravan. These merchants, traveling in small trains only, took the Mexican coach road from Chihuahua southeastward through Mapimí, Parras, Saltillo, Monterrey, and Matamoros to the port of Brazos Santiago, on the Gulf of Mexico near the mouth of the Río Grande. From there they returned to the United States in one of the packet boats from New Orleans.[28] Meanwhile, the outbound caravans from Missouri with cargoes for the interior of Mexico were channeled as before through the customs house at Santa Fé.

[27] *Ibid.;* Kendall, *Narrative of the Texan Santa Fé Expedition,* I, 120–21; Grant Foreman, *Advancing the Frontier, 1830–1860,* 164–65.

[28] Wetmore to Cass, Franklin, Mo., October 11, 1831, *Missouri Historical Review,* Vol. VIII, No. 4 (July, 1914), 181–82.

6.

Commercial Controls
and Contraband

THE TRAVAILS of merchant caravans on the Santa Fé Trail
and the Camino Real were small enough when compared to
the vexations of Mexican law and its enforcement. On arriving in the republic, overland traders were subjected to all
manner of official imposition. The inspection of cargo, manifests, destination certificates, passports, and safe-conduct passes,
and, of course, the evaluation and taxation of merchandise
were all mere formalities. But there were occasions when, as
a result of international tensions quite beyond their own control, they suffered imprisonment and confiscation of their
goods. Even the American consuls at Santa Fé were not im-
mune to such oppression.[1] Still, although unjust, the Mexican

1 Although four consuls were appointed from Washington to reside at
Santa Fé, none of them was recognized by the Mexican government, and only

authorities were also corrupt, and their own indulgence frequently permitted an evasion of both the formal and financial obligations of the merchants.

Passports were first required of the traders in 1825, when the state governors of Mexico were ordered to report the arrival of every foreigner, and a supplementary act in 1830 required the deportation of all arriving without them. But because of the large number and temporary status of foreigners in New Mexico, an exception to the rule was allowed to apply there. For merchants and others who did not establish residence, the state governor could waive the passport requirement.[2]

Manifests for incoming cargoes, however, had to account for all packages, their certified value, and the persons to whom they were consigned; and a Spanish translation of these documents had to be presented in duplicate by the traders to the customs office at Santa Fé. One copy of the manifest was filed at that office and the other retained by the trader for presentation to the authorities at Chihuahua or whatever city was

---

one seems to have filed reports with the Department of State or otherwise made his functions known. Augustus Storrs, appointed March 8, 1825, was at Santa Fé in September of the same year, but was without record after that date. James Davis, of Alabama, was named to succeed him on March 29, 1830, but did not assume his duties, and the same was true for Ceran St. Vrain, of Missouri, who was appointed May 12, 1834. Finally, Manuel Alvarez was appointed on March 21, 1839, and when he reached Santa Fé in July of that year, he found no American flag, coat-of-arms, consular seal, or other accoutrements of the office. Although never granted an *exequatur* by the Mexican government, Alvarez served as acting consul until the American occupation of New Mexico in 1846. Storrs to Gov. Narbona, Santa Fé, September 23, 1825, A.S.R.E., L-E-1055, I, 149–50; Davis to Pres. Andrew Jackson, Russellville, Ala., October 20, 1830, and Alvarez to Secretary of State John Forsyth, Santa Fé, September 20, 1839, U.S.N.A., Consular Despatches, Santa Fé, I; Chief Clerk of the Department of State to Sen. T. B. Catron, Washington, October 18, 1913, M.N.M., Read Collection, Folder D.

2 Ministro de Relaciones to Gov. José Antonio Chávez, Mexico City, April 13, 1831, A.S.R.E., L-E-1070, Tomo XXII, 190.

designated as the final destination of the merchandise. The value of the goods was declared for tax purposes, but it bore little relation to what the trader had paid or even to what the New Mexican officials collected. Apparently the customs records of that state merely justified the amount of revenue which it actually sent to the national treasury, and the true value of the so-called Santa Fé trade was never accurately recorded.

Even the tariff rates were ephemeral. Only after a most careful study of Mexican legislation can the various imposts levied on foreign commerce and the fluctuation of their rates be reconstructed, and even then the findings are to little avail. In the first place, there was a time-lag between the enactment of a tariff schedule at Mexico City and its publication at Santa Fé or Chihuahua; in the second place, the enforcement of the supposedly current rate was often at the whim of the governor or the local collector; and, finally, the official rate, either current or obsolete, was frequently nullified by a secret *arreglo*, or "arrangement," which the traders were able to make with the local authorities.[3]

In theory there were two major taxes on imported merchandise, the *derecho de internación* (or *de arancel*) and the *derecho de consumo*. The former constituted the national duties, supposedly based on the value of the goods as declared in the manifest, levied according to the current tariff schedule, and assessed at the maritime or inland ports of entry. These duties were first collected at Santa Fé in 1823, when the rate on cotton textiles, the main importation at that time, was 15 per cent ad valorem.[4] The *derecho de consumo* was an excise tax levied on imported goods by the individual states of the republic and could be assessed at the point of entry, of initial sale, or of final

---

[3] Gregg, *Commerce of the Prairies*, 79–80, 336.
[4] Storrs to Narbona, Santa Fé, September 23, 1825, A.S.R.E., L-E-1055, I, 149–50; Albert William Bork, *Nuevos aspectos del comercio entre Nuevo México y Misuri, 1822–1846*, 41.

destination. The *consumo* rate was 3 per cent in 1824, 5 per cent in 1829, 6 per cent in 1832, 5 per cent again and 20 per cent for a short time only in 1839, and 15 per cent in 1843.[5] As in the case of the *internación* duty, however, the amount collected did not always coincide with the prevailing legal rate. The records at Santa Fé show another tax, the ancient *alcabala,* as having been collected, but this was legally an excise tax on the exchange of domestic goods, and it appears to have been only the New Mexican designation for the *derecho de consumo.* According to reports of their own countrymen, the collectors at Santa Fé were notoriously ignorant of the law and untrained for their duties.[6]

By virtue of a special concession from the central government, the domestic produce of New Mexico with the exception of silver and gold remained free of export duty. All bullion taken out of the country, however, had to pay the *derecho de extracción de oro y plata,* and this was borne chiefly by the American traders. As established in 1827, this duty amounted to 2 per cent on all wrought or coined gold and 3.5 per cent on silver in the same form.[7] Until 1828 the exportation of gold and silver in dust or bars was not legally allowed, and although permission was later granted, it was temporarily suspended again for silver in 1835.[8] But as bullion constituted a vital part of their return cargo, American merchants soon found ways and means of smuggling it out of the country, sometimes by

5 *Legislación mexicana ó colección completa de las disposiciones legislativas expedidas desde la independencia de la república,* compiled by Manuel Dublán and José María Lozano, I, 748-49; II, 151, 283, 435; III, 667, 763; IV, 641.

6 Barreiro, "Ojeada sobre Nuevo México," translated in Carroll and Haggard (eds.), *Three New Mexican Chronicles,* 64-65; Bork, *Nuevos aspectos del comercio entre Nuevo México y Misuri,* 73.

7 Tariff schedule of November 16, 1827, *Legislación mexicana,* II, 26-46.

8 Decree of July 19, 1828, and Treasury circular of September 9, 1835, *ibid.,* II, 75-76; III, 71-72.

packing it in false, oversized axletrees which they attached to their wagons.[9]

The ever changing rates of the national tariff, the "arrangements" between traders and collectors, the incompetence of the customs officials, and, no doubt, the devious means by which the traders disguised the true value of their wares, all tended to confound the revenue system. From 1839 to 1844, the blustering Governor Armijo solved the problem in an arbitrarily simplified manner. Without regard to the prevailing national tariff or to the manifested value of the merchandise, he imposed a flat rate of $500 per wagonload on all imports. As the average legal duties amounted to from $1,000 to $2,000 per load, this arbitrary rate was hardly disadvantageous to the traders, and, as a matter of fact, it led to a further reduction of their payments through the importation of more expensive goods and the transportation of them in oversize wagons. These devices and the consequent reduction of the revenue collected induced Governor Armijo to return soon afterward to the ad valorem system.[10] In 1844, Governor Mariano Martínez reverted to the flat per-wagon rate, raised it to $750, and required a formal inspection of the cargo, but in the following year the rate was reduced to $500 again.[11] As far as the national treasury was concerned, the arbitrary rate was no improvement at all. The annual revenue from this system amounted to from $40,000 to $80,000, according to one estimate, and because of embezzlement, only half of this sum ever reached Mexico City.[12] Indeed, the independence of New Mexico from national

9 David H. Coyner, *The Lost Trappers*, 216–17.

10 Gregg, *Commerce of the Prairies*, 79–80; Kendall, *Narrative of the Texan Santa Fé Expedition*, I, 351.

11 Webb, *Adventures in the Santa Fé Trade*, 56; Alvarez to Walker, Independence, June 18, 1845, M.N.M., Read Collection, Alvarez Letter Book.

12 Gregg, *Commerce of the Prairies*, 336.

regulation was such that from 1838 to 1840 the Santa Fé customs office never filed a report to the central treasury.[13]

In addition to the regular national and state import duties, the traders had also to pay a per diem tax on their retail shops in Santa Fé and an arrival duty of ten dollars on each mule load of their merchandise, both of which were subjects of much complaint in 1831.[14] Early in 1839, moreover, a new retail tax was levied by the municipal government to help support a war then being waged on the Navajo Indians. Since this new burden fell equally on Mexican and American merchants, there was at first no cause for complaint, but in November of that year native merchants were specifically exempted, and the tax was then borne only by foreigners and naturalized citizens. Complaining to the Governor, the Americans pointed out that this not only violated Article 9 of the Treaty of 1831, but was also grossly unfair to the several traders who, as naturalized citizens of Mexico, had lent both money and military service to the government during the prevailing emergency. The state government then agreed to exempt the naturalized citizens who could show proof of their service, but it gave foreign merchants only the right to appeal their cases to the municipalities.[15] According to Manuel Alvarez, the acting consul for the United States at Santa Fé,[16] this was a deliberate attempt to drive Americans from the New Mexican trade.

13 *Memoria de la Hacienda Nacional* (title varies), issues for 1838 to 1840, *passim;* Bork, *Nuevos aspectos del comercio entre Nuevo México y Misuri,* 75.

14 Wetmore to Cass, Franklin, October 11, 1831, *Missouri Historical Review,* Vol. VIII, No. 4 (July, 1914), 182–83.

15 Memorial to Gov. Armijo endorsed by John Scholly, Lewis Lee, John Fournier, J. K. Dormston, Manuel Alvarez, Charles Blummer, Benjamin Wilson, and Josiah Gregg, Santa Fé, December 2, 1839 (translated copy); Guadalupe Miranda to Alvarez, Santa Fé, December 3, 1839; Alvarez, Memorial to Daniel Webster, Washington, February 2, 1842, U.S.N.A., Cons. Desp., Santa Fé, I.

16 Manuel Alvarez was born in Abelgas, Spain, in 1794, and came to New York in 1823. He entered the Santa Fé trade in 1824, renounced his Spanish nationality in 1834, was appointed consul at Santa Fé in 1839, and became an

By this time a large number of wealthy Mexicans were buying goods in the United States for the local market, and in clearing the customs house at Santa Fé, they were accorded preferential consideration. José Chávez y Castillo, for instance, was charged only $1,200 in duties on eleven wagonloads of goods in the summer of 1840, while an American trader was assessed $1,286 for only three wagonloads.[17] Many months passed before equal treatment of native and foreign merchants was restored in compliance with the Treaty of 1831, and the latter were never reimbursed for their payment of the discriminatory municipal retail tax. For a short time, in fact, all foreigners were prohibited from engaging in the retail business in New Mexico except those naturalized, married to Mexicans, or residing in the republic with their families.[18] This, however, was an outgrowth of severe international tension of political and military character, and cannot be charged entirely to economic nationalism.

The occasion was the arrival of the Texan–Santa Fé expedition in 1841 and the reprisal in 1842 and 1843 for its ill treatment by the Mexicans. As previously pointed out, the

American citizen in 1842. Shortly after reaching Santa Fé for the first time, he opened a store there and continued as a trader for over thirty years, building up one of the largest mercantile businesses in New Mexico. On occasion he left Santa Fé to purchase goods in the United States and report to the Secretary of State, and in the winter of 1843–44 visited London and Paris to buy merchandise. His status was changed from consul to commercial agent in 1846, he was elected lieutenant governor of the Territory of New Mexico in 1850, and died at Santa Fé in 1856. Alvarez to Forsyth, Santa Fé, September 20, 1839; to Webster, Washington, February 2 and March 4, 1842; and to Buchanan, Independence, June 18, 1845, U.S.N.A., Cons. Desp., Santa Fé, I; certificate of citizenship, April 9, 1842, and appointment as commercial agent, March 18, 1846, M.N.M., Read Collection, Folders A and B; Lansing Bloom, "Ledgers of a Santa Fé Trader," *New Mexico Historical Review*, Vol. XXI, No. 2 (April, 1946), 135–39.

[17] Alvarez, Memorial to Webster, Washington, February 2, 1842, U.S.N.A., Cons. Desp., Santa Fé, I.

[18] 28 Cong., 1 sess., *Senate Exec. Doc. No. 1*, pp. 31–32; Bieber (ed.), in Webb, *Adventures in the Santa Fé Trade*, 25.

expedition from Texas was looked upon by the New Mexicans as a military invasion, and American merchants in Santa Fé at the time became the victims of both mob and official hysteria. Already subjected to individual attacks on their persons and property, a record of which their consul subsequently submitted to their government,[19] the Americans were condemned as a group when several of them were implicated in the invasion by the statements of two of its deserters. As Governor Armijo assumed command of the militia and prepared to intercept the main body of the intruders, Manuel Alvarez asked for permission to go out and parley with the Texas commander, to inform him that American lives and property must be respected. Armijo, however, forbade him or any other foreigner to leave the city until his own return. A state of emergency existed, and the ensuing injustices to Americans may properly be considered as the effects of security measures rather than of outright tyranny, although the consul made no such point in his report to Washington. An exceptional instance of sheer terrorism, however, was perpetrated against Alvarez himself, and this circumstance may have colored his over-all view of the tense situation.

Shortly after Armijo and the militia left the city to intercept the Texans, one of his nephews, an ensign named Tomás Martín, returned to the plaza, removed one of the previously captured Texans from jail, brought him to Alvarez's home, and began to abuse the consul. Martín and his captive were then joined by two other soldiers and eventually by a menacing crowd which clamored for Alvarez's death. According to the consul, Martín tried to stab him to death, and did inflict a deep facial wound, but was deterred by the timely arrival of Guadalupe Miranda, the state secretary, who dispersed the assail-

[19] Alvarez, Memorial to Webster, Washington, February 2, 1842, U.S.N.A., Cons. Desp., Santa Fé, I.

ants.[20] Even though Martín went unpunished, the intervention of Miranda indicates that the attack was not officially inspired. But the anti-American campaign continued.

A week later a caravan belonging to James Giddings[21] and Reuben Gentry[22] arrived from Missouri, and Gentry, then residing in Santa Fé, was refused a pass to go out and take charge of the incoming wagons. About the same time, three Americans, who were on a business mission from Bent's Fort and who were carrying proper credentials, were arrested and incarcerated at Santa Fé. At Taos, Francis Lecompte, an American citizen, was clubbed to death while resisting arrest on charges which he, being a deaf mute, was unable to understand. A few days later Charles Bent,[23] arriving from his fort on the Arkansas River, was arrested and temporarily imprisoned, and about the same time a mob entered and robbed George Gould's

---

20 *Ibid.*, 20–23.

21 James Giddings was born in Kentucky about 1812, entered the Santa Fé trade about 1835, and became a resident merchant there from 1840 to 1853, when he established a ranch on the Pecos River in present Baca County. He was still there in June, 1865. Bieber (ed.), in Webb, *Adventures in the Santa Fé Trade*, 97n.

22 Reuben Gentry, of Kentucky, was born about 1817 according to his *carta de seguridad* and entered the inland trade with Mexico at least as early as 1839, when he accompanied the Giddings-Patterson train from Independence to Chihuahua. In 1843 he freighted goods to Zacatecas for the English firm of Kerford and Jenkins and was still with that company in 1846. He was probably the brother of Nicolas Gentry, known as "Old Contraband," who was a Santa Fé trader as early as 1825 and was interned for a time at Chihuahua for customs violation in 1845. *Carta de Seguridad* for Reuben Gentry, September 15, 1842, U.S.N.A., Consulate General, Mexico, Miscellaneous Record Books, II, 137; San Francisco *Review*, September 28, 1883; Gibson, *Journey of a Soldier*, 327–28; Webb, *Adventures in the Santa Fé Trade*, 81, 132.

23 Charles Bent, of Missouri, was born in 1789, engaged in the Santa Fé and Rocky Mountain trade in 1828, and helped his brother William build Bent's Fort on the upper Arkansas in 1832. He married a New Mexican and resided at Taos, became a captain of scouts with the American army of occupation in 1846, and was the first American governor of New Mexico, but was murdered shortly after his appointment during the abortive revolt against the Americans at Taos in 1847. Leroy R. Hafen (ed.), in *Ruxton of the Rockies*, 191n.

house at Taos. Gould was not only denied redress by the justice of the peace, but was also refused permission to leave the country.[24]

Nor did the abuses cease when the danger of the invasion had passed. The goods of Thomas Rowland, a resident of San Miguel del Vado but absent at the time, were confiscated by the local justice of the peace on the grounds that he was a known friend of the Texans.[25]

Unable to obtain redress for the abused Americans, or even recognition of his own status as consul, Alvarez requested his passport on September 29, 1841. Denied even this after much haggling, he left for the United States without it. Before reaching Independence on December 13, he lost forty of his sixty-seven horses and mules and two of his fifteen traveling companions, mostly from cold and exposure. Finally, he arrived in Washington, where he described to the secretary of state the dire predicament of the traders in New Mexico.[26]

Suspicion against the Americans in New Mexico continued, and the hostility of Governor Armijo increased, but now for personal as well as political reasons. The Americans, after all, were his competitors in the overland trade. In the summer of 1842 a large amount of merchandise which Armijo himself had ordered was lost on a Missouri River steamboat, and on learning of this, he became intensely excited against all American residents of New Mexico. As one of its most important merchants, Armijo had been struggling for some time to monopolize the commerce of his province, according to Alvarez,

[24] Alvarez, Memorial to Webster, Washington, February 2, 1842, pp. 25–27, U.S.N.A., Cons. Desp., Santa Fé, I.

[25] His brother, John Rowland, having been appointed by the Texans to to seek an amicable reception for their expedition, had fled after its capture to California with several other Americans. Obituary of John Rowland, Los Angeles *Express*, October 16, 1873, and Los Angeles *Herald*, October 23, 1873.

[26] Alvarez, Memorial to Webster, Washington, February 2, 1842, p. 29, U.S.N.A., Cons. Desp., Santa Fé, I.

From W. W. H. Davis's *El Gringo*

Cathedral of El Paso del Norte

City of Chihuahua, about 1850

and his mistreatment of Americans was designed to make them abandon the trade in disgust.[27] By the spring of 1843 this harrying of American traders, now intensified in retaliation for a second invasion from Texas, had slowed the Santa Fé trade to a mere trickle. Many entrepreneurs, both Mexican and American, were abandoning it altogether.

The apprehension of the Americans was justifiably intensified when one band of Texans raided the frontier village of Mora, another robbed and murdered Antonio José Chávez while he was on his way to Missouri, and still another defeated and captured an advance guard of New Mexican militia on the Cimarron Cut-off. Accused of collusion with the marauders, several American residents were ordered to appear at Santa Fé for examination and were put to considerable inconvenience. Alvarez, who had returned to Santa Fé in the spring of 1842 and was again on his way back to the United States to plead the cause of the American traders in the early summer of 1843, met a band of Texans near the Arkansas crossing, but was allowed to pass. However, the regular caravan from Missouri was more seriously threatened. Made up about equally of American and Mexican traders, it was confronted a short distance beyond the Arkansas by the marauders, but Captain Philip St. George Cooke's troops, who had escorted it to the Arkansas, crossed over into Mexican territory, arrested and disarmed the Texans, and permitted the caravan to reach Santa Fé in safety.[28]

In retaliation for the hostilities of the Texans and the supposed collusion of American citizens, the central government of Mexico, by a decree closing the frontier customs houses, ordered the overland trade with the United States stopped as

[27] Alvarez to the Secretary of State, Independence, July 1, 1843, U.S.N.A., Cons. Desp., Santa Fé, I.

[28] Ibid.; Gregg, Commerce of the Prairies, 337–43.

of September 23, 1843.[29] This arbitrary measure met with considerable opposition, not only in the United States but in New Mexico and Chihuahua as well. One trader, Josiah Gregg, predicted that a revolution would break out in New Mexico if the customs house there remained closed, and offered to invest his money in a store to be situated at the Arkansas crossing, where the Americans could sell their goods without leaving their own territory.[30] Actually, however, the Mexican embargo had little adverse effect on the trade. Imposed in September, 1843, after the caravans of that year had already reached Santa Fé, it was repealed in the following spring,[31] just in time for the outfitting of the first trains of that season. Moreover, the total value of American merchandise reaching Santa Fé in 1843 and 1844 was approximately $650,000, which was well over that of any two previous years, and the trade continued to increase thereafter.[32]

Contrary to the general tone of the consular reports, abuses in the overland trade were not always originated by the Mexicans, nor were they always disadvantageous to the Americans. Both official and private records attest to a thriving contraband trade and also to an institutionalized system of evasion of duties through outright bribery. Mexican government reports complain of these irregularities, American consular letters admit their prevalence, and the journals of the traders themselves boastfully supply the details.

The establishment of customs houses well out on the frontier, at Taos in the north and San Miguel del Vado in the east, was ordered by the central government time and again, but Santa Fé remained the only active port of entry for New

[29] Decree of August 7, 1843, *Legislación mexicana*, IV, 507.
[30] Gregg to Alvarez, New York, December 26, 1843, in *Diary and Letters of Josiah Gregg*, I, 138–39.
[31] Decree of March 31, 1844, *Legislación mexicana*, IV, 752.
[32] See Gregg's table, above.

Mexico, and American traders took full advantage of its inadequacy. According to José Agustín Escudero, a government spokesman from Chihuahua, the overland traders frequently transferred the loads of their wagons to mule trains on reaching the frontier of New Mexico and sent them over little-used trails to Chihuahua and other interior markets without passing through Santa Fé or paying the national duties at all.[33] Just when this irregularity first came to the attention of the central government is uncertain, but it was at least suspected by 1831, when a disgruntled Missouri trader offered to turn informer.

In the fall of that year a Dr. Peter Harris (or Peter Harris Estes, as he sometimes signed his name) had just returned to his home in Liberty, Missouri, from a disappointing venture in the Santa Fé trade. In order to recoup his losses, he wrote the President of Mexico offering for a handsome price to supply startling information on the manner and extent of the fraudulent American practices. Hinting at evasions amounting to one million dollars and collusions involving a Masonic conspiracy, he was, he said, risking his own life in volunteering this information. Anticlimactically, the matter was referred to the Mexican consul at St. Louis, whose ensuing correspondence with the informer was handicapped by the latter's inability to read Spanish and by the misdirection of a number of the letters. Finally, when Harris (or Estes) insisted on a reward of half of what his knowledge would save the Mexican government in revenue, one thousand dollars in advance, and direct communication with the President, the government of Mexico dropped the whole affair.[34]

[33] Escudero, annotations, in Carroll and Haggard (eds.), *Three New Mexican Chronicles*, 65–66.

[34] The correspondence on this subject, dating from December 24, 1831, to November 17, 1832, appears as "Propuesta de Peter H. Estes, de Liberty, Missouri, para servirse como espía de México relativo al comercio de Nuevo México, Años de 1831–1832," A.S.R.E., Legajo 44-6-22.

If these negotiations failed to open official eyes, the frauds were certainly known by the close of 1835. By that time the Mexican treasury officials were complaining bitterly that copious amounts of American goods were being introduced through the frontiers of both New Mexico and Chihuahua without paying duties, and ten years later goods imported through New Mexico were reportedly being sold in Chihuahua and Durango at prices which would have been ruinous to the merchants if full duties had been paid. The militia company stationed at San Miguel del Vado was then ordered to redouble its vigilance over incoming caravans, for it had come to the attention of the commandant at Santa Fé that after reaching the frontier, the wagons were being reloaded in such a manner as to reduce the legal duties.[35]

This latter device is explained in the correspondence and memoirs of the traders themselves. As the duty was to be collected according to the number of wagonloads entered rather than to the quality or quantity of the merchandise itself, a number of wagons were freed on entering New Mexico by overloading others, and the emptied ones were then either left behind or burned. As iron was extremely scarce in New Mexico and brought unusually high prices there, the parts made of this material were salvaged from the discarded wagons, taken to Santa Fé as part of the regular cargo, and sometimes sold there for enough to pay the entire duties on the cargo of the overloaded wagons. If troops from New Mexico were expected to meet the incoming trains and escort them to Santa

35 Ministro de Hacienda to Director General de Rentas, Mexico City, December 17, 1835, (copy) in "Documentos estadísticos redactados por Manuel Payno y Bustamante," II, 73 (MS), Archivo Histórico de Hacienda (hereinafter cited as A.H.H.), Legajo 117-1; Ambrosio Armijo to Administrador de la Aduana Fronteriza, Santa Fé, September 1, 1845, and Comandante de la Partida to Alferez Ramón Sena, Santa Fé, October 21, 1845, M.N.M., Twitchell Collection, 8231, 8321.

Fé, the transfer of cargo was made, before their arrival, near the Arkansas crossing. Otherwise, it took place much farther along the road, at Mora or San Miguel del Vado.[36]

Even more notorious than this practice was the *arreglo*, wherein goods legally entered at Santa Fé still evaded at least part of the prescribed national duties. In 1824, before the per-wagon rate was arbitrarily imposed in New Mexico, Meredith Marmaduke[37] found the customs collector "an astonishingly obliging man as a public officer,"[38] and in 1831 Gregg learned that he was moved by an "actuated sympathy" for the American merchants, causing them to open only a few packages so as to show "the least discrepancy with the manifest." This "arrangement" sometimes amounted to a division of the legal duties into three parts: one for the government, one for the collector, and one for the merchant himself.[39] In 1842, Alvarez admitted that notwithstanding the general discrimination against American merchants at Santa Fé, "we all pay less than the tariff calls for."[40]

Even more explicit was James Webb.[41] His company, arriv-

[36] Charles Bent to Alvarez, Taos, November 12, 1844, M.N.M., Alvarez Papers, 1839–45; Coyner, *The Lost Trappers*, 216–17; Ruxton, *Adventures in Mexico and the Rocky Mountains*, 152–53; obituary of Henry J. Cainiffe, San Francisco *Review*, August 2, 1884.

[37] Meredith Miles Marmaduke, who was born in Virginia in 1791, served as a colonel of militia in the War of 1812 and came to Missouri about 1824. He engaged in the Santa Fé trade from that year to about 1830, held several offices in Missouri including that of lieutenant governor (1840) and governor (1844), and died in 1864. K. L. Gregg (ed.), in *The Road to Santa Fé*, 251. See also note 38 below.

[38] "Santa Fé Trail: M. M. Marmaduke Journal," *Missouri Historical Review*, Vol. VI, No. 1 (October, 1911), 8.

[39] Gregg, *Commerce of the Prairies*, 79.

[40] Alvarez, Memorial to Webster, Washington, February 2, 1842, p. 6, U.S.N.A., Cons. Desp., Santa Fé, I.

[41] James Josiah Webb was born in Connecticut in 1818 and came to Missouri in 1843, where he entered the overland trade in 1844. He made three trips to Santa Fé in partnership with George P. Doan between 1845 and 1848, accompanied Albert Speyer to Chihuahua and San Juan de los Lagos in 1846, and

ing in 1844 as "recognized and confessed contrabandists," passed a number of prohibited articles through customs after a week of negotiations with Governor Mariano Martínez. Two of his party, Samuel Wethered[42] and Thomas Caldwell,[43] having previously befriended Martínez in Chihuahua, were allowed to open retail shops in Santa Fé in violation of an existing law which restricted foreign traders to wholesale transactions. In 1845, Webb's caravan passed the customs inspection with little trouble, the officers being "satisfied by small loans of money which were never paid or expected to be, and small presents of some kind to which they would take a fancy, generally amounting to $25 or $100, according to circumstances and number of wagons entered." Again, in 1846, Webb made an *arreglo,* this time with Governor Armijo, whereby one of his loaded wagons was exempted from duties, the others were charged only at a reduced rate, and all were permitted to proceed to Chihuahua and other interior markets under certification that duties had been paid in full.[44] Captain Cooke thought it surprising that American merchants preferred clearing their

was in partnership with William S. Messervy from 1850 to 1853 and thereafter with John M. Kingsbury. Elected to the New Mexico legislative assembly in 1856, he left the territory for the last time in 1857, was elected to the U. S. Senate from Connecticut in 1863, retired as a gentleman farmer in that state shortly afterwards, and died there in 1889. Webb, *Adventures in the Santa Fé Trade, passim;* "The Papers of James J. Webb, Santa Fé Merchant, 1844–1861," *Washington University Studies,* Vol. XI, No. 2 (1924), 255–305.

42 Samuel Wethered, of Baltimore, Maryland, was in the Santa Fé trade at least as early as 1839 and until the early 1850's, in association with Thomas Caldwell from 1844 to 1847. Bieber (ed.), in Webb, *Adventures in the Santa Fé Trade,* 45.

43 Thomas J. Caldwell, of Baltimore, Maryland, was born about 1818 according to his *carta de seguridad,* entered the Mexican trade about 1840, was in Chihuahua by 1843, served as an interpreter for Colonel Doniphan from late 1846 to February, 1847, and then returned to Missouri. *Carta de Seguridad,* April 3, 1843, U.S.N.A., Cons. Gen., Mex., Misc. Rec. Books, II, 214; Bieber (ed.), in Webb, *Adventures in the Santa Fé Trade,* 45n.; F. S. Edwards, *A Campaign in New Mexico,* 244.

44 Webb, *Adventures in the Santa Fé Trade,* 57, 81–82, 86–89, 138.

goods at Santa Fé rather than at the interior cities, to which three-fourths of their goods were consigned in 1846,[45] but the curious amenability of the New Mexican authorities no doubt justified the preference.

In order to pass the interior customs offices, it was necessary to obtain important papers at Santa Fé. In addition to a copy of the entire list of merchandise that had to accompany the cargo, there were also the *guía* and *tornaguía*. The *guía* was a mercantile passport bearing the signature, place, and date of the official issuing it, the name of the merchant, the number of packages in his cargo, a specification of which were of foreign and which were of domestic origin, the value of the merchandise, its destination, the name of the person to whom it was consigned, and the number of days allowed for remitting the certification of its final arrival. Only three destinations were permitted, and the merchant could sell his goods at these only. The *guía* was required not only on leaving the port of entry, but also on taking goods from one state to another and, except in New Mexico, from one town to another within a state. Thus, from El Paso del Norte on southward, every important town had its revenue officers, and the same consignment of goods sometimes had to pay the *derecho de consumo,* or internal duties, six times before it was finally sold. The *tornaguía,* a certification that the merchandise had reached its proper destination, had to be endorsed by another merchant at that point and returned within a specified time to the port of entry. Failure to meet this requirement subjected the endorser to a forfeiture equal to the full amount of the duties on the consignment. In drawing up the *guía,* invoice, passport, and *tornaguía,* great care was required, for the slightest mistake or emendation might subject the merchandise to confiscation. The same penalty was also imposed by law on any cargo found

45 Cooke, *The Conquest of New Mexico and California,* 33.

off the main road to its proper destination unless unavoidably detoured.[46]

After leaving Santa Fé, the merchant train was next halted for clearance at El Paso del Norte, where a customs house was supposedly established in 1835,[47] but the journals of the traders make only slight mention of an inspection or assessment there. After 1842, as a matter of fact, merchants arriving late in the year were granted special favor. A presidential decree gave the town an annual fair, lasting from December 8 to 16, with all the privileges and exemptions enjoyed by the great fair of San Juan de los Lagos in the interior. All goods brought to town within a month before the fair opened were permitted the same exemption from the *alcabala,* or sales tax, and from certain other imposts if kept in the warehouse under the surveillance of the revenue officers.[48] A frequent imposition at El Paso del Norte, however, was the inspection and seizure of horses and mules by the local citizenry. According to Mexican custom, the ownership of such animals was ascertained by the *fierro,* or brand, unless this mark was accompanied by the *venta,* another mark signifying its legal release. Without full knowledge of this custom, American traders frequently purchased horses or mules at Santa Fé, which had been previously stolen from the south by Indians, only to have them legally claimed at El Paso del Norte by citizens carrying the appropriate branding irons. According to Gregg, it was customary for each arriving train to be surrounded by a crowd of villagers who carefully examined every horse and mule and attempted

[46] A sample *guía* form appears in M.N.M., Twitchell Collection, 7757. See also Gregg, *Commerce of the Prairies,* 265–66, 286–87.

[47] Decree of October 23, 1845. Another order to the same purpose on February 17, 1837, suggests that the customs house was not in existence until at least the latter date. *Legislación mexicana,* III, 87, 281.

[48] Decree of August 26, 1842, *ibid.,* IV, 256.

to produce the matching iron. Albert Speyer lost fifteen mules in this manner and James Webb three in 1846.[49]

At the city of Chihuahua, the destination of a large proportion of the merchandise, a full-scale customs service was maintained. Unfortunately, however, the records of this office and also those of the American consulate were subsequently destroyed by fire,[50] and the few reports made by the latter and still extant provide only fragmentary information. As at Santa Fé, the consuls appointed by the United States were not granted *exequaturs* by the Mexican government and were thus in fact merely commercial agents. Furthermore, many who were appointed did not remain long at the post, and their functions were often handled by other resident merchants acting in their behalf.[51]

[49] Gregg, *Commerce of the Prairies*, 132-33, 203; Webb, *Adventures in the Santa Fé Trade*, 191-93.

[50] Consular reports from Chihuahua date from 1825, but the early records of the post were destroyed by fire in 1922, and only six of its communications to Washington exist in the Department of State files for the period prior to 1848. Ralph G. Lounsbury, "Materials in the National Archives for the History of New Mexico Before 1848," *New Mexico Historical Review*, Vol. XXI, No. 3 (July, 1946), 251-52.

[51] Joshua Pilcher, the first appointee, started for Chihuahua in August of 1826, the year after his appointment, but turned back because of illness and subsequently resigned without assuming office; Charles M. Webber, of Tennessee, appointed in 1827, declined to serve; and John Ward, appointed in 1829, was the first to actually fill the post, reaching Chihuahua in the following year. Among other resident merchants who held the position or acted in that capacity were John S. Langham in 1833, Charles W. Davis in 1839, Benjamin Riddells in 1840 and again in 1844, William S. Messervy in 1841, James Wiley Magoffin, off and on for several years, Edward J. Glasgow from 1846 to 1848, and Alfonso C. Anderson for a time during Glasgow's absence. Pilcher to Secretary of State Henry Clay, St. Louis, Mo., August 18, 1826, Webber to Clay, Columbia, Tenn., November 27, 1827, Ward to Secretary of State Martin Van Buren, Chihuahua, November 30, 1830, and George C. Bestor to the Secretary of State, Peoria, Ill., July 30, 1839, U.S.N.A., Cons. Letters, Chihuahua, I; William D. Jones to Davis, Mexico City, February 27, 1839, John Black to Benito Riddells, Mexico City, January 6, 1841, January 20, 1844, and February 28, 1844, and Black to Messervy, Mexico City, October 15, 1841, Letter Book, I, 389-90; III, 18, 211, 230;

The first official complaint against the treatment of American merchants in Chihuahua was filed by John Ward[52] in 1830, but it was vague and general, being accompanied by a more detailed memorial drawn up by the traders themselves (unfortunately now missing from the consular records). Ward reported a "hostile disposition" against Americans stemming from their taking so much money out of the country and the suspected attempt of their government to revolutionize and annex the province of Texas. The resident merchants were much aggrieved by their subjection to forced loans, by the "perfectly arbitrary" proceedings in the local courts, by the prevailing prejudice against the Protestant religion, and by the recent enactment of laws restricting American business.[53] Although Ward did not so specify, the objectionable laws seem to have been those which raised the export tax on gold and silver in 1828 from 2 per cent and 3.5 per cent, respectively, to 7 per cent on each; which enlarged the list of prohibited goods in 1829; which permitted the states in 1829 and 1830 to raise the *derecho de consumo* from 3 per cent to 5 per cent; and which in 1830 required the deportation of foreigners without passports.[54] At least one American resident was already in seri-

---

Magoffin to Jones, Chihuahua, October 17, 1838, January 30 and March 9, 1839, Correspondence, 1829–41; Anderson to Black, Chihuahua, January 19, 1847, Correspondence, 1845–48.

52 John Ward, of Missouri, was probably the "Juan Worde" listed as a trader among thirty-two Americans who arrived at Santa Fé in 1825. On his return from Mexico in 1841, he was reputedly a rich man, practically owning the town of Rocheport, Missouri, but a draft on his St. Louis bank account backfired the same year. He was still in business at Chihuahua in 1847. Estado que manifiesta los estrangeros que han arribado al Territorio de Nuevo México de los Estados Unidos del Norte, Año de 1825, A.S.R.E., L-E-1075, Tomo XXI, 95; David Waldo to Alvarez, Independence, April 20, 1841, M.N.M., Alvarez Papers, 1839–45; Anderson to Black, Chihuahua, January 19, 1847, U.S.N.A., Cons. Gen., Mex., Corresp., 1845–48.

53 Ward to Van Buren, Chihuahua, November 30, U.S.N.A., Cons. Letters, Chihuahua, I.

ous trouble. James Collins[55] was arrested at Chihuahua in 1830 for refusing to pay duties on his goods and for showing disrespect toward the local *alcalde,* and was imprisoned for twelve hours and held under house arrest at his store for thirty days.[56] Such discrimination against American residents should have been prevented by the Treaty of 1831, but in 1839 Charles Davis[57] complained of several new laws oppressive to his countrymen. Among these was a new forced contribution to help finance a current war with France but which largely exempted Mexican merchants. Although assured by the consul general at Mexico City that this was indeed contrary to Article 9 of the recent treaty, Davis was also informed that no official protest could be lodged without more specific complaint and substantiation.[58]

The resident merchants were also much aggrieved by a new law, promulgated September 23, 1843, and made effective

[54] Decrees of July 19, 1828, May 22, 1829, August 22, 1829, and August 24, 1830, *Legislación mexicana,* II, 75, 151, 283; *Niles' Weekly Register,* Vol. XXXVI, 354; Ministro de Gobernación to Gov. Chávez, Mexico City, April 13, 1831, A.S.R.E., L-E-1070, XXII, 190.

[55] James "Squire" Collins, of Missouri, was born about 1801 according to his *carta de seguridad,* was a justice of the peace at Franklin and then a resident of Booneville, a Santa Fé trader in 1827, and a merchant at Chihuahua as early as 1830. He was chief interpreter for Colonel Doniphan in 1847, the principal owner and editor of the Santa Fé *Gazette* in the 1850's, superintendent of Indian affairs for New Mexico from 1857 to 1863, and afterwards in charge of the government depository at Santa Fé. In the latter office he was found shot to death with the vault door open. *Carta de Seguridad,* February 1, 1845, U.S.N.A., Cons. Gen., Mex., Misc. Rec. Books, III, 123; Connelley (ed.), in *Doniphan's Expedition,* 91–92n., 417n.; Bieber (ed.), in Webb, *Adventures in the Santa Fé Trade,* 77n.

[56] Gov. José Ysidro Madero to Ministro de Relaciones, Chihuahua, April 12, 1831, A.S.R.E., Legajo 5–1–7595.

[57] Charles W. Davis had been consul at Guaymas, Parral, and Chihuahua, and was still in Mexico in 1844. Davis to Black, Chihuahua, May 11, 1844, U.S.N.A., Cons. Gen., Mex., Corresp., 1842–44. See also note 58 below.

[58] Davis to Jones, Parral, February 3, 1839, and Jones to Davis, Mexico City, February 27, 1839, U.S.N.A., Cons. Gen. Mex., Corresp., 1829–41, Letter Book I, 389–90.

April 11, 1844, which prohibited foreigners from exercising the retail trade unless they were naturalized citizens, married to Mexicans, or resident in Mexico with their own families. Jesse Sutton[59] and Dr. George East complained that their shop had been ordered closed six days before the law became effective and that, although given an extension of eighteen days, they had considerable difficulty in disposing of their goods. Having a great amount on hand, they tried to sell it by the piece, gross, and dozen, but they were informed that they could sell only by the package. As most of their goods were already unpackaged, they were faced with having to sell the entire stock at one stroke, and this, they complained, would be entirely ruinous.[60] The objectionable restriction seems to have been repealed in the following year, shortly after a revolution overthrew the national administration.

Still another imposition, although quite a legal one, required that each foreign merchant obtain a *carta de seguridad,* or safe-conduct pass, in order to travel or reside within the republic and subjecting him to a fine or imprisonment for being without it. The pass cost the applicant three dollars and was obtained from the central authorities through the consulate at Mexico City, which had to certify his national citizenship. The *carta de seguridad* was valid for only one year and was supposedly nontransferable, for it specified the color of the bearer's eyes, hair, beard, and complexion, the shape of his nose, his height and age, and identifying marks if any ex-

---

59 Jesse B. Sutton was a Santa Fé trader from about 1830 to 1845, a partner of Josiah Gregg from 1831 to at least 1835, a merchant at Chihuahua as early as 1839, and a resident of San Francisco, California, from about 1849 to 1858. Gregg, *Commerce of the Prairies,* 95, 309; Fulton (ed.), in *Diary and Letters of Josiah Gregg,* II, 354n.; Manifiesto No. 43, Aduana de Nuevo México, Santa Fé, August 8, 1830, A.H.H., Legajo 1167-2.

60 Sutton and East to Black, Chihuahua, May 4, 1844, U.S.N.A., Cons. Gen., Mex., Corresp., 1842-44.

isted. There was considerable inconvenience in obtaining this pass, for it was unsafe to send the fee in cash by the regular mails, and few of the merchants at Chihuahua had acquaintances in Mexico City on whom they could draw funds. Furthermore, the consul general could obtain passes only upon proof from the trader that he had arrived in the republic within thirty days of his application or on payment of a $20 fine. One merchant requested, without effect, that arrangements be made allowing the governor to issue the passes directly to the merchants in his state.[61]

With all its requirements of manifests, *guías,* passports, and safe-conduct passes, the Mexican government was still unable to enforce trade regulations at Chihuahua. There is no indication that collusion between customs officers and traders was as disastrous to the revenue system there as it was at Santa Fé, but the *arreglo* seems to have existed nonetheless. When Gregg arrived with a caravan from Santa Fé in October, 1839, he was surprised by the leniency of the collector, especially since he had experienced a more severe test in 1837. The changed situation, he learned, was due to the expected return of the Mexican caravan which had blazed a new trail through Texas and Indian Territory the previous spring. Since a special reduction of duties had already been guaranteed to its proprietors, the usual strict treatment of the Americans would have been too glaring a contrast.[62] A more compromising "arrangement" was made with the officers by Speyer in 1844. Before entering Chihuahua with a legitimate cargo, he had hidden four wagon-

61 In 1844 the pass cost four dollars, half of which was for the consular fee. A form for the *carta de seguridad* appears in U.S.N.A., Cons. Gen., Mex., Misc. Rec. Books, I, 248. See also Black to Robert L. Reid, Mexico City, April 24, 1841, Black to East, Mexico City, October 21, 1843, Black to Riddells, Mexico City, January 20, 1844, and Black to Charles Bent, Mexico City, April 10, 1844, Letter Books, III, 34–35, 193–94, 211, 248–49; and John McKnight to Black, Chihuahua, October 18, 1841, Corresp., 1829–41.

62 Gregg, *Commerce of the Prairies,* 277.

loads of contraband goods near the Rancho de Sacramento, and afterwards, through the good offices of Benjamin Riddells, the American consul, managed to induce the customs house guard to pass the prohibited cargo. For this special consideration Speyer paid one hundred dollars to the officer and one dollar, a pair of shoes, and a bottle of whiskey to each of the ten soldiers.[63]

Almost every American trader who brought his own goods to Chihuahua after the spring of 1842 did so in violation of a federal law which seems never to have been enforced in the north. American wagons, carrying heavier loads and having much narrower tires than those of Mexican manufacture, had apparently been damaging the surface of the national highways. At any rate a presidential decree which became effective in May, 1842, prohibited all wagons carrying loads of more than two hundred *arrobas* (about five thousand pounds) or having tires less than eight inches in width from traveling the public roads.[64]

Curiously enough, the protests which followed this announcement came not from the American merchants but from the authorities of Chihuahua. The governor, legislative assembly, council of state, and chamber of commerce all demanded special consideration for the merchants of Chihuahua. According to their argument, the narrower tires of American wagons did little if any damage to the roads of northern Mexico, and for that matter these were natural roads, not maintained at public expense. Furthermore, ever since 1832, when the Apaches launched their current war against the inhabitants of Chihuahua, transportation had become utterly dependent upon American wagons. Caravans of wagons could better protect themselves against Indian attack than could mule trains; and

[63] Hobbs, *Wild Life in the Far West,* 77.
[64] Decree of January 15, 1842, *Legislación mexicana,* IV, 97.

wagons of Mexican manufacture, which met the new specifications, were rare in Chihuahua, as were also wagon makers and iron for their construction. For this reason most of the merchants had purchased American wagons, and there were now more than one hundred of them operating in Chihuahua. Finally, since the Comanches as well as the Apaches were now on the warpath, the protection offered by American wagons was considered all the more vital.[65] In response to these arguments the central government granted the Mexican merchants in Chihuahua a year of grace, dating from May, 1843, and in a few individual cases special exemption from the ruling for the next three years.[66] But there is no record of any American's being either exempted or prosecuted under the new regulation, even though all continued to use their oversize wagons with narrow tires. The authorities of Chihuahua apparently made no effort at all to enforce the federal policy.

The Apache war about which the authorities complained in 1842 raged unabated for several years, and the roads of northern Mexico were plagued by the murdering and plundering of the enemy. Mexican merchants came to rely not only on the readily fortified wagons but also, whenever possible, on the company of American caravans. Military escorts were simply not available for all of their trains, for these came and went at all seasons and traveled not only the Camino Real but also the lesser roads of the country. For many years, therefore, the government of Chihuahua tried to solve the problem by less

[65] Pedro Olivares and Francisco Holguín, Memorial to Pres. Santa Anna, Chihuahua, September 24, 1842; Gov. Mariano Martínez to Ministro de Relaciones, Chihuahua, September 28, 1842; Gov. José Mariano Monterde to same, Chihuahua, May 19, 1843; Luís Zuloaga to same, Chihuahua, May 24, 1843; José Cordero and Francisco Márquez, Memorial to Pres. Santa Anna, Chihuahua, May 25, 1846, A.G.N., Fomento-Caminos, Tomo XIII, Expediente 283.

[66] Ministro de Gobernación to Gov. Monterde, Mexico City, May 30, 1843, and various permits granted to Manuel Aguilar, Francisco Gutiérrez, and others from 1843 to 1847, A.G.N., Fomento-Caminos, XIII, Exped. 283.

[147]

formal means—a methodical extermination of the Apache people—and, although many Americans criticized this barbarous reprisal, many also aided and abetted it. In 1839 or 1840, the governor, promising a stipulated sum for each Apache scalp taken, engaged the services of about one hundred American teamsters and hunters who happened to be in the state, including a number of Shawnee and Delaware Indians. Led by a notorious borderland adventurer named James Kirker,[67] this party attacked an Apache encampment early in February, 1840, and brought in fifteen scalps and twenty prisoners. Except for the news that they were about to embark on another such raid, nothing more of the gory business appears in the consular reports,[68] but some details are furnished by other accounts.

Traveling under heavy guard with other captives from the Texan Santa Fé Expedition, George Kendall met one of the scalp hunters near the Presidio of Carrizal in November of 1841. This was Charley Tirrell, a half-blood Delaware, who was returning from still another raid near by. Tirrell informed

[67] James Kirker was born in Belfast, Ireland, in 1793, came to the United States in 1810, and engaged in the fur trade out of St. Louis. Reaching Santa Fé in 1825, he worked the Santa Rita copper mine in northern Chihuahua with Nathaniel Pryor sometime before 1827, led a band of Shawnees which became involved with William Dryden in an alleged attempt to assassinate Governor Armijo in 1839, and then fled to Chihuahua. According to one report, he became chieftain of an Apache band which stole mules in Chihuahua and sold them in New Mexico, had a price on his head of $9,000, but finally made peace with the governor of Chihuahua. He led a party of American Apache-scalp hunters which collected a huge bounty in Chihuahua from 1839 to 1841, and again after a retirement in Correlitos, Sonora, from 1845 to 1846, served as a scout for Colonel Doniphan from 1846 to 1848, led a party of goldseekers to California in 1849, and died there at a cabin near Mount Diablo in 1852 or 1853. List of Americans in Santa Fé in 1825 (copy), M.N.M., Read Collection, Folder A; J. J. Warner, "Reminiscences of Early California" (MS), The Bancroft Library; Hobbs, *Wild Life in the Far West*, 81–82; Bancroft, *History of New Mexico and Arizona*, 321–22; Hafen (ed.), in *Ruxton of the Rockies*, 148n.

[68] Davis to Black, Parral, February 17, 1840, U.S.N.A., Cons. Gen., Mex., Corresp., 1829–41.

Kendall that earlier forays had been successful, but that Kirker had been accused of collecting the bounty on Mexican as well as Apache scalps. Thereupon the governor had modified the arrangement so as to provide a regular wage of one dollar a day for the hunters instead of a reward for each scalp, and so Kirker had gone into retirement. He was then thought to have been hiding out in Sonora and aiding the Apaches against the Mexicans, but all attempts to arrest him had failed. About twelve Shawnees and Delawares had remained in the governor's service, but their leader, a famous scout named Shawnee Spybuck, had been killed in the encounter with the Apaches just concluded near Carrizal.[69] A much more detailed and fascinating description of these lurid activities is provided by an American teamster, James Hobbs,[70] who supposedly took part in these forays, but his information is so garbled chronologically as to be largely unreliable.[71]

[69] Kendall, *Narrative of the Texan Santa Fé Expedition*, II, 56–59.

[70] James Hobbs, according to his own memoirs, was born in the Shawnee Nation in 1819, joined Charles Bent's trappers in 1835, and was captured and held by the Comanches from 1835 to 1839. He accompanied Albert Speyer as a teamster from Santa Fé to Chihuahua and San Juan de los Lagos in 1840 or 1841, and was associated with Kirker's scalp hunters in 1841, then became a freighter for a British firm at Zacatecas. He remained in the interior trade of Mexico until 1847, served Colonel Doniphan as a dispatch carrier in 1847, went to California, and later became involved in the French occupation at Mexico City. Hobbs, *Wild Life in the Far West*.

[71] Confusing the separate campaigns against the Apaches of 1839–40 and 1845–46, Hobbs states that he, Shawnee Spybuck, and other Shawnees and Delawares joined Albert Speyer after the loss of his mules in the snowstorm at Willow Bar (which was in 1844, three years after Spybuck's death!) and accompanied him to Chihuahua as hunters and scouts. While Speyer was storekeeping in Chihuahua, Hobbs, the hunters, and a number of other Americans in the city, making a party of about 170, joined Kirker in a contract with Governor Angel Trías (who did not take office until 1845) wherein they were allowed all stolen horses and mules they could recover from the Apaches and also $50 for each scalp. They also made an arrangement with a wealthy merchant named Pores (presumably J. Calistro Porras), who had just lost all of his mules and merchandise and all but one of his men to the Apaches, allowing them half of the animals and merchandise they could recover.

Overtaking the culprits near the headwaters of the Yaqui River, they am-

Whatever success the scalp hunters had in reducing the strength of the Apaches in 1840 and 1841, they were as great a menace as ever in 1845, and by 1846 they were overrunning the entire states of Chihuahua and Durango, killing and plundering not only on the roads but even in the towns. In this desperate situation the governor of Chihuahua called Kirker and his followers out of retirement. About 150 men were now recruited, a bounty of fifty dollars a scalp was now offered, and funds for its payment were raised by private subscription rather than government appropriation as in the past. In July and August of 1846, Kirker's hunters, aided by the Mexican citizenry and under cover of an official truce, massacred at least three bands of Apaches: 130 at La Muralla, 18 at San Buenaventura, and 170 at Galeana. Neither women nor children were spared, and their scalps hanging from poles were marched into the city of Chihuahua to the accompaniment of martial music in a procession led by the governor and the

---

bushed them and returned with a booty consisting of 182 scalps (including that of their own Mexican guide), nineteen Apache women, a number of captive Mexican women and children, 300 head of stolen sheep and goats, a large number of horses, and most of Porras' mules and merchandise, notably excepting a quantity of liquor which they consumed on the way back. Their own losses were only three men, two Shawnees, and their Mexican guide. The returning heroes were met outside of Chihuahua by the Governor and his wife, a band of musicians, and hundreds of the townspeople, who escorted them into the city; the Governor held a ball in their honor, Stevenson and Riddells gave a dinner at their hotel, Speyer providing the dress suits, and the local *cantinas* allowed the Shawnees and Delawares to get uproariously drunk.

However, the state treasury was able to pay for only 40 of the 182 scalps taken, not to mention those of the 19 women which were still intact, and the Governor's pledge of the tobacco-monopoly revenue to cover the remainder did not satisfy the hunters. Furthermore, several Mexican citizens tried to repossess the recovered horses and mules which bore their brands, and so Hobbs and his Indian comrades left for Santa Fé and Bent's Fort. Kirker remained, but when Hobbs later returned to Chihuahua, he found that scalp hunting was not paying the Irishman enough to live on, and the Americans there were so annoyed with the Governor for welshing on his payments that, although Apache depredations now extended into the city itself, they refused to serve further. *Ibid.*, 59–60, 66, 82–112.

priests. An English traveler who learned of the Galeana massacre from an eyewitness saw the grim evidence himself, 170 gory tresses dangling from the *portales* opposite the main entrance to the city's cathedral.[72]

By this time, according to an American soldier, Kirker and his comrades had run up a bill for $30,000, and the governor had not only repudiated the debt but even threatened to throw the hunters in prison. Most of the Shawnees and Delawares had returned to the United States, but some remained with Kirker, who again retired to Sonora. On learning of the war between the United States and Mexico, Kirker joined Colonel Doniphan's column on its march down the Río Grande from Santa Fé in December of the same year.[73]

[72]Ruxton, *Adventures in Mexico and the Rocky Mountains*, 151, 153–54; *El Sonorense*, June 24, 1846, quoted in "Documents for the History of Chihuahua," II, 35 (MS), The Bancroft Library.
[73]F. S. Edwards, *A Campaign in New Mexico*, 62; Meredith T. Moore to Connelley (ed.), in *Doniphan's Expedition*, 388n.

7.

Profit and Loss in Wartime

THE MOUNTING American claims against Mexico arising out
of maritime and overland commerce, the inability and unwill-
ingness of Mexico to give satisfaction, and especially the ex-
pansionist designs of the United States on Mexican territory
made war between the two countries inevitable. When the
United States formally annexed Texas in 1845 and recognized
its claim of territory west and south to the Río Grande, only
a border incident was required to produce open hostilities, and
this occurred in the spring of 1846. The land between the
Nueces and the Río Grande was occupied almost simultaneous-
ly by American and Mexican troops, and the blood of both
was soon shed on the disputed soil. As of May 13, 1846, by
proclamation of President James K. Polk, a state of war existed.

By the time this momentous news reached Independence,
Missouri, most of the overland merchants had completed their
spring purchases and were already making up their trains.

They could ill afford to abandon their enterprise at this late date, and fortunately for them the military policy of their government did not require it. Instead of placing an embargo on the caravan trade, the government mobilized an army to protect it, to occupy New Mexico, and thereby to eliminate the tariff charges at Santa Fé. The Army of the West, as it was called, consisted of 1,700 men—mainly volunteers and largely mounted—under the command of Colonel Stephen W. Kearny, who was shortly promoted to the rank of general.[1]

As Kearny's forces did not leave Fort Leavenworth until June, they were unable to escort the first merchants who crossed the plains that season, and the haste with which some of these traveled suggests that they were much more interested in early profits than in military protection. Among those who left in advance of the army were James J. Webb and his partner, George P. Doan.[2] Their five wagons, accompanied by three more under William S. McKnight and an undisclosed number under Norris Colburn, James B. Turley, Juan Armijo, and some others, left Independence on May 9. Governor Manuel Armijo's train, which carried arms and ammunition as well as merchandise, left some days earlier. Also in advance of the army were the wagons of George Peacock, Benjamin Pruett, Charles Blummer, others by the name of Rallston, Aubry, Hill, Mayer, and Wieck, and, most important of all to the Army of the West, the Prussian merchant, Albert Speyer.[3]

During the preceding season Speyer had taken an order for arms from the governor of Chihuahua as well as one for mer-

1 Ralph P. Bieber (ed.), in *Marching with the Army of the West: The Journals of Abraham R. Johnston, 1846; Marcellus Ball Edwards, 1846–47; and Philip Gooch Ferguson, 1847–48*, 23–26.

2 George P. Doan was born in the British West Indies, resided at St. Louis, where his father owned a wholesale dry goods store, and was a partner of James J. Webb from 1845 to 1848. Bieber (ed.), in Webb, *Adventures in the Santa Fé Trade*, 116n.

3 *Ibid.*, 179, 183; Bieber (ed.), in Gibson, *Journey of a Soldier*, 41n.

[153]

chandise from Armijo, and his train of about twenty-five wagons which left Independence shortly after the declaration of war carried not only goods valued at about $70,000 but also two wagonloads of Mississippi Jägers with ammunition to fit.[4] About three weeks after Speyer's departure, Colonel Kearny sent two companies of dragoons to intercept him, but the contraband train had a sufficient head start to outrun its pursuers. Speyer's haste to reach Santa Fé ahead of the Army of the West was inspired not only by the questionable nature of his cargo, but also by his desire to reach the richer markets of the interior, which an American occupation of New Mexico would likely prevent. He further realized that a very large caravan of traders would arrive in one body behind the American army and flood the New Mexican market before he could dispose of his own goods at favorable prices. Reaching Santa Fé about the end of June, Speyer paid approximately $7,500 in duties, bought out a large portion of the consignment he carried for Armijo, and obtained a *guía* for the southern markets. He had assumed quite correctly that the United States would blockade the maritime ports of Mexico and keep the majority of the overland traders behind Kearny's forces, all of which would cause a shortage of foreign goods in the interior and higher prices for his own wares.[5]

Notwithstanding the state of war and the impending invasion of New Mexico, Governor Armijo pursued an obliging policy, admitting not only the merchandise of neutrals such as Speyer but also those of Americans who arrived in advance of the Army of the West. Webb and Doan, who reached Santa

[4] Webb, *Adventures in the Santa Fé Trade*, 180–81, 186, 206–207; Wislizenus, *Memoir of a Tour to Northern Mexico*, 5; Bieber (ed.), in Gibson, *Journey of a Soldier*, 41n.; Drumm (ed.), in Susan Magoffin, *Down the Santa Fé Trail*, 97n.

[5] Webb, *Adventures in the Santa Fé Trade*, 180–81, 186; Col. Stephen W. Kearny to Capt. Benjamin Moore, June 5, 1846, in Bieber (ed.), *Marching with the Army of the West*, 114n.; Marcellus B. Edwards, journal, in *ibid.*, 112.

Fé half a day behind Speyer, also carried goods for the interior markets and expected some security of travel from Doan's British passport. However, Doan suffered an injury which forced him to remain behind, and Webb, being an enemy alien, had to place their goods in Speyer's custody and travel as a common teamster under his protection. Speyer carried both Prussian and British passports.[6]

After about a week of preparations in Santa Fé, Speyer's train left for the south on July 5, accompanied by the wagons of Webb and Doan. While traveling down the Río Grande, their progress was slowed by heavy rains; while they were encamped on the Jornada del Muerto, a keg of gunpowder exploded and destroyed one of their wagons; and at El Paso del Norte they were relieved of several of their mules by due process of the *fierro* law. Otherwise they met with little unexpected inconvenience until they reached the valley of Encinillas.[7] There on about August 26 they were overtaken by Armijo and his military escort and informed that Kearny's forces had captured Santa Fé. While Speyer's American teamsters were still rejoicing over this news and also marveling at the speed of Armijo's travel (about 550 miles in nine days), they were arrested and disarmed at the Hacienda del Peñol by two companies of Mexican infantry. For a time Webb considered rearming the teamsters from the two wagons loaded with muskets; but after conferring with the Mexican officers, Speyer decided to acquiesce, and the next day they were escorted along with Armijo's party to the city of Chihuahua. The two wagons with arms which Speyer had purchased for the governor of Chihuahua were confiscated, but none of the men were permitted to enter the city for fifteen days, except Speyer, his Spanish clerk Lorenzo Oliver, and other non-Americans. When

6 Webb, *Adventures in the Santa Fé Trade*, 181, 186–87.
7 *Ibid.*, 188–98; Wislizenus, *Memoir of a Tour to Northern Mexico*, 34–46.

the teamsters were finally brought into the city, they were detained with the wagons at the Plaza de Toros for another fifteen days. Speyer was permitted to file a claim for payment for the confiscated arms and was also allowed to open a retail store and sell his other merchandise, but Webb and the other Americans were interned as enemy aliens throughout the month of September.[8]

Meanwhile, more than three hundred American wagons with an aggregate cargo worth over one million dollars were being held up at three points along the Santa Fé Trail—at Pawnee Fork, at the Arkansas crossing, and at Bent's Fort—and forced to fall in behind Kearny's Army of the West. Among the more important merchants with this caravan was Samuel Magoffin.[9] Accompanying his train of fourteen wagons was his bride, Susan Shelby Magoffin, whose diary adds a charming touch to the records of both the military and the commercial invasion. Samuel's brother, James Wiley Magoffin, was traveling well ahead of his own train, which was now under the supervision of his brother-in-law, Gabriel Valdés, and another brother, William Magoffin. In the same company were the wagons of Samuel Owens and his partner, James Aull, both of whom were to meet unexpected death in Chihuahua. On the road ahead were those of other prominent merchants: Edward J. Glasgow, whose partner, Dr. Henry Connelly, would be up from Chihuahua to meet him at Santa Fé; Solomon Houck,[10] who had just made a quick purchase of goods

8 Webb, *Adventures in the Santa Fé Trade,* 201–10.

9 Samuel Magoffin, of Kentucky, was born in 1801, entered the overland trade from Missouri with his elder and more illustrious brother at least as early as 1830, and remained in the business until 1847. In Mexico he was known as "Don Manuel." After returning to Missouri from Chihuahua in 1847, he purchased a large estate near Lexington, Kentucky, entered the real estate business there after 1852, served in the Confederate Army during the Civil War, and died in 1888. Drumm (ed.), in Susan Magoffin, *Down the Santa Fé Trail,* xx–xxi.

10 Solomon Houck was born about 1803 according to his *carta de seguridad,*

in June after a trip from Santa Fé to Independence of only twenty-one days; Francis McManus;[11] a number of Mexican merchants; and Manuel X. Harmony, a naturalized American citizen from Spain representing the New York importing firm of P. Harmony, Nephews and Company and conducting over $38,000 worth of goods in twelve wagons. Harmony's subsequent claims against the United States government for property seized by the army en route to Chihuahua sheds much light on the experiences of the entire caravan.[12]

Throughout the month of July one wagon train after another pulled into Bent's Fort on the upper Arkansas, and it was not until the beginning of August that any of them were permitted to leave for Santa Fé. Even the Army of the West remained at the fort until then, awaiting a report from the Magoffin mission.

James Wiley Magoffin arrived at Bent's Fort on July 26, five days ahead of his own wagons, but his business was more official than commercial. From Chihuahua he had returned to Independence on May 21 with a season's profit of $40,000, and there he had found an urgent request awaiting him. Senator Benton wanted him to come to Washington at once. On

entered the inland trade with Mexico in the 1820's, was at Chihuahua as early as 1841, became a naturalized Mexican citizen sometime before 1846. He had made sixteen trips across the plains by 1849 and was still in the Mexican trade in 1852. William G. Dryden, Solomon Houck, and B. F. Broaddus to the Consul General, Chihuahua, September 12, 1841, U.S.N.A., Cons. Gen., Mex., Corresp., 1829–41; Houck to Alvarez, Valverde, November 30, 1846, M.N.M., Alvarez Papers, 1846; Hobbs, *Wild Life in the Far West*, 118; Bieber (ed.), in Webb, *Adventures in the Santa Fé Trade*, 129n.

11 Francis McManus was born about 1816 according to his *carta de seguridad* and was a Chihuahua trader from at least 1842 to 1847. *Carta de Seguridad*, February 18, 1842, U.S.N.A., Cons. Gen., Mex., Misc. Rec. Books, II, 72; Webb, *Adventures in the Santa Fé Trade*, 277.

12 30 Cong., 1 sess., *House Report No. 458;* Susan Magoffin, *Down the Santa Fé Trail*, 2–4, 24–25, 50, 72, 78–84. Dr. David Waldo, a veteran Santa Fé trader, also accompanied the caravan but not as a merchant, having joined the Missouri Volunteers in Kearny's army. Drumm (ed.), in *ibid.*, 82n.

reaching that city, he was presented by Benton to President Polk, and for an hour on June 15 they discussed the prospects of a successful invasion of Mexico's northern provinces. Two days later Magoffin met with the President again, this time in the presence of Secretary of War William L. Marcy, and both agreed that Magoffin's experience and connections could be of real value to the army—not only in obtaining supplies but also in aligning the Mexican people with the United States.[13] Accordingly, Magoffin was commissioned as a colonel of cavalry, provided with letters of recommendation, and sent to Bent's Fort for assignment. The letters, one to Colonel Kearny and another to General John Wool, who was to march on Chihuahua from Texas, both indicated that the President was impressed with Magoffin's character, intelligence, and patriotism, and that owing to his knowledge of northern Mexico, he might render "important services" to the military operations.[14]

At Bent's Fort on August 2, Colonel Kearny sent Magoffin and Captain Philip St. George Cooke with an escort of twelve dragoons and under a flag of truce to confer with Governor Armijo at Santa Fé. Accompanying them for some reason, perhaps as Cooke's interpreter, was José González, a busines associate of Magoffin. Captain Cooke bore a letter from Kearny stating that the American intention was to take possession of that part of New Mexico lying east of the Río Grande, which the United States claimed as belonging to the recently annexed state of Texas; that his own disposition was friendly towards all in New Mexico who would accept the occupation peacefully; that the inhabitants would be guaranteed against moles-

[13] *The Diary of James K. Polk,* ed. by Milo Milton Quaife, I, 472, 474-75; Drumm (ed.), in Susan Magoffin, *Down the Santa Fe Trail,* xviii.

[14] William L. Marcy to Col. Kearny and to Gen. John Wool, Washington, June 18, 1846, *The Magoffin Papers* [*Publications of the Historical Society of New Mexico,* No. 24], 42-43.

tation of their persons, property, and religion; but that Kearny had forces available to overcome any resistance which Armijo might mount; and that any bloodshed resulting would be the Governor's own responsibility.[15] After a ten-day trip, during which Magoffin's seemingly inexhaustible supply of Irish wit and red claret kept the entire party in high spirits, the truce team arrived at Santa Fé on August 12. So as not to betray his own official capacity, Magoffin remained aloof from the preliminary discussions, and Kearny's terms were presented to the Governor by Captain Cooke. That night, however, Magoffin joined the Captain, and in a secret conference with the Governor seemingly convinced him that armed resistance to the American occupation would be both unwise and futile. González played no part in the negotiations, but remained intoxicated during the entire proceedings.[16]

During the next few days Magoffin held extensive conversations with several other military and civilian dignitaries, assuring them also of Kearny's peaceful intentions and the folly of resistance. He had learned from Dr. Connelly, recently arrived from Chihuahua, that the Lieutenant Governor had already made public his intention to fight. Colonel Diego Archuleta was also Armijo's second in military command and supposedly had one thousand of the best troops in New Mexico under his own control. If he should carry out his threat, Armijo would be compelled to follow suit. Magoffin therefore employed special persuasion to conciliate the young Colonel, informing him that the United States claimed only the territory to the Río Grande and that should he acquiesce in its

15 Kearny to Armijo, Bent's Fort, August 1, 1846, (certified Spanish copy), A.S.R.E., L-E-1085, Tomo XXXI, 175.

16 Magoffin to Marcy, Santa Fé, August 26, 1846, and Capt. Philip St. George Cooke to Magoffin, Philadelphia, February 21, 1849, *Magoffin Papers*, 43–44, 60–62; Cooke, *The Conquest of New Mexico and California*, 6–31.

occupation by the Americans, he might well seize the western part of the territory for himself.[17] This had the desired effect.

For the sake of appearance at least, Armijo displayed a strong inclination to defend New Mexico. He sent his official reply to Kearny's headquarters with Captain Cooke and his escort, who left Santa Fé on August 13, accompanied by Dr. Connelly. In his reply Armijo denied the legality of the American claim to New Mexico, asserted that he had more than enough forces for a successful resistance, that the people were behind him, and that it was his duty to lead them. He did, however, offer to confer with Kearny at Las Vegas and arrive at a reasonable settlement, provided that the American forces did not advance.[18]

After accompanying this reply to Kearny, Dr. Connelly returned to Santa Fé with a report on the numbers and equipment of the American army that unnerved many of the New Mexican officials.[19] Meanwhile, on August 14, Armijo began mobilizing his forces at Apache Pass, a canyon of the Pecos through which the road passed about thirteen miles from Santa Fé. By August 16 his force there was at full strength, and he was further supported by a large body of civilian dignitaries. A council of war was held, and all who spoke except Armijo himself exhibited an eagerness to fight. Armijo, however, professed a lack of confidence in the inexperienced volunteers and, after sending them home, ordered the artillery and his own elite dragoons into full retreat.[20] With the latter he passed

17 Magoffin to Marcy, Santa Fé, August 26, 1846; Henry Connelly, notarized deposition, Chihuahua, September 20, 1848; Cooke to Magoffin, Philadelphia, February 21, 1849; and Magoffin to George W. Crawford, Washington, April 4, 1849, *Magoffin Papers*, 43–44, 46–47, 59–60, 60–62; Thomas Hart Benton, *Thirty Years' View*, II, 683.

18 Armijo to Kearny, Santa Fé, August 12, 1846, (certified Spanish copy), A.S.R.E., L-E-1085, XXXI, 176–77.

19 Connelley (ed.), in *Doniphan's Expedition*, 281n.; Drumm (ed.), in Susan Magoffin, *Down the Santa Fé Trail*, 105n.

through Santa Fé and on toward Chihuahua in forced marches in order, as he later asserted, to join reinforcements which he had requested from Chihuahua and Durango.[21] Within forty-eight hours after the retreat from Apache Pass, all of the New Mexican troops were in their homes, and Kearny's Army of the West entered Santa Fé unopposed on August 18.[22]

Whether the "bloodless conquest" of Santa Fé was due principally to Magoffin's machinations or to other causes has long been questioned by historians. The evidence weighs heavily in favor of the veteran merchant, but is by no means conclusive. The one document which, according to Magoffin himself, would have established the efficacy of his influence beyond all doubt was captured by the Mexicans, and thus when he subsequently presented evidence in support of his claim for remuneration, it did not enter the records.[23]

Kearny's occupation of Santa Fé wrought great changes. All of New Mexico—not just that part claimed by Texas—was

20 Report of the citizens of New Mexico to the President of Mexico, Santa Fé, September 26, 1846, A.S.R.E., L-E-1088, XXXIV, 270–82.

21 Armijo's version was that the volunteers expressed an indisposition to fight, that all retreated from the pass except himself and two hundred regulars, and that several of the regulars deserted the next day, August 17, leaving him with only seventy dragoons and the artillery, an insufficient force with which to make a stand. Armijo to the Ministro de Relaciones, Chihuahua, September 8, 1846, A.S.R.E., L-E-1085, XXXI, 171–79.

22 Magoffin to Marcy, Santa Fé, August 26, 1846, *Magoffin Papers*, 43–44.

23 Magoffin's influence over Armijo and especially over Archuleta is asserted in his itemized statement of services rendered the United States from June 18, 1846, to February, 1849, and the supporting documents, in *ibid.*, 43–50, 59–62. Senator Benton, relying on these depositions and on personal conversations with Magoffin also pleads his case, but his own antipathy toward Kearny probably prejudiced him unduly. Benton, *Thirty Years' View*, II, 683. On the other hand, Magoffin's influence in effecting the "bloodless conquest" is not even mentioned in Kearny's letter to Armijo of August 1, 1846, in Armijo's reply of August 12, in the report of the citizens of New Mexico to the President of Mexico, September 26, or in Armijo's report to the Ministro de Relaciones, September 8 (all previously cited). Nor does the American consul mention Magoffin in his official report on the occupation. Alvarez to Buchanan, Santa Fé, September 4, 1846, U.S.N.A., Cons. Desp., Santa Fé, I.

declared to be United States territory. Santa Fé, moreover, now teemed with American troops, both regulars and undisciplined volunteers, and shortly afterwards with more American merchants than it had ever known. Their huge caravans, strung out for miles along the road over Raton Pass, filtered into the city in gradual stages. Samuel Magoffin's train arrived on August 30, twelve days behind the troops, and his brother's wagons entered on September 26, almost four weeks later.[24] Meanwhile, on or about September 2, James Magoffin had left for the south to smooth the way for General Wool's invasion of Chihuahua from the east.[25]

For some distance down the Río Grande, Magoffin was accompanied by Kearny, now a general, who was making a tour of the principal towns, but beyond Tomé his party included only himself and his friend González in a carriage and about six other Mexicans on horseback whom he had hired as an escort. Beyond the Jornada del Muerto, somewhere below the new settlement of Doña Ana, they were attacked by Apaches. Magoffin, González, and perhaps others survived, but their carriage, mules, and baggage were carried off. Then, when they finally reached El Paso del Norte, they were arrested and imprisoned on suspicion of espionage. From two Mexican merchants, Antonio Jáquez and Jesús Palacios, recently returned from Santa Fé, the authorities had learned that Magoffin was the chief cause of the collapse of New Mexico's defense.[26] For

24 Susan Magoffin, *Down the Santa Fé Trail*, 71–102, 146.

25 *Ibid.*, 107–108.

26 *Ibid.*, 107–108, 151–52, 169; Connelley, notarized deposition, Chihuahua, September 20, 1848, *Magoffin Papers*, 59–60; M. B. Edwards, journal, in Bieber (ed.), *Marching with the Army of the West*, 219. Susan Magoffin was informed that President Polk's letter (actually Secretary Marcy's) recommending Magoffin to General Wool was found on his person and was being used as evidence against him, which may have been true, but Edwards' information that Kearny's letter to Wool had been taken by the Apaches and turned over to the Mexican authorities is much less likely.

the moment the evidence against him was inconclusive, but more was in the making.

Sometime before September 25, when General Kearny left for California, he gave the merchants at Santa Fé permission to proceed southward to the interior markets of Mexico, under military protection as far as the southernmost settlements but at their own risk thereafter.[27] The Army of the West, counting on selling treasury drafts to the traders for hard money, had not brought sufficient specie for paying the troops, but the merchants were also short of silver, for they could obtain little from New Mexican customers, and they accepted the army script only at reduced value. This situation, which was later to become more aggravated, probably accounted for Kearny's leniency in allowing the merchants to seek the more lucrative markets in the south.[28]

Also, before his departure, Kearny wrote a letter to the Secretary of War for Magoffin, recounting his services in the capture of New Mexico for future presentation in support of his claim for remuneration—or so Magoffin subsequently asserted. This letter was supposedly entrusted to his brother Samuel, who in turn sent it with Dr. Connelly for delivery to Magoffin at Chihuahua. Dr. Connelly was among the first merchants who started down the Camino Real, and early in October he, Francis McManus, and George P. Doan went on ahead of the others to ascertain at Chihuahua how they would

[27] Petition of the merchants to Col. Alexander Doniphan, Valverde, December 9, 1846, 30 Cong., 1 sess., *House Report No. 458*, p. 46.

[28] Doniphan later reported that money in New Mexico was confined to "a few American traders—who I regret to say are generally American only in name. They are Mexicans in feeling, & Jews in principle—and the few drafts that were attempted to be cashed for the Qr. Mrs. Department, they were the first to depreciate; & although they are making some remittances, they ask from 10 to 25 per cent to make an exchange alike accommodating to them & us." Doniphan to Marcy, Santa Fé, October 20, 1846, quoted by Bieber (ed.), in Gibson, *Journey of a Soldier,* 250n.

be received. On reaching El Paso del Norte, however, Connelly, McManus, and Doan were arrested. They were searched, imprisoned, and later—along with Magoffin and González, who had been previously captured there—removed to Chihuahua and confined in that city. Among the papers seized by the Mexican authorities was General Kearny's alleged report on Magoffin's secret services which Connelly carried,[29] and as the penalty for espionage in wartime was death, the doom of Magoffin seemed now to have been sealed.

Meanwhile, the main caravan of merchants remained behind in rendezvous among the cottonwoods near the ruins of Valverde, about 150 miles south of Santa Fé, where they were isolated from their markets and exposed to enemy attack. Not only had their envoys to Chihuahua been captured and interned, but the new commander of the troops, Colonel Alexander W. Doniphan, whom Kearny had left to push on toward Chihuahua with the Missouri Volunteers, was too busy with the Navajos to offer them adequate protection. When troops finally did arrive, their needs caused such a drain on the resources of the camp that the subsistence of the merchants and teamsters themselves was in peril. Not knowing when, if ever, they could proceed to Chihuahua, the traders dug in at Valverde for the winter, erecting for their shelter tents, log shanties, and thatched huts. The wagons were drawn up into corrals and sunk to their hubs for protection against enemy attack, and the stock was driven into the enclosure each night. There were from three to four hundred traders, teamsters, and other hired hands in the rendezvous, the advance guard of Colonel

29 Samuel C. Owens to his wife, Valverde, October 20, 1846, quoted in *ibid.*, 263n.; Magoffin to Crawford, Washington, April 4, 1849; Magoffin, itemized statement, 1849; and Connelly, notarized deposition, Chihuahua, September 20, 1848, *Magoffin Papers*, 46–47, 50, 59–60; Susan Magoffin, *Down the Santa Fé Trail*, 169.

Doniphan's column forming a separate camp three or four miles upstream on the west side of the river. The unexpected expenses of the merchants in standing by threatened to consume all of their prospective profits before the end of October, and by the middle of November some had consumed all of their provisions.[30]

Rumor from the south on November 17 informed the traders that calico goods were selling in Chihuahua at 37½ cents per *vara,* which was a third more than they had anticipated and 27½ cents more than the original cost; and that finer cloth, costing about 25 cents a *vara,* was selling in Chihuahua at two dollars. As each wagon contained from $2,000 to $3,000 worth of goods, the merchants were extremely eager to reach that market. The rumor also indicated that all of the traders at Chihuahua except Magoffin and González were being allowed perfect liberty.[31] Five days later, the English traveler George Ruxton arrived from the south with further news. Albert Speyer had been permitted to proceed from Chihuahua to the more interior cities, but his American teamsters had been arrested, and twenty-one of them who had escaped while being conducted to Durango had become lost in the desert, where some died of fatigue and thirst. A circular addressed by Governor Trías to the customs officers of the state with verbal amplification declared that if the traders in New Mexico would dismiss their American teamsters, replace them with Mexicans, and pay the *derecho de consumo* at El Paso del Norte together with the same *derecho de arancel* that had been charged at Santa Fé the preceding year, they would be per-

---

[30] Abert, "Report," 30 Cong., 1 sess., *House Exec. Doc. No. 31,* pp. 499–502; John Taylor Hughes, diary, in Connelley (ed.), *Doniphan's Expedition,* 82; Owens to his wife, Valverde, October 20, 1846, quoted by Bieber (ed.), in Gibson, *Journey of a Soldier,* 263n.

[31] Abert, "Report," 30 Cong., 1 sess., *House Exec. Doc. No. 31,* pp. 499–500·

mitted to enter the city of Chihuahua and sell their goods free of further molestation.[32]

The reaction to this offer was varied. Several merchants looked upon the specifications as a ruse which would enable Governor Trías to confiscate their goods. Others, including some who had as much as $150,000 tied up in merchandise, were willing to risk the Governor's good faith in spite of his well-known anti-American prejudices, and the foreign merchants—Spanish, Mexican, and English—were most eager to take advantage of his offer. With its inventory of forty-five wagonloads the English company of Kerford and Jenkins decided to dismiss its American teamsters and proceed with Mexican hands. Solomon Houck, who enjoyed citizenship privileges in both the United States and Mexico, wrote to the American consul at Santa Fé for his Mexican naturalization papers.

The ultimate decision, however, did not belong to the merchants. A rumor of an impending attack by the Mexicans threw the rendezvous into confusion on November 25, and although it proved to be a false alarm, the army restrained the traders from breaking camp and ordered them to remain in their fortified position. The merchants were now completely bewildered. Glasgow, Owens, and several others started back to Santa Fé on November 30 to ascertain from Colonel Doniphan just how they were to be affected by military policy.[33]

Without waiting for a clarification, the forty-five wagons of Kerford and Jenkins, followed shortly by those of Francisco Elguea, a Spanish merchant of Chihuahua, broke camp and started south. Both were halted by troops a few days later, how-

---

[32] *Ibid.*, 500; Ruxton, *Adventures in Mexico and the Rocky Mountains*, 174; Cornelius Davy to J. S. Phelps, Washington, March 22, 1848, in 30 Cong., 1 sess., *House Report No. 458*, p. 45.

[33] Houck to Alvarez, Valverde, November 30, 1846, M.N.M., Alvarez Papers, 1846; Hughes, diary, in Connelley (ed.), *Doniphan's Expedition*, 81–83; Abert, "Report," 30 Cong., 1 sess., *House Exec. Doc. No. 31*, p. 504.

ever, and a guard of twenty-four soldiers was then stationed at Valverde. All of the merchants—American and foreign—were ordered to proceed no farther until the arrival of Colonel Doniphan and his full command. At this turn of affairs the merchants drew up a petition to the captain of the guard at Valverde, asking that the Kerford and Jenkins train be allowed to proceed. It, they pleaded, had an immense stock of goods from England which, having been imported under the Drawback Act of 1845, was entirely duty-free. If these low-cost goods were held up and permitted to enter Chihuahua at the same time as those of the other merchants, they would all be ruined from the competition. On the other hand, if that train was permitted to proceed now, the goods of Kerford and Jenkins could pass on through to the richer markets of Durango and Zacatecas and leave that of Chihuahua unaffected. These arguments failed to impress the captain, who merely increased the guard.[34]

On December 9 the merchants drew up a second petition, this time addressing it to Colonel Doniphan himself. Most of them, they pleaded, carried foreign goods imported expressly for the Mexican market, received in the United States after the war had begun but previously consigned to Mexico by special permission of the secretary of the treasury. General Kearny, before leaving New Mexico, had assured a number of them that they might proceed with their goods to Chihuahua with military protection through the southernmost New Mexican settlement, and they had thus come to Valverde in good faith, there to await assurances of the Mexican government before proceeding farther. They had no idea that they would be hindered by the American army. Their provisions were now almost exhausted, the country around Valverde had been drained of forage and supplies by the troops, and with severe winter

[34] Hughes, diary, in Connelley (ed.), *Doniphan's Expedition*, 83–84; Abert, "Report," 30 Cong., 1 sess., *House Exec. Doc. No. 31*, 504–505.

setting in they would be subjected to starvation if further detained. A number of animals had already perished from the cold, their men were about to desert for lack of pay, and their property was exposed to Indian depredations. Whereas they now faced financial ruin, all would profit if those who so wished were allowed to go on to Chihuahua, for their goods would reach markets throughout the country and would not be in competition with those who followed later behind the army. The introduction of their goods into Mexico would be of no military advantage to the enemy, they concluded, for the duties charged against them would be slight.[35]

But again commercial considerations failed to sway the military mind. The traders were allowed to move down the road a few miles to Fray Cristóbal camp on December 14, but notwithstanding the efforts of some to elude the guard, they were held there until Colonel Doniphan arrived on December 19. Then, falling in behind the army, they were allowed to march over the Jornada del Muerto.[36]

Beyond the Jornada word was received that a large Mexican force was advancing from El Paso del Norte, and on December 24, Colonel Doniphan requested the merchants to raise a battalion from their own ranks, but, there being no assurance of pay, no volunteers were forthcoming.[37] The next day, Christmas, the first military engagement took place a few miles above the Rancho del Bracito. About 1,200 Mexican troops met Doni-

[35] Petition to Col. Doniphan, Valverde, December 9, 1846, by Owens & Aull, Manuel X. Harmony, Solomon Houck, Francisco Elguea, J. Calistro Porras, Thomas F. McManers, Alexander Ferguson, Hoffman & Barney, Kerford & Jenkins, Cornelius Davy, and William H. Glasgow, 30 Cong., 1 sess., *House Report No. 458,* pp. 46–48.

[36] Hughes, diary, in Connelley (ed.), *Doniphan's Expedition,* 86; M.B. Edwards, journal, in Bieber (ed.), *Marching with the Army of the West,* 219; Ruxton, *Adventures in Mexico and the Rocky Mountains,* 183.

[37] Hughes, diary, in Connelley (ed.), *Doniphan's Expedition,* 87; M. B. Edwards, journal, in Bieber (ed.), *Marching with the Army of the West,* 238.

phan's advance force of about 450 and, after an exchange of fire lasting only thirty minutes, were put to flight. The only trader who participated was Thomas Caldwell, who had enlisted as an interpreter.[38] Shortly after dark on the same day, however, the old trapper and scalp hunter James Kirker and half a dozen of his Delaware comrades arrived and enlisted as military scouts.[39]

After the battle of Bracito, December 25, the Mexican forces retreated steadily in the face of the American advance until they reached the Hacienda de Sacramento, about twenty miles north of Chihuahua. Doniphan's column occupied El Paso del Norte without resistance on December 27. There, while the army searched the town for arms and spies, the traders opened their goods and did a thriving business for more than a month, exchanging their wares for corn, wood, hay, and cattle, which they sold in turn to the army. Their unique disposition to barter brought customers thronging from all parts of the countryside.[40] Meanwhile, in their anxiety to reach Chihuahua, several traders moved down the river road toward the Presidio of San Elizeario, and on February 3, 1847, troops were sent to restrain them. Fifteen miles beyond the presidio, Elguea's train was overtaken and forced to return, but the wagons of Kerford and Jenkins, under the supervision of Reuben Gentry, made their escape, reached Chihuahua ahead of the American forces, and proceeded to the firm's main store at Durango.[41]

[38] *Ibid.*, 228–36.
[39] *Ibid.*, 238. According to one of the traders, Doniphan accepted Kirker's services with some reservation on account of the hunter's checkered past, and although he was sent ahead as a scout, others went along to watch him carefully and to shoot him in case of treachery. However, he proved entirely faithful. Edward J. Glasgow to William E. Connelley, Governor's Island, N. Y., November 27, 1906, in Connelley (ed.), *Doniphan's Expedition*, 102n.
[40] F. S. Edwards, *A Campaign in New Mexico*, 91.
[41] Gibson, *Journey of a Soldier*, 325–28.

When the army moved down to the presidio on February 8, there were about 315 merchant wagons in its rear; and the next day, with a view toward converting them from a military liability to an asset, Doniphan ordered the merchants and teamsters to organize themselves into two companies of infantry of seventy-five men each and report to his headquarters immediately. This being a command rather than a request, as on December 24, almost all of the merchants complied. Manuel Harmony, however, protested vigorously and refused to enlist, but his mules, horses, wagons, and goods were forcibly commandeered. On February 11, the other traders met and elected officers: Edward Glasgow, captain of Company A; Henry Skillman, captain of Company B; and Samuel Owens, major of the entire battalion. Both companies were ordered to remain with their wagons until further notice and hold themselves in readiness at all times.[42]

A few days before the caravan left the presidio, a large number of oxen were stolen from the train of Houck, Ewing, Bray and Company by three Apaches, but Solomon Houck recovered most of them and took an Apache scalp in the process.[43] The Spaniard Harmony and the Mexican Porras[44] at-

[42] Doniphan to the merchants, Presidio, February 9, 1847, and Harmony, claim, in 30 Cong., 1 sess., *House Report No. 458*, pp. 15–16; Doniphan to Adj. Gen. Jones, Chihuahua, March 4, 1847, 30 Cong., 1 sess., *Senate Exec. Doc. No. 1*, I, 498–502; M. B. Edwards, journal, in Bieber (ed.), *Marching with the Army of the West*, 244, 248. Under Captain Edward Glasgow in Company A, William H. Glasgow was elected first lieutenant and Calvin Huston and H. C. Harrison second lieutenants; under Captain Skillman in Company B, Manlius F. Branham was elected first lieutenant and John Howard and A. F. Francisco second lieutenants. Bieber (ed.), in Gibson, *Journey of a Soldier*, 332n.

[43] M. B. Edwards, journal, in Bieber (ed.), *Marching with the Army of the West*, 248; Gibson, *Journey of a Soldier*, 331.

[44] J. Calistro Porras was one of the signers of the Valverde petition of December 9, 1846 (note 35 above). Hobbs, referring to him as "Pores" (Hughes calls him "Porus"), describes him as a rich Mexican merchant of Chihuahua who sent a pack train of sixty or eighty mules to the west coast for goods every year and had property reportedly worth two million dollars. Hobbs, *Wild Life*

tempted to remain behind at the presidio by hiding their mules and reporting them stolen by the Indians, hoping thereby, as the troops believed, to await the outcome of the battle for Chihuahua and enter the city a friend of the winner. They were forced to fall in behind the army, however, and the march got under way.[45]

From the Presidio of San Elizeario to the Hacienda of Sacramento, a march of about 235 miles in fifteen days, little of importance occurred. James Collins, who had replaced Caldwell, and another interpreter named Henderson were sent ahead with Kirker and a scouting party of only twenty men. Finding the Presidio of Carrizal occupied only by civilians, they captured it by themselves.[46] Kirker then proceeded to the Laguna de Encinillas and reported back that about one thousand Mexican troops were preparing to make a stand there. This proved false, but his next report, from the Rancho de Sacramento, was the real thing. A large force was digging in there, and its artillery emplacements and other fortifications, observed and charted by one of the Delaware scouts, were made known to Doniphan in Kirker's report.[47]

With this information Doniphan now ordered the trader wagons to be formed in four parallel columns about thirty feet apart, so as to screen his troops and artillery train, which then marched on Sacramento in three enclosed files. The battle, on

in the Far West, 83, 95; Hughes, diary, in Connelley (ed.), Doniphan's Expedition, 99.

[45] Col. David D. Mitchell to Porras and Harmony, February 10, 1847, 30 Cong., 1 sess., House Report No. 458, p. 16; M. B. Edwards, journal, in Bieber (ed.), Marching with the Army of the West, 249.

[46] Ibid., 252–53; Hughes, diary, in Connelley (ed.), Doniphan's Expedition, 99.

[47] Ibid., 101; Connelley, in ibid., 388–89n.; M. B. Edwards, journal, in Bieber (ed.), Marching with the Army of the West, 256–57. James Hobbs, an associate of Kirker's Indian scouts, takes personal credit for charting the fortifications of Sacramento and delivering the map to Doniphan after a daring ride through enemy territory. Hobbs, Wild Life in the Far West, 121–27.

February 28, 1847, was more fiercely contested than that of El Bracito, but the outcome was the same. The trader and teamster battalion remained behind the front to guard the supplies, but were under fire from Mexican artillery throughout the engagement. In storming the heights and capturing the enemy position, the American troops lost only one killed and ten wounded, although one of the latter died soon afterwards. The Mexicans, according to Doniphan's report, lost three hundred killed, about the same number wounded, and forty taken prisoner. As the result of an ill-understood order, the merchant-major Samuel Owens charged a Mexican battery almost singlehanded and died at the parapets. He, Collins, Henderson, Kirker, and another scout named Anderson were cited for gallantry in the action.[48] On March 1, the day after the battle, Francis McManus, who had been captured with Connelly and Doan the preceding fall, arrived with word that the Mexican forces had retreated beyond Chihuahua, whereupon Doniphan's troops and the merchant caravan marched into the undefended city.[49]

For several months prior to the capture of Chihuahua, American merchants and teamsters there had presented the state with a delicate problem. If it granted them freedom of trade, the revenues would be increased and the roads made safer from Indian attacks, but at the same time the presence of such a large number of well-armed enemy aliens would constitute a veritable "fifth column" for the invasion. Governor José María de Irigoyen had pursued a moderate policy toward

[48] Doniphan to Jones, Chihuahua, March 4, 1847, 30 Cong., 1 sess., *Senate Exec. Doc. No. 1*, I, 498–502; M. B. Edwards, journal, in Bieber (ed.), *Marching with the Army of the West*, 260–70; Hughes, narrative, in Connelley (ed.), *Doniphan's Expedition*, 418; Glasgow to Connelley, August 13, 1906, and Meredith T. Moore, statement to Connelley, *ibid.*, 398n., 418n.

[49] M. B. Edwards, journal, in Bieber (ed.), *Marching with the Army of the West*, 270.

the Americans, allowing them to travel under arms and without Mexican guards, but only in small numbers, limiting these by a strict enforcement of the passport regulations. His successor, Angel Trías, who took office August 25, 1846, simply interned all enemy aliens as fast as they arrived. In September he removed most of them to the village of Cusihuiriachic, about seventy miles southwest of Chihuahua, leaving Alfonso C. Anderson to represent their interests in the city.[50]

James Webb and the American teamsters with Albert Speyer, who reached Chihuahua about the first of September, were interned by Governor Trías for about a month and then were allowed to accompany Speyer's train as far as the Hacienda del Río Florido, where they were again detained. Speyer himself, having ample passport protection, was allowed to carry his goods to Durango, Aguascalientes, and to the annual fair at San Juan de los Lagos, but only after hiring a full complement of Mexican teamsters. In order to accompany him, Webb again had to place his goods and person in Speyer's hands and also obtain a falsified safe-conduct pass. When their train left for the south, about October 1, it was accompanied by the American teamsters, a heavy Mexican guard, several Chihuahua families, and Manuel Armijo, who was on his way to Mexico City to report on his precipitant retreat from Santa Fé. Armijo had acquired seven wagons laden with imported cotton goods which he expected to sell along the way. At the Hacienda

50 Gov. Irigoyen to the Ministro de Relaciones, Chihuahua, August 4, 1846; Gov. Trías to the same, Chihuahua, February 3, 1847, A.S.R.E., L-E-1086, XXXII, 84–85, and L-E-1088, XXXIV, 108. There were twenty American merchants interned at Cusihuiriachic for whom Anderson had to obtain safe-conduct passes at the beginning of 1847: George East, David Douglas, George Wethered, Robert Carlisle, James Buchanan, Joseph W. Henry, George Stilts, James Littleton, John Ward, Lewis Dutton, William Messervy, George Litchliter, John Fristoe, Lewis Flotte, James Johnson, Thomas Moore, John Patton, James Rogers, Lewis Sheets, and Archibald Stevenson. Anderson to Black, Chihuahua, January 10, 1847, U.S.N.A., Cons. Gen., Mex., Corresp., 1845–48.

del Río Florido, where the American teamsters were to be interned, the military escort turned back to Chihuahua, and Speyer, in conspiracy with the proprietor of the hacienda, allowed the internees to continue with him to Durango. Then, at La Zarca, twenty-one of them with Speyer's connivance made a dash for freedom. They tried to reach the Río Grande by crossing the Bolsón de Mapimí, but after traveling fourteen days in that arid desert, mostly without provisions, eleven of them perished from thirst and fatigue, and the other ten, changing course, finally reached Guajuquilla (now Jiménez de Hidalgo), where they were subsequently rescued by American troops.[51] Their tragic experience was to weigh heavily on the Prussian merchant when he was later brought to trial by the American military authorities.

Meanwhile, other American merchants were arriving at Chihuahua under arrest. James Magoffin and José González, who had been captured at El Paso del Norte in September, were transferred to a prison at Chihuahua along with Connelly, McManus, and Doan, who had been taken at the same place in October. Doan, being protected by his English passport, was freed, and early in December he reached San Juan de los Lagos, where he joined his partner Webb at the fair.[52] González managed to escape, and after being recaptured at El Paso del Norte, got away again and reached Samuel Magoffin's train at the Valverde rendezvous on December 20.[53] The others were held at Chihuahua, and James Magoffin was scheduled to go on trial for his life, the captured report on his services in New Mexico constituting a veritable death warrant.

But no trial was held. Owing to Magoffin's personal prestige

---

[51] Webb, *Adventures in the Santa Fé Trade*, 209–32; Ruxton, *Adventures in Mexico and the Rocky Mountains*, 110, 118–19; John T. Hughes to Miller, Chihuahua, April 25, 1847, in Connelley (ed.), *Doniphan's Expedition*, 461–62n.
[52] Webb, *Adventures in the Santa Fé Trade*, 250.
[53] Susan Magoffin, *Down the Santa Fé Trail*, 178–79.

in Chihuahua, a well-placed bribe, and perhaps the luck of the Irish, the incriminating evidence disappeared before the trial was to begin, and the case against him collapsed. As Magoffin himself later reported with no further elaboration, the military judge confronted him with the letter before other authorities had seen it. "We understood one another; he told me to tear it up, which I did in his presence, for I was a prisoner and it was not safe for either of us that I should keep it. That affair cost me $3,800, and deprived me of General Kearny's statement to lay before the Government."[54] Captain Cooke's oft-quoted statement that Magoffin managed to "dissolve all charges, prosecutions, and enmities in three thousand three hundred and ninety-two bottles of Champagne wine (by a close computation)," is not supported by Magoffin's own accounting.[55] Although acquitted of the espionage charges, Magoffin was nonetheless held as an enemy alien until the end of the war (nine months by his own reckoning), and when the other American merchants were taken to Cusihuiriachic, he was sent to Durango and was the only one of the merchants not released when Doniphan occupied Chihuahua.[56]

Meanwhile, after the fair of San Juan de los Lagos, which lasted from December 1 to 12, Albert Speyer went to Zacatecas to sell the remainder of his goods and Webb and Doan returned to Chihuahua. There Webb was fined three times

[54] Magoffin, itemized statement, 1849, *Magoffin Papers*, 50.

[55] Cooke, *The Conquest of New Mexico and California*, 44n. Magoffin's claim does list $2,000 for claret and champagne, but this was for the entertainment of military and civilian authorities and influential citizens at Santa Fé and Durango as well as Chihuahua and for "promoting the interests of the United States." Magoffin, itemized statement, 1849, *Magoffin Papers*, 47–49. According to a relative of Magoffin's, the sentence was suspended at the request of Governor Armijo, who was related to Magoffin's wife. Robert B. McAfee to the Secretary of War, Harrodsburg, Ky., June 22, 1847, *ibid.*, 47. Senator Benton gives the same version as that in Magoffin's claim but with some embellishment. Benton, *Thirty Years' View*, II, 684.

[56] Magoffin, itemized statement, 1849, *Magoffin Papers*, 48–49.

for improperly entering his wagons, but he was also permitted to freight domestic goods to and from Durango. Doan was allowed to go to the west coast for additional foreign goods. About ten days before the battle of Sacramento, some fifteen or twenty Americans were rounded up and sent to Cusihuiriachic, but about ten others, including Webb, Alfonso Anderson, Francis McManus, and George Carter, succeeded in hiding out in the city. The authorities promised the populace a free appropriation of all of their property and goods if the Mexicans prevailed at Sacramento. As news of the impending battle arrived, John Potts, the English manager of the Chihuahua mint, gave the Americans refuge in his building, and they waited on the roof for news of the outcome. From this vantage point they could hear the cannonading, and after one false report of a Mexican victory, the true results became apparent. Governor Trías and his retreating army galloped back to the city and, scarcely halting for refreshment, sped on to Parral. Doniphan's cavalry arrived on March 1, and his infantry, followed by the merchant train, entered the city the next day.[57]

A few days after the occupation began, Speyer arrived from Zacatecas. He was immediately arrested by the American military authorities and charged with carrying contraband arms to the enemy and with responsibility for the tragic plight of his American teamsters. Lieutenant Colonel David D. Mitchell told Webb that they planned to hang him if he was found guilty, but Speyer entertained his captors nightly with whist parties and wine and gave them the run of his store. Many silver ornaments and curios disappeared from his shelves, according to Webb, and when the trial was held about two weeks later, he was honorably acquitted. According to the Missouri press, the court found that Speyer had carried only six kegs of powder and sixty muskets from Independence, which were not

57 Webb, *Adventures in the Santa Fé Trade*, 261–73.

[176]

considered contraband of war. Webb, of course, knew better, but agreed with the court that in outrunning the dragoons that pursued him across the plains, Speyer was merely trying to protect his investment by reaching the Mexican markets ahead of his competitors, and that in releasing his American teamsters at La Zarca, he was merely acting in their own best interests.[58]

The retreat of the Mexican troops to Parral, meanwhile, was accompanied on March 5 by the release of the American merchants held at Cusihuiriachic, leaving only James Magoffin, who was now held at Durango.[59] But the crisis had not passed. What was to become of them when Doniphan's column marched away to its next military objective? On March 7, at the request of the leading merchants, Doniphan sent Henry Connelly under military escort to arrange a truce with Governor Trías at Parral. Doniphan proposed to reinstate Trías in office, evacuate the city, and require the traders to pay the regular duties on their goods on condition that Trías release Magoffin and guarantee the American merchants at Chihuahua full protection of their lives, property, and commercial pursuits. But while awaiting the results of these overtures, he made preliminary arrangements for a full withdrawal, and the merchants were thrown into a near panic. Connelly returned from Parral on March 18 with three commissioners carrying counterproposals from Trías. The Governor would guarantee the traders full protection only on condition that the American forces evacuate the city immediately, leaving behind all materiel captured at Sacramento and paying liberally for all damage done to the city since the beginning of the occupation. These conditions were rejected on March 20, and the negotiations were broken off at the request, according to Doniphan,

[58] *Ibid.*, 275–76; Bieber (ed.), quoting the *Daily Missouri Republican* of May 18, 1847, in *ibid.*, 275–76 n.
[59] Wislizenus, *Memoir of a Tour to Northern Mexico*, 54.

of the American merchants. They felt that they could prevail upon him to protect them "as long as there was a shirt-tail full of goods in the City."[60]

On the same day negotiations were broken off, Doniphan sent James Collins under military escort to find General Wool and request further orders, advising him that his own position in Chihuahua was exceedingly embarrassing. His troops were tired, restless, and eager to join the General's command, but the merchants, having several hundred thousand dollars at stake, were so violently opposed to his departure that he could not reasonably leave the city for several days. He was willing to extend his protection as far as practicable, but he objected to remaining in Chihuahua as a mere wagon guard.[61] While awaiting the return of this mission, the merchants became steadily more apprehensive. On April 2 a decree issued from Parral announced that no goods introduced under protection of the American army could be transported or sold by Americans in any of the unoccupied portions of the state, and that even Mexican merchants and those of neutral nations could not carry or sell goods acquired after the battle of Sacramento.[62] The market was thus limited to the city and its environs, and throughout the month of April the American traders, established on the main streets of Chihuahua, exerted every means they knew to dispose of their immense stock of goods. Most of them were able to sell their heaviest packages, but only at considerable sacrifice.[63]

[60] Doniphan to Capt. David Waldo, Liberty, Mo., January 10, 1848, in Ralph Emerson Twitchell, *The Military Occupation of New Mexico, 1846–1851*, 327–29; Hughes, diary, in Connelley (ed.), *Doniphan's Expedition*, 107–108; M. B. Edwards, journal, in Bieber (ed.), *Marching with the Army of the West*, 275.

[61] Doniphan to Wool, Chihuahua, March 20, 1847, in Connelley (ed.), *Doniphan's Expedition*, 445n.

[62] Acting-Gov. Laureano Muñoz, decree, Parral, April 2, 1847, (English translation) in 30 Cong., 1 sess., *House Report No. 458*, pp. 28–29.

Collins and his escort found General Wool at Saltillo on April 2, picked up orders for Doniphan and an additional escort of twenty-six Arkansas volunteers, and retraced their 500-mile route to Chihuahua in fourteen days, arriving on April 23. With them was Josiah Gregg, who had started from Independence with Samuel Owens' train in the spring of 1846 but had quit to enlist in Wool's army. At Chihuahua, Gregg found lodging in the American hotel run by Riddells and Stevenson and visited his old trader friends in the city. He was shocked to learn of Owens' death and was further horrified at the raucous behavior of the Missouri volunteers during their occupation of the city.[64]

The apprehension of all of the traders was heightened by the military orders from Saltillo. Chihuahua was to be evacuated entirely, Doniphan's forces were to repair at once to Saltillo, and the traders could accompany them or remain behind at their own option.[65] In preparation for his departure, Doniphan made a final call on the Mexican authorities of the city and, threatening to return and chastise them if necessary, made them promise to respect the lives and property of those merchants who remained. Most of the Americans and other foreign residents, however, had little confidence in this pledge. The first battalion left the city on April 26, but the merchants protested so vehemently that the other forces remained two days longer. Even then, however, most of the traders were still not prepared to move.[66] Samuel Magoffin, having still on hand some 311 bales of his brother's goods, sold them to the English-

[63] Webb, *Adventures in the Santa Fé Trade*, 277; Hughes, narrative, in Connelley (ed.), *Doniphan's Expedition*, 465–66.

[64] *Diary and Letters of Josiah Gregg*, II, 79, 89–101.

[65] Extract of orders from Gen. Zachary Taylor to Doniphan, 30 Cong., 1 sess., *House Report No. 458*, p. 38.

[66] *Diary and Letters of Josiah Gregg*, II, 104–105; Wislizenus, *Memoir of a Tour to Northern Mexico*, 61.

man John Potts at a sacrifice, for half of their freight costs and a guarantee against further customs charges. As soon as the American troops had left the city, the Mexican authorities called upon Potts to pay $15,698.96 in duties on these goods, and after his release from Durango, James Magoffin had to repay him this amount.[67] Christopher Branham and others sold out their remaining goods by accepting the first offer of José Cordero.[68] Solomon Houck, hoping to do better, waited two days before offering his goods at the same price, but Cordero reduced his offer. When Houck refused to sell until the following day, Cordero lowered it again, and when Houck finally agreed to terms, he was "out about $2,500 by his smartness."[69]

Most of the Americans decided to leave with Doniphan's troops on April 28, and they returned to the United States by way of Saltillo, Monterrey, and the port of Brazos de Santiago, where they took separate steamers to New Orleans in June. Samuel Magoffin, who remained at Monterrey for some months, sent his bullion ahead with George East, John Fristoe, and Josiah Gregg, who took a total of $36,000 in bullion to the Philadelphia mint.[70] Some thirty or forty traders, including Webb, Houck, Branham, Cornelius Davy, and Ebenezer W. Pomeroy, left within a week of the army's departure, but took the Camino Real to Santa Fé. Edward and William Glasgow,

[67] Potts, notarized deposition, Chihuahua, October 1, 1848, *Magoffin Papers*, 63.

[68] José Cordero was one of the wealthiest merchants of Chihuahua, a political enemy of Governor Trías, and a great friend of the Americans, to whom he frequently lent money. After the war he lent the state government $24,000, and in 1852 served a short term as governor, at which time he was also a landed proprietor and considered the richest man in the state. González Flores, *Chihuahua de la independencie a la revolución*, 92, 101; Hobbs, *Wild Life in the Far West*, 131; Webb, *Adventures in the Santa Fé Trade*, 277–78; Bartlett, *Personal Narrative of Explorations*, II, 427.

[69] Webb, *Adventures in the Santa Fé Trade*, 277–78.

[70] *Diary and Letters of Josiah Gregg*, II, 107–57; Susan Magoffin, *Down the Santa Fé Trail*, 230–60.

Connelly, McManus, and James Aull remained behind, as did the Englishman Doan, who had returned to the city from Guadalajara with a cargo of domestic goods just before Webb's departure. Except for Doan and Aull, those who remained, trusting to the protection of the Chihuahua authorities, were all long-time residents of the city who knew the language and customs and were accepted for all practical purposes as Mexican citizens.[71]

Colonel Doniphan had left with Connelly a written statement for the municipal authorities which asserted that if a treaty were made between the state government and the American residents for their protection, he would use his influence to prevent a reoccupation of the city by American troops. Negotiations between the municipal and state authorities for such an agreement got under way immediately, and a treaty was concluded on April 30, 1847. It stipulated that the American troops evacuate the city immediately (which they had already done), that Doniphan use his efforts to prevent its future reoccupation, that the American merchants pay duties fixed by the state on all their goods (both sold and unsold) which had been introduced under military protection, and that the authorities respect the persons and property of the merchants as though they were citizens of the state.[72] Only one outrage marred the observance of this pact, and it was committed by irresponsible elements.

On June 23, 1847, four Mexicans broke into the store of James Aull, killed him, and made off with $5,000 in money

[71] Webb, *Adventures in the Santa Fé Trade*, 281–84; Ebenezer W. Pomeroy to Robert Aull, Santa Fé, May 29, 1847, in "Letters of James and Robert Aull," *Missouri Historical Society Collection*, V, 295–96; Hughes, narrative, in Connelley (ed.), *Doniphan's Expedition*, 468.

[72] Doniphan to Waldo, Liberty, Mo., January 10, 1848, in Twitchell, *Military Occupation of New Mexico*, 327–29; Hughes, narrative, in Connelley (ed.), *Doniphan's Expedition*, 468; George C. Furber, *Twelve Months' Volunteer*, 454–55; González Flores, *Chihuahua de la independencia a la revolución*, 78–79.

and merchandise. The assassins were later apprehended and imprisoned, and Aull, like his partner, who had died more gloriously on the field of Sacramento, was buried at Chihuahua.[73] The settlement of the Owens and Aull estate involved the good offices of several merchants at Chihuahua. Robert Aull had been named executor in the will, but he was in Missouri. Fortunately, a brother-in-law, Ebenezer Pomeroy, was still at Santa Fé when news of the tragedy arrived, and he returned on August 28 in company with Joseph P. Hamelin, Doan, and John Howard to take possession of the property. Connelly was appointed defender of the estate, and Edward Glasgow, John Potts, and some Mexican citizens were named trustees. With the aid of Hamelin and Doan, Pomeroy opened three retail shops at Chihuahua and sent some of the goods to Durango, but they were unable to liquidate the complete stock until the early part of 1848. On the initial investment of $70,-000, James Aull had recovered and sent back $16,000 before his death. Pomeroy and his associates realized on the balance of the estate over $45,000 in specie, and returned about $6,000 worth of mules and wagons and $16,000 in drawback duty credits against the United States government. Pomeroy, Glasgow, and Hamelin arrived at Lexington, Missouri, with the final returns on July 4, 1848.[74]

Meanwhile, shortly after Aull's death, James Wiley Magoffin was finally released from his internment, but not without another costly bribe. In order to cross the palm of the military auditor of Durango, he had to borrow $1,600 from John Bel-

73 Hughes, narrative, in Connelley (ed.), *Doniphan's Expedition*, 468; Bieber (ed.), in "Letters of James and Robert Aull," *Missouri Historical Society Collection*, V, 296n.

74 Pomeroy to Robert Aull, Santa Fé, May 29, 1847, to same, Chihuahua, November 15, 22, and 27, 1847; Hamelin to Robert Aull, Chihuahua, October 31, 1847; Robert Aull to Siter Price & Co., Lexington, Mo., February 15, March 25, April 4, and July 14, 1848, in *ibid.*, 295–307.

den, a merchant of that city. Samuel and Susan Shelby Magoffin learned the good news at Saltillo on August 20, 1847, from a Mr. Chapman of Parras, whom Belden had written, believing them to be already out of the country.[75] When he returned to the United States, James Magoffin filed a claim for his expenses and services amounting to $37,798.96, of which an even $30,000 was allowed by the government.[76]

One final episode involving the traders occurred before the hostilities between the United States and Mexico ceased. As General Sterling Price's army marched south from Santa Fé to occupy Chihuahua for a second time, James Collins was riding to meet it with a dispatch from General Wool. Collins was captured at El Paso del Norte and taken to Chihuahua for trial as a spy, but with the aid of Ebenezer Pomeroy he escaped from his prison cell, and by the middle of February, 1848, made his way back to El Paso del Norte, where he reached Price's command.[77] The latter then occupied Chihuahua, on March 7, pursued Governor Trías and the state militia to Santa Cruz de Rosales, about sixty miles to the south, and forced their surrender on March 15.[78] This campaign, however, had no bearing on the outcome of the war, for the peace treaty of Guadalupe-Hidalgo had already been signed, on February 2, and it was ratified by the United States Senate on March 16. The only effect of the renewal of hostilities in Chihuahua was the further anxiety of the remaining American merchants.

[75] Susan Magoffin, *Down the Santa Fé Trail,* 249; Magoffin, itemized statement, 1849, *Magoffin Papers,* 48–49. James Hobbs gives a fanciful account of his own part in obtaining Magoffin's release *before* Doniphan's arrival at Chihuahua and asserts that the Magoffin brothers made up a purse of $500 for him, and that James Magoffin gave him a pair of Colt revolvers. Hobbs, *Wild Life in the Far West,* 116–31.

[76] Secretary of War George W. Crawford to the President, Washington, April 1, 1849, *Magoffin Papers,* 50–56.

[77] Philip Gooch Ferguson, journal, in Bieber (ed.), *Marching with the Army of the West,* 352–53.

[78] *Ibid.,* 355–58.

8.

The Significance

In 1848 the Treaty of Guadalupe-Hidalgo brought an end not only to the Mexican War but also to an era. Thereafter the Chihuahua Trail—although developing from a wagon trace into a stage road, into a railway, and ultimately into a paved automobile highway—was only one of several major inland trade routes between the United States and Mexico. Its principal rival was a shorter road through Texas. The heyday of the Camino Real was the quarter of a century immediately following the independence of Mexico from Spain. During that era its commercial traffic significantly altered the political and economic growth of the United States and, to a lesser extent, the social and economic growth as well. It also raised the standard of living of the New Mexicans, made them more dependent upon the Americans, and facilitated the military invasion which changed their very citizenship. These historical influences can readily be demonstrated, but the volume and

[184]

value of the trade which wrought these changes can never be accurately measured.

Since its first publication in 1844 and revision in the following year, the statistical table prepared by Josiah Gregg[1] has remained the most reliable quantitative analysis available. Admittedly based on rude estimates rather than strict accounting, Gregg's figures are derived from information submitted to him personally by other traders and from their reports to the frontier Missouri newspapers, which annually announced the departure of the caravans. A notable weakness of these sources was that most of the merchants, being in debt for their goods and conveyances, were loath to publicize the true extent of their current investments. Indeed, a number of discrepancies between Gregg's figures and those found in the newspapers were pointed out by a prominent Missouri historian in 1917.[2] An attempt was made more recently, in 1944, to calculate the annual value from the official customs records and to collate it with Gregg's statistics, but the result was unsatisfactory. In the first place, the Mexican treasury figures represented not necessarily what was collected at Santa Fé but only what was sent to Mexico City, which was seldom if ever the same. In the second place, they represented fiscal years (ending June 30), while Gregg's figures were for calendar years, and as the imports were not evenly distributed over the months, no accurate collation is possible. In the third place, the national treasury received no reports from Santa Fé until 1825, only fragmentary reports for 1836, 1837, and 1841, and none at all for 1838, 1839, 1840, and 1844 or thereafter, leaving important gaps for those years. Finally, the tariff itself varied according to the category of the goods imported, and the entire schedule

1 See above, Chapter III.
2 Stephens, "Missouri and the Santa Fé Trade," *Missouri Historical Review*, Vol. XI, No. 3 (April, 1917), 295–97.

of rates changed from year to year, making it impossible to compute an official evaluation even for the years when returns were complete.[3]

It was my original purpose to determine the value of the trade from a more direct source: the manifests filled out by the traders themselves and filed at the customs office. However, an investigation of these files at Santa Fé showed them to be incomplete, and a fuller study of the methods of assessing and collecting duties led to a conviction that even a complete file of manifests would furnish only shaky evidence at best. The concealment of goods by the traders and the "arrangements" which they made with the collectors rendered all such documentation little more reliable than the monthly reports of the latter to the governor and his annual reports to the national treasury, which are also incompletely preserved.[4] The treasury reports of the United States are without information on the subject because no export duty was levied on the American goods, and, unfortunately, the consuls at Santa Fé and Chihuahua saw no reason to keep records on the extent of the trade. The ledgers of the traders themselves would offer another evaluation, but only a few of them have survived. Thus, the rough estimates of one public-spirited trader remain the most complete and systematic analysis of the volume and value of the Santa Fé and Chihuahua trade.

The returns from Mexico were chiefly in specie and bullion

---

3 Bork, *Nuevos aspectos del comercio entre Nuevo México y Misuri*, 68–71. Gregg's estimate of the value for 1830, for example, was $120,000, while the official report for the fiscal year 1830–31, which would coincide closely with the caravan season of 1830, shows that the *derecho de consumo* collections amounted to 1,977 pesos, which at the legal rate of 5 per cent would put the total value of goods entered at only $39,540. Estado de Ingresos, Nuevo México, July 1, 1830–June 30, 1831, A.H.H., Legajo 1167–2.

4 Various *manifiestos, guías, libros de carga y data,* and *estados de corte de caja,* arranged chronologically with other documents in M.N.M., Twitchell Collection.

—some gold dust but mostly silver bars and coin—but it is impossible to calculate how much they were worth from year to year. The traders were even more close-mouthed on this score than on their investment in goods, and so only fragmentary reports were publicized: $180,000 for 1824, at least $200,000 for 1829, $100,000 in 1832 from one company alone, and more than $200,000 in 1834 for another single company.[5] Almost as incomplete and probably less reliable were the statistics reported by the New Mexican customs house, thanks both to official negligence and private evasion. During the fiscal year 1834–35, for instance, Santa Fé reported collections on the export of specie amounting to only $403 which, at the prevailing duty rate of 3.5 per cent would indicate that only $1,141 were exported in that season.[6] For the calendar year 1842 collections were reported on only $49,656 worth of silver and for 1843 on only $46,950.[7] Not all of the remainder escaped taxation, however, for the Chihuahua traders frequently returned by way of the Gulf of Mexico and cleared their money through Brazos de Santiago instead of Santa Fé.

In addition to the silver coin which the traders received for goods retailed, a considerable amount of money in silver bars was obtained from their wholesale operations and from purchases from mine operators. These bars, weighing between fifty and eighty pounds each and worth one to two thousand dollars, were assayed by authorized Mexican agents and were

[5] Storrs to Benton, Franklin, Mo., November, 1824, *Niles' Weekly Register*, XXIX, 312–16; Stephens, "Missouri and the Santa Fé Trade," *Missouri Historical Review*, Vol. XI, No. 4 (July, 1917), 305–306; Dorothy B. Dorsey, "The Panic and Depression of 1837–43," *ibid.*, Vol. XXX, No. 2 (January, 1936), 132–61.

[6] Libro de Carga y Data, 1834–35, Aduana Fronteriza de Nuevo México, A.H.H., Legajo 176–2.

[7] *Memoria de la Hacienda Nacional de la República 1844*, part 2. The exportation of bullion was prohibited altogether by law between 1822 and 1828 and again after 1835, but a large amount was annually smuggled out by traders. Gregg, *Commerce of the Prairies*, 296–97; *Legislación mexicana*, II, 75; III, 72–73.

stamped with their proper weight and fineness, making them a convenient form of currency for large transactions. As they usually brought 10 per cent above their nominal value when presented at a United States mint, some traders in Chihuahua and Durango made special trips to the mines expressly to buy silver bars.[8] On their return to the United States, they presented their bullion to the mint at Philadelphia. That of New Orleans was closer to their circuit of operations, but, as Gregg tells us, it had a bad reputation among the merchants of his acquaintance.[9]

Probably the most vital influence of the overland trade on the economy of the United States was the stabilizing effect which this Mexican silver exercised, especially on the monetary system of Missouri. Before the beginning of the trade, Missouri, like other western states and territories, suffered acutely from a shortage of hard money, a rapid depreciation of "wild cat" bank notes, and a wide circulation of counterfeit paper bills, all of which embarrassed even the most ordinary business transactions. The influx of Mexican silver from the Santa Fé and Chihuahua trade admirably shored up this shaky monetary system. By the close of 1824, the Mexican peso had reached Missouri in such numbers and was circulating so freely that it was accepted by the federal land office in Franklin at par weight with the American dollar; by 1828 it was more common in the western counties of Missouri than the dollar itself; and by 1831 it constituted the principal circulating medium for the entire state. Although never legal tender in the strictest sense, the peso contained 374 grains of fine silver as compared to only 371.25 for the American dollar, and was therefore preferred at this time to the national coinage by most of the people in the western communities.[10]

[8] Gregg, *Commerce of the Prairies*, 296–97.
[9] *Diary and Letters of Josiah Gregg*, II, 156.

The abundant influx of Mexican silver made Missouri unique among the agricultural states in its popular preference for "hard" money, and it may well have influenced Senator Benton's own well-known proclivities for sound currency. More significantly, it enabled Missouri to weather more easily than other states the Panic of 1837 and the six-year depression which followed. When the crash came, Missouri was the only state in the Union without one or more state-incorporated banks, and only after the depreciated bank notes of neighboring states flooded it and threatened to drive out hard money did the legislature establish such an institution of its own. The Bank of Missouri, founded in 1837, gained a reputation as being one of the soundest state banks in the nation. Serving as a depository for the silver of returning traders, it was able to pay in specie from the very beginning, and its notes commanded a premium of 7.5 per cent over those of other western banks. During a "run" in 1839, it was saved from probable disaster by the timely deposit of $45,000 in silver by returning overland merchants.[11]

Another branch of the American economy which the Mexican trade stimulated was the mule-breeding industry, especially in Missouri, where it reached a celebrated pre-eminence. As early as 1823, some four hundred jacks, jennets, and mules were brought to Missouri by a returning caravan; in 1824, over six hundred; in 1827, eight hundred; and in 1832, thirteen hundred. Many of these and their offspring were shipped to the southern plantations, where there was quickly developed a preference for mules over horses as draft animals. Until mid-century little breeding was done in Missouri itself, but it was an important center of the mule trade, which itself was a

[10] Stephens, "Missouri and the Santa Fé Trade," *Missouri Historical Review*, Vol. XI, No. 4 (July, 1917), 306–309.
[11] *Ibid.*, 310–11.

profitable enterprise during the early years. In 1829 jacks and jennets purchased in Chihuahua and Sonora at from seven to ten dollars a head brought sixty dollars in the United States.[12] By 1840 they were selling at a sacrifice, and after the outbreak of war with Mexico, on account of the unusual demands of the American army, the New Mexican and Chihuahua prices were raised from forty to seventy-five dollars.[13] Meanwhile, in the 1830's, the so-called Missouri mule made its appearance. The Mexican jack when bred with the American mare produced a larger and stronger mule than that raised in Mexico, and the offspring of an American stallion and a Mexican jennet was considered superior to the *macho,* its Mexican counterpart. However, all of the mules, jacks, jennets, and horses entering the United States for this industry did not arrive by way of the Chihuahua and Santa Fé trails. Virginia relied largely on jacks and jennets from Cuba; New Orleans and Natchez bought large herds driven from the Mexican state of Tamaulipas; and others were brought overland from the missions of California by the mountain men.[14] By the 1850's, when Missouri became recognized around the world as a "mule kingdom," it produced an even larger animal than before. At that time most of the jacks came from Kentucky, where they were carefully bred from Spanish, Cuban, and Maltese stock. The Missouri mule soon won a preference over that of Mexico for farm work and wagon pulling, but the smaller

12 R. W. H. Hardy, *Travels in the Interior of Mexico,* 459; Pattie, *The Personal Adventures of James O. Pattie,* 108; Frederick A. Culmer (ed.), "Selling Mules Down South in 1835," *Missouri Historical Review,* Vol. XXIV, No. 4 (July, 1930), 537–49.

13 Waldo to Alvarez, Independence, April 20, 1841, M.N.M., Alvarez Papers, 1839–45; Harmony claim, 30 Cong., 1 sess., *House Report No. 458,* pp. 7, 27; Hughes, diary, in Connelley (ed.), *Doniphan's Expedition,* 96; Cooke, *The Conquest of New Mexico and California,* 83.

14 *Niles' Weekly Register,* Vol. XXIX (October 15, 1825), 100; George Frederick Ruxton, *Life in the Far West,* 138ff.; James Westfall Thompson, *A History of Livestock Raising in the United States, 1607–1860,* 76–77.

Mexican animal found an important place in the pack trains of the United States Army.[15]

Early attempts to introduce New Mexican sheep into Missouri were less rewarding. Sheep, the chief export of that province to the interior of Mexico, could be purchased from the poorer *rancheros* for from fifty to seventy-five cents a head, and wool, which brought fifteen cents or more a pound in Missouri, could be bought in New Mexico for from three to four cents. It was inferior in quality to that produced by American sheep, however, and failed to compete successfully. The sheep of New Mexico were far more celebrated for their meat than for their fleece.[16]

The intellectual and social influences of the inland trade are more difficult to assess. In an era of national expansion—"manifest destiny" as it was then known—it was only natural that the American public craved information and inspiration from the land to the west of the settled frontier, and it was likewise fitting that the letters, diaries, and memoirs of early adventurers in the new land should find their way into print. It was from these personal narratives that a new genre of American literature was born—the "western." But before the "dime novels," "penny dreadfuls," and other lurid fiction made their appearance—replete with Indian attacks on wagon trains, scalpings, stampedes, buffalo hunts, prairie fires, desert mirages, dark-eyed señoritas, half-breed villains, and fair-haired heroes—the factual raw materials had first to be reported. The Oregon Trail had its Francis Parkman, the Rocky Mountain fur trade its George Ruxton, and the Santa Fé trade its Josiah Gregg. Zebulon Pike's factual *Expeditions* (1810) must be con-

[15] Dorsey, "The Panic and Depression of 1837–43," *Missouri Historical Review*, Vol. XXX, No. 2 (January, 1936), 135n.; "Missouri Jack Passes His 'Physical,'" *ibid.*, Vol. XXXVI, No. 3 (April, 1942), 341–42; F. S. Edwards, *A Campaign in New Mexico*, 55; Daly, *Manual of Pack Transportation*, 17.

[16] Gregg, *Commerce of the Prairies*, 133–35.

sidered the pioneer effort, and George Kendall's graphic *Narrative of the Texan Santa Fé Expedition* (1844) an important complement, but Gregg's *Commerce of the Prairies* (1844) was the finest and fullest description. It was an adventure story, nature study, historical treatise, travel guide, and handbook for traders, all rolled in one. Other memoirs of traders and travelers on the Chihuahua Trail which caught the public fancy and were forerunners of the "western" were James O. Pattie's *Personal Narrative* (1833), Ruxton's *Adventures in Mexico and the Rocky Mountains* (1847), and John Taylor Hughes' *Doniphan's Expedition* (1847).[17]

The social influences of the trade stem not only from the widespread effects of this literature but also from the first-hand contacts of teamsters and traders with the people of northern Mexico. And the attitudes which they developed demonstrated that international contact in itself does not always promote international harmony. Although some of the veteran traders such as the Magoffins became tolerant of the striking cultural differences between their hosts and the people back home, most of the Anglo-Americans showed a prejudice against the Spanish culture as deep and bitter as that of their ancestors in Elizabethan England. By declaration or intimation they pictured the Mexican as superficially polite and generous, but more often undependable, treacherous, dishonest, and addicted to gambling, inebriation, promiscuity, and other vices which were frowned upon, although practiced none the less, in their own homeland. The Roman Catholicism of the Mexican was extremely abhorrent to the predominant Protestantism of these frontiersmen. Although they were hostile toward such prevalent Mexican forms of amusement as the bullfight, cockfight, and rodeo in its original form, they fully enjoyed

[17] *Literary History of the United States,* edited by Robert Spiller and others, II, 764–67, 771–72.

the *fandangos* and card games. The Mexicans, on the other hand, looked upon the *americanos* as political expansionists, economic materialists, religious heretics, and cultural barbarians. Yet a most striking result was the frequent intermarriage of the two nationalities. Most of the resident American merchants married into Mexican families, learned the Spanish language, and remained on good terms with the people of the country even after the outbreak of war.

As has already been demonstrated, the main political influence of the inland trade was in paving the way for the American "bloodless conquest" of New Mexico. A quarter-century of New Mexican association with American traders had not only brought about an economic dependence on them, but also a measure of respect and admiration, especially for their ability to deal effectively with hostile Indians. The influence of James Magoffin and Henry Connelly in dissuading Governor Armijo and Colonel Archuleta from resisting the Army of the West has already been discussed, as have the services of the Trader Battalion to Doniphan's column. Of perhaps equal importance was the fact that when New Mexico was annexed to the United States and made an organized territory, a surprisingly large number of American traders became the political as well as commercial leaders of the new commonwealth.[18] Had they not done so, and had new faces appeared from the East to govern it, the Spanish-speaking population might have received a much less sympathetic treatment and have been slower to accept the new order.

The influences of the trade on Mexico itself were much

[18] For example, David Waldo became an official translator for the army of occupation; Henry Connelly, a member of the territorial legislative council and twice territorial governor; Charles Bent, territorial governor; Manuel Alvarez, territorial lieutenant governor; James Josiah Webb, a member of the legislative assembly; and James Collins, federal superintendent of Indian affairs and depositor for New Mexico. See biographical notes above.

more pronounced. The most significant change was the reorientation of New Mexico's trade. Previously its commerce was entirely with Chihuahua and the other cities to the south. Unfavorably balanced, it drained away New Mexico's short supply of gold and silver coin and thus compounded the poverty of the province. The overland trade from the United States, while adversely affecting the internal trade of central and coastal Mexico, was a boon to the frontier. Now, thanks to greater competition among the merchants, lower taxes, and fewer losses to Indian raids, the expensive imports from the south were more cheaply obtained from the east. Especially after the passage of the Drawback Act of 1845, the overland caravans brought, at prices much lower than those of Veracruz and Mexico City, not only the domestic manufactures of the United States but also the superior products of Europe. The resulting loss of profits to Mexican importers and freighters constituted a corresponding gain to the New Mexicans. Now they were able to buy immense quantities of imported dry goods and hardware and sell them to the interior in competition with those entering from Veracruz, Tampico, Mazatlán, Guaymas, and Acapulco. Moreover, the New Mexicans were now in a position to demand specie from the south for these wares, and the imbalance of their interior trade was thereby reversed.

By 1839 several wealthy New Mexican merchants were taking their own trains to the United States to buy at wholesale for the Mexican market. Less is known of these traders than of those of Missouri, but their importance was fully as great. Most of the *ricos* of the province—the Chávez, Perea, Ortiz, and Otero families—became merchants as well as feudal lords. José Chávez y Castillo, who became acting governor of New Mexico in 1848, purchased eleven wagonloads of dry goods in the United States in 1840 and a large consignment of English goods in New York in 1846.[19] Mention has already been made of Antonio José Chávez, who was robbed and murdered on the Santa Fé Trail in 1843. His brother, Mariano Chávez, of Padillas, sent $26,474 worth of imported goods from Santa Fé to Chihuahua in 1844, and during the same season several other New Mexicans carried American goods to the south, principally to Chihuahua, Durango, Zacatecas, and Aguascalientes. Among these were the brothers José and Juan Perea with goods valued at $25,128, Antonio J. Ortiz with two consignments ($17,878 and $2,102), Antonio José Otero with another two ($2,341 and $2,385), Manuel Antonio Otero ($2,326), Santiago Flores ($5,837), José Salazar ($892), Governor Manuel Armijo ($10,309), and Ambrosio Armijo ($18,049).[20] The Governor was buying goods from the United States at least as early as the summer of 1841, when he lost over $18,000 worth of merchandise being shipped from St. Louis to Independence.[21] By 1845 he had run up an outstanding debt of $6,000 and nineteen ounces of gold with P. Harmony, Nephews and Company of New York.[22]

Even more important than the enrichment of the merchants of New Mexico was the elevation of the standard of living of their customers, which was brought about by the large-scale introduction of both necessities and luxuries at lower prices. Before the trade from Missouri was developed, the New Mexicans, except for the *ricos,* were not only virtually without real money but also without almost any kind of cloth-

[19] Alvarez, Memorial to Webster, Washington, February 2, 1842, pp. 5–6, U.S.N.A., Cons. Desp., Santa Fé, I; Harmony, Nephews & Company to Secretary of the Treasury R. J. Walker, New York, May 30, 1846, and Walker to C. W. Lawrence, New York, June 10, 1846, in 30 Cong., 1 sess., *House Report No. 458,* pp. 62–63.

[20] *Guías* and *facturas,* M.N.M., Twitchell Collection, 7771, 7823, 8244, and 8256.

[21] Alvarez to Webster, Santa Fé, December 18, 1842, U.S.N.A., Cons. Desp., Santa Fé, I.

[22] Alvarez to the Secretary of State, Independence, July 1, 1843, U.S.N.A., Cons. Desp., Santa Fé, I.

ing except leather and homespun, and almost without iron or steel tools of any kind. There was not a single printing press in the province, and there was a deplorable scarcity not only of books but also of paper. Medical supplies other than native herbs and potions were equally rare.[23]

Within a few years after 1821, however, most of these needs were available in quantity. The market was soon flooded with textiles of almost every kind: broadcloth, cotton prints, shirting, drills, muslin, bandana, cords, denim, flannel, taffeta, calico, percale, cambric, pongee, velvet, velveteen, nankeen, lawns, linen, silk, and cashmir. Almost every conceivable article of clothing and personal adornment became readily available.[24] And by the 1840's the women of New Mexico and Chihuahua were aping even the styles set in Paris. Curiously enough, the fashion leader in New Mexico was not one of the provincial aristocracy but Gertrúdiz Barcelo, a notorious *monte* dealer.[25]

Little imagination is necessary to visualize the effect on domestic industry of the wholesale introduction of tools. Now there were iron and steel implements for carpentry, housekeeping, farming, and hunting. There were also the common drugs of the day: alum, Seidlitz powders, Epsom salts, cologne, saffron, cream of tartar, sulphur, balsam, spirits of nitrate, cathartic salts, bicarbonate of soda, emetic tartar, and assorted pills for various ailments.[26]

The new trade brought in comforts to the mind as well as the body. Books, although not in great quantity, began to make their appearance in Santa Fé assortments. Josiah Gregg,

23 Various *guías* and *facturas* in M.N.M., Twitchell Collection.
24 *Ibid.*
25 Kendall, *Narrative of the Texan Santa Fé Expedition,* I, 318 n.; Bartlett, *Personal Narrative of Explorations,* II, 428.
26 Various manifest listings in M.N.M., Twitchell Collection, and in A.H.H., Aduana de Nuevo Mexico.

for instance, brought in 1,141 books in one year (1834). Although several of these were for his own use to while away the winter hours at his Santa Fé store and only 30 of them were in the Spanish language, over 700 were designed for use in primary schools. William Hooke introduced 22 books that same year; Hiram Smith, 10; and Philip Houck, 24.[27] New Mexico's first printing press fully equipped with type was also imported from the United States in 1834, by Gregg and his partner, Jesse B. Sutton. It was entered duty-free and was almost immediately put to use by Father José Antonio Martínez of Taos, who during four weeks of the same year published the province's first newspaper, *El Crepúsculo*. This publication lapsed after Martínez's election to the national congress, but the press continued in operation and produced several primers, catechisms, and loose-leaves.[28]

The introduction of American wagons was another boon to northern Mexico. Previously the only vehicles available to the ordinary people were the homemade oxcarts fashioned entirely of wood whose wheels were so irregular, axles so ill fitting, and total construction so unwieldy that two oxen were required to pull a load easily drawn by one in a conveyance of American manufacture. Since the American traders returned to the east with little cargo, they needed only a few of their wagons and sold the others with their regular goods. The native merchants were eager buyers, but so were those from the south, for in 1843 there were more than one hundred American wagons owned and operated by the citizens of the state of Chihuahua.[29]

27 Manifiesto de José Sutton y Josiah Gregg, Santa Fé, July 29, 1834, A.H.H., Legajo 176–3; Bork, *Nuevos aspectos del comercio entre Nuevo México y Misuri*, 85–86.
28 *Ibid.*, 82–84.
29 Gov. Monterde to Ministro de Relaciones, Chihuahua, May 19, 1843, A.G.N., Fomento-Caminos, XIII, Exped. 283.

American wagons were veritable fortresses on wheels and, together with superior American firearms and the undaunted confidence of American traders and teamsters, gave their caravans something of an immunity against Indian attack on the Camino Real. Real security from Indian raids had never been provided by Mexican authority, either local or national, and Mexican trains, large or small, were forever the victims of marauding Apaches and Navajos. Such was the reputation of the caravans from Missouri that Mexican traders often delayed their departures until they could accompany American merchants, and the provincial governments sometimes availed themselves of the same protection for important mail and money shipments. Samuel Magoffin's wagons were chartered by the government at Chihuahua to carry the Santa Fé garrison's pay roll in 1842, one Mexican sergeant and five soldiers constituting the "official" escort.[30] To some extent, then, the well-armed American caravans served to patrol the highways and keep the hostile tribes in check.

The annexation of Texas in 1845, the temporary occupation of Nuevo León, Coahuila, and Chihuahua during the next two years, and especially the acquisition by the United States of additional Mexican territory in 1848, reoriented the trade of northern Mexico once more. North of the Río Grande ford the Camino Real was now an American road, and El Paso del Norte replaced Santa Fé as the Mexican port of entry. However, with Texas now a recognized part of the United States, many of the American traders now took a short cut through that state. The Chihuahua Trail of Texas stretched from Indianola on the western shore of Galveston Bay through San Antonio and the Davis Mountains to El Paso. From San Antonio, other wagon roads took a more southerly direction,

---

[30] *Carta de Seguridad* for Sgt. Pedro Sandoval, Chihuahua, March 1, 1842, M.N.M., Alvarez Papers, 1839–45.

crossing the Río Grande at Del Río and Eagle Pass and reaching Chihuahua by way of Monclova and Guajoquilla. These routes were well established by 1851 and flourished until superseded by the Galveston, Harrisburg and San Antonio Railroad in 1877 and the Southern Pacific shortly thereafter.[31]

The Santa Fé Trail remained the most important route linking the Mississippi Valley with New Mexico until the completion in 1880 of the Atchison, Topeka and Santa Fe Railroad from Chicago to the Río Grande. This line, curiously enough, by-passed Santa Fé itself, but in the same year the Denver and Rio Grande Western completed a track to the city from the north, and the A. T. and S. F. finished a spur line to it from Lamy, in the south. Both were later abandoned.

The Chihuahua Trail was superseded by rails in 1882. In that year the A. T. and S. F. extended its track from Santo Domingo on the upper Río Grande to El Paso, Texas, where by crossing the river it connected with the just completed Mexican Central Railroad. The latter, originating at Mexico City, followed the old Camino Real all the way north through Chihuahua to Ciudad Juárez, the former El Paso del Norte. For anyone who might care to follow the historic Chihuahua Trail today, there is a choice of three convenient means of travel. One can now ride along it, with some local deviations, by train, automobile, or airplane.

The railroad from Santa Fé, depending upon slopes of minimum grade and towns of maximum importance, passes to the east and south of the old trail to Santo Domingo and

[31]Part of this road was pioneered by Henry Connelly's party from Chihuahua in 1839–40, part by Gen. John Wool's column in 1846–47, and part by Major John Polk Campbell, who returned from Chihuahua by way of Texas in 1847 with thirty-eight men. Wislizenus, *Memoir of a Tour in Northern Mexico*, map opp. p. 112; Hughes, narrative, in Connelley (ed.), *Doniphan's Expedition*, 451–52; Mrs. Ruth Campbell Owen, letter to the editor, quoted in *ibid.*, 451–52n.

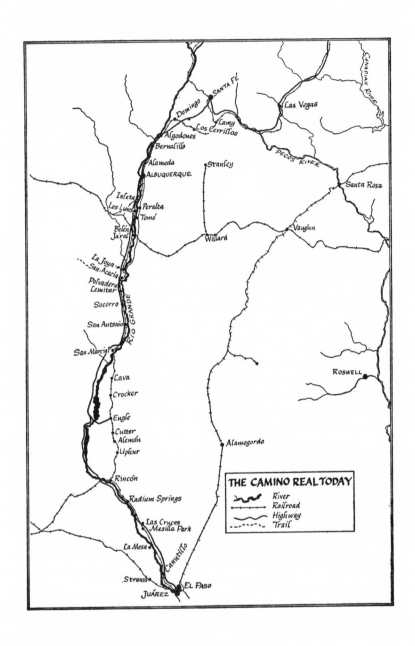

THE CAMINO REAL TODAY

~~~~~ River
+—+—+— Railroad
——— Highway
‑ ‑ ‑ ‑ Trail

JUÁREZ   • Isleta

Mesa   • San Elizario
            • Fabens
Samalayuca   • Tornillo

Los Médanos

Calendaria

      • Ranchería

      • Lucero

San José

Carrizal • • Ahumada

Santa Rosa •   • Nuevo

      • Moctezuma

Alsacia
El Sueco
      • Gallego

      • Arados

Encinillas

      • El Sauz
      • Terrazas

Nombre de Dios •
      CHIHUAHUA

RÍO GRANDE

Guadalupe

RÍO CONCHOS

RÍO CHUVISCAR

THE CAMINO REAL TODAY

River
Railroad
Highway
Trail

follows the west bank of the Río Grande between Isleta and San Marcial, but otherwise it is not far off of the historic track of the caravans, even over the Jornada del Muerto. Since the great sand dunes have become stabilized on the way directly south of El Paso, the railway passes through Samalayuca and follows the Jornada de los Médanos rather than detouring by way of San Elizeario and the Jornada de Cantarrecio. Along the entire way from Santa Fé to Chihuahua many of the names of old campsites still live as those of the railroad stations.

For those traveling by automobile there is pavement over the entire route, U. S. Highway 85 from Santa Fé to El Paso and Mexico's Camino 45 from Ciudad Juárez to Chihuahua and on to Mexico City. But the highway is less respectful of the original trail than is the railroad. Although following it more closely out of Santa Fé, it by-passes Santo Domingo and strikes the river at Algodones instead. Moreover, on its course down the valley of the Río Grande it passes over to the west bank twice, following that side between Albuquerque and Arrey and between Derry and Radium Springs, thereby avoiding the desolate Jornada del Muerto. By taking state highway 47 south of Albuquerque, one can drive on pavement over more of the original trail, but only as far as La Joya. Beyond that point, over the old Paso de Contadero and Jornada del Muerto, only primitive roads and trails are found. Beyond El Paso the Mexican highway follows the Jornada de los Médanos, as does the railroad, and continues along the old wagon trace as far as the valley of Encinillas. In order to take the alternate road from El Paso, along the right bank of the Río Grande and around the great sand dunes, one may follow Mexico's Route 2 downstream, but only for about forty miles. Thereafter a dirt road continues along the dunes to Tinajas de Cantarrecio, and from there to Lucero, where the main highway is joined again, there is only a trail. In the valley of

Encinillas the highway veers to the west and passes around that side of the Laguna de Encinillas before rejoining the old route at El Sauz and continuing along it to Chihuahua.

Finally, of course, one may take a commercial airline and by so doing get a bird's-eye view of the Chihuahua Trail. From Santa Fé the plane flies almost due south to the beacon at Otto and then almost due west to Albuquerque. But from there on to Radium Springs the course is almost directly over the old road, passing in a straight line south-southwest to the beacon at Engle, on the Jornada del Muerto, and then south-southeast over Radium Springs, near the old river camp of Robledo. As the flight continues in the same direction to a beacon seventeen miles west of El Paso before landing at that field, most of the river road south of the Jornada is left somewhat to the east, and as the old trail from El Paso to Chihuahua bows slightly while the airline is straight, the flight leaves much of it a few miles to the west.

In summary, the Chihuahua Trail exerted several significant influences on a strategically important region. The wagon trace blazed by Oñate's emigrant train at the close of the sixteenth century from the mining camps of northern Mexico to the Pueblo towns on the upper Río Grande proved to be not only the most feasible route thither but also the very life line of a new frontier civilization. Over this trail passed the mission and merchant caravans which kept New Mexico alive in the seventeenth and eighteenth centuries. By means of a near monopoly of this traffic, the merchants of Chihuahua impoverished the province, but their stranglehold was broken by merchants from Missouri early in the nineteenth century. At first these so-called "Santa Fé traders" exchanged only the produce of Missouri for that of New Mexico, but within a few years they were buying better goods more cheaply in the distant

Atlantic seaports of the United States and Europe and, by following the Camino Real beyond Santa Fé, were selling in the larger and richer cities of the Mexican interior.

By availing themselves of larger wagons, sturdier draft animals, greater capital, longer credit terms, and more effective government protection, they developed a complex and far-flung business whose volume and value increased almost annually. By resorting to contraband and connivance, they subverted the restrictions imposed on them by the Mexican government. By underselling the merchants of the interior, they provided New Mexico with sufficient necessities and luxuries to raise its standard of living and weaken its dependence upon central Mexico. By taking payment in silver, they bolstered the economy of their homeland. And by recording and publishing their exciting experiences in the West, they helped give birth to a new genre of American literature.

During the war between the United States and Mexico their road to Chihuahua facilitated the American invasion, and their own influence over the people and governments of northern Mexico was turned to American military advantage. After the war many of them participated actively in the administration of the conquered territory, and by so doing rendered less difficult and painful to both sides the pacification of New Mexico. Finally, their historic wagon road between Santa Fé and Chihuahua was not forgotten in the onward march of civilization, but remained instead essentially the route still followed by the most modern means of transportation.

Bibliography

I. MANUSCRIPTS

a. *Archivo General y Pública de la Nación, Mexico City*

i. *Provincias Internas*

Jacobo Ugarte y Loyola to the Audiencia of Mexico, Encinillas, March 2, 1787, Tomo XIII, Expediente 1.

Ministro de la Real Hacienda, *pago de libranza,* Chihuahua, January 1, 1788, Tomo XIII, Expediente 3.

ii. *Fomento-Caminos*

Secretario del Interior to Secretario de la Junta del Estado, Chihuahua, November 8, 1838 (certified copy), Tomo XI, Expediente 225.

Gov. Bernardo Revilla to Ministro de Gobernación, Chihuahua, November 20, 1838, Tomo XI, Expediente 225.

George East, John Patton, Lucian Thurston, and Riley Jackson to the Governor, Chihuahua, January 4, 1839, Tomo XI, Expediente 225.

Lucas Alamán to Ministro de Gobernación, Mexico City, February 19, 1839, Tomo XI, Expediente 225.

Ministro de Relaciones Exteriores to Ministro de Gobernación, Mexico City, April 2, 1839, Tomo XI, Expediente 225.

Ministro de Relaciones Exteriores to Ministro de Gobernación, Mexico City, April 16, 1839, Tomo XI, Expediente 225.

Gov. Manuel Armijo to Ministro de Gobernación, Santa Fé, September 26, 1839, Tomo XI, Expediente 225.

José Antonio Chávez to Ministro de Gobernación, Santa Fé, October 11, 1839, Tomo XI, Expediente 225.

Ministro de Guerra y Marina to Ministro de Relaciones Exteriores, Mexico City, May 21, 1840, Tomo XI, Expediente 225.

Pedro Olivares and Francisco Holguín, Memorial to Pres. Antonio López de Santa Anna, Chihuahua, September 24, 1842, Tomo XIII, Expediente 283.

Gov. Mariano Martínez to Ministro de Relaciones, Chihuahua, September 28, 1842, Tomo XIII, Expediente 283.

Gov. José Mariano Monterde to Ministro de Relaciones, Chihuahua, May 19, 1843, Tomo XIII, Expediente 283.

Luís Zuloaga to Ministro de Relaciones, Chihuahua, May 24, 1843, Tomo XIII, Expediente 283.

Ministro de Gobernación to Gov. José Mariano Monterde, Mexico City, May 30, 1843, Tomo XIII, Expediente 283.

José Cordero and Francisco Márquez, Memorial to Pres. Antonio López de Santa Anna, Chihuahua, May 25, 1846, Tomo XIII, Expediente 283.

b. *Archivo Histórico de Hacienda, Mexico City*

Estado de Ingresos, Aduana de Nuevo México, Santa Fé, July 1, 1830–June 30, 1831, Legajo 1167–2.

Manifiesto No. 42, Aduana de Nuevo México, Santa Fé, August 8, 1830, Legajo 1167–2.

Libro de Carga y Data, 1834–35, Aduana de Nuevo México, Legajo 176–2.

Manifiesto de José Sutton y Josias Gregg, Aduana de Nuevo México, Santa Fé, July 29, 1834, Legajo 176–3.

Documentos estadísticos redactados por Manuel Payno y Bustamante, Tomo II, Legajo 117–1.

c. *Archivo de la Secretaría de Relaciones Exteriores, Mexico City*

Gov. José de Urquidi to Ministro de Relaciones, Chihuahua, May 13, 1825, L-E-1055, Tomo I, 129–36.

Augustus Storrs to Gov. Antonio Narbona, Santa Fé, September 23, 1825, L-E-1055, Tomo I, 149–50.

Estado que manifiesta los estrangeros que han arribado al territorio de Nuevo México de los Estados Unidos del Norte, Año de 1825, L-E-1075, Tomo XXI, 95.

Gov. Antonio Narbona to Ministro de Relaciones, Santa Fé, March 4, 1826, L-E-1055, Tomo I, 160–61.

Gov. José Ysidro Madero to Ministro de Relaciones, Chihuahua, April 12, 1831, Legajo 5–1–7595.

Ministro de Relaciones to Gov. José Antonio Chávez, Mexico City, April 13, 1831, L-E-1070, Tomo XXII, 190.

Propuesta de Peter H. Estes, de Liberty, Missouri, para servirse como espía de México relativo al comercio estrangero de Nuevo México, Años de 1831–32, Legajo 44–6–22.

Col. Stephen W. Kearny to Gov. Manuel Armijo, Bent's Fort, August 1, 1846 (certified copy in Spanish), L-E-1085, Tomo XXXI, 175.

Gov. José María de Irigoyen to Ministro de Relaciones, Chihuahua, August 4, 1846, L-E-1086, Tomo XXXII, 84–85.

Gov. Manuel Armijo to Col. Stephen W. Kearny, Santa Fé, August 12, 1846 (certified copy in Spanish), L-E-1085, Tomo XXXI, 176–77.

Gov. Manuel Armijo to Ministro de Relaciones, Chihuahua, September 8, 1846, L-E-1085, Tomo XXXI, 171–79.

Report of the citizens of New Mexico to the President of Mexico,

Santa Fé, September 26, 1846, L-E-1088, Tomo XXXIV, 270–82.

Gov. Angel Trías to Ministro de Relaciones, Chihuahua, February 3, 1847, L-E-1088, Tomo XXXIV, 108.

d. *National Archives, Washington*

i. *Consular Letters, Chihuahua*

Joshua Pilcher to Secretary of State Henry Clay, St. Louis, Mo., August 18, 1826, Vol. I.

Charles M. Webber to Secretary of State Henry Clay, Columbia, Tenn., November 27, 1827, Vol. I.

John Ward to Secretary of State Martin Van Buren, Chihuahua, November 30, 1830, Vol. I.

George C. Bestor to the Secretary of State, Peoria, Ill., July 30, 1839, Vol. I.

ii. *Consular Dispatches, Santa Fé*

James Davis to President Andrew Jackson, Russellville, Ala., October 20, 1830, Vol. I.

Manuel Alvarez to Secretary of State John Forsyth, Santa Fé, September 20, 1839, Vol. I.

Memorial to Governor Armijo endorsed by John Scholly, Lewis Lee, John Fournier, J. K. Dormston, Manuel Alvarez, Charles Blummer, Benjamin Wilson, and Josiah Gregg, Santa Fé, December 2, 1839 (copy in English), Vol. I.

Secretario del Estado Guadalupe Miranda to Manuel Alvarez, Santa Fé, December 3, 1839, Vol. I.

Manuel Alvarez, Memorial to Secretary of State Daniel Webster, Washington, February 2, 1842, Vol. I.

Manuel Alvarez to Secretary of State Daniel Webster, Washington, March 4, 1842, Vol. I.

Manuel Alvarez to Secretary of State Daniel Webster, Santa Fé, December 18, 1842, Vol. I.

Manuel Alvarez to the Secretary of State, Independence, Mo., July 1, 1843, Vol. I.

Manuel Alvarez to Secretary of State James Buchanan, Independence, Mo., June 18, 1845, Vol. I.

Manuel Alvarez to Secretary of State James Buchanan, Santa Fé, September 4, 1846, Vol. I.

iii. *Consulate General, Mexico*

(a). *Correspondence, 1829–41, 1842–44, 1845–48*

George East to Consul General William D. Jones, Chihuahua, February 20, 1838.

James Wiley Magoffin to Consul General William D. Jones, Chihuahua, October 17, 1838.

James Wiley Magoffin to Consul General William D. Jones, Chihuahua, January 30, 1839.

Charles W. Davis to Consul General William D. Jones, Parral, February 3, 1839.

James Wiley Magoffin to Consul General William D. Jones, Chihuahua, March 9, 1839.

Charles W. Davis to Consul General John Black, Parral, February 17, 1840.

William G. Dryden, Solomon Houck, and B. F. Broaddus to the Consul General, Chihuahua, September 12, 1841.

John McKnight to Consul General John Black, Chihuahua, October 18, 1841.

George East to Consul General John Black, Chihuahua, October 2, 1843.

Henry Connelly to Consul General John Black, Chihuahua, March 18, 1844.

Jesse B. Sutton and George East to Consul General John Black, Chihuahua, May 4, 1844.

Charles W. Davis to Consul General John Black, Chihuahua, May 11, 1844.

Alfonso C. Anderson to Consul General John Black, Chihuahua, January 10, 1847.

Alfonso C. Anderson to Consul General John Black, Chihuahua, January 19, 1847.

(b). *Letter Books*

William D. Jones to Charles W. Davis, Mexico City, February 27, 1839, Vol. I, 389.

William D. Jones to Stephen Curcier, Mexico City, August 28, 1839, Vol. II, 91–92.

John Black to Benito Riddells, Mexico City, January 6, 1841, Vol. III, 18.

John Black to Robert L. Reid, Mexico City, April 24, 1841, Vol. III, 34–35.

John Black to William S. Messervy, Mexico City, October 15, 1841, Vol. III, 48.

John Black to George East, Mexico City, October 21, 1843, Vol. III, 193–94.

John Black to Benito Riddells, Mexico City, January 20, 1844, Vol. III, 211.

John Black to Benito Riddells, Mexico City, February 28, 1844, Vol. III, 230.

John Black to Charles Bent, Mexico City, April 10, 1844, Vol. III, 248–49.

(c). *Miscellaneous Record Books*

Carta de Seguridad form, Vol. I, 248.

Carta de Seguridad for George East, January 1, 1841, Vol I, 340.

Carta de Seguridad for Hugh Stevenson, January 1, 1841, Vol I, 342.

Carta de Seguridad for Benjamin Riddells, January 1, 1841, Vol I, 343.

Carta de Seguridad for Francis McManus, February 18, 1842, Vol. II, 72.

Carta de Seguridad for Reuben Gentry, September 15, 1842, Vol. II, 137.

Carta de Seguridad for Thomas Caldwell, April 3, 1843, Vol. II, 214.

Carta de Seguridad for George East, October 20, 1843, Vol. II, 251.

Carta de Seguridad for James Collins, February 1, 1845, Vol. III, 123.

Carta de Seguridad for Hugh Stevenson, January 19, 1846, Vol. III, 187.

e. *Museum of New Mexico, Governor's Palace, Santa Fé*

i. *Spanish Archives*

Gov. Marqués de la Penuela, proclamation, Santa Fé, May 10, 1712, archive 17.

Juan Joseph Aramburu, declaration, n. p., April 5, 1749, archive 506.

Gov. José Rubio to Gov. Francisco Trebol Navarro, Chihuahua, January 20, 1778, archive 711.

Gov. Francisco Trebol Navarro, proclamation, Santa Fé, March 31, 1778, archive 726.

Gov. Fernando de la Concha to Jacobo Ugarte y Loyola, Santa Fé, June 15, 1789, archive 1049.

Pedro Ramos de Verea, Antonio de Yribaren, Diego Ventura Márquez, Ventura de Porto, Sabino Diego de la Pedruesa, Francisco Manuel de Elguea, Andrés Manuel Martínez, Pablo de Ochoa, Joseph Suárez, Pedro Yrigoyen, Mariano Barulto, and Joseph Mariano Solís, contract, Chihuahua, October 18, 1790 (certified copy), archive 1120.

Gov. Fernando Chacón to Pedro de Nava, El Paso del Norte, August 30, 1800, archive 1503.

Gov. Fernando Chacón to Pedro de Nava, El Paso del Norte, October 17, 1800, archive 1512.

Gov. Fernando Chacón to the Consulado of Veracruz, Santa Fé, August 28, 1803, archive 1670 a.

Nemesio Salcedo to Gov. Joaquín Real Alancaster, Chihuahua, September 9, 1805, archive 1889.

Gov. Joaquín Real Alancaster to Nemesio Salcedo, Santa Fé, November 20, 1805, archive 1925.

Nemesio Salcedo to Gov. Joaquín Real Alancaster, Chihuahua, March 5, 1806, archive 1972.

Gov. José Manrrique to Nemesio Salcedo, Santa Fé, April 1, 1809, archive 2218.

Gov. José Manrrique to Nemesio Salcedo, Santa Fé, March 31, 1810, archive 2311.

Nemesio Salcedo to Gov. José Manrrique, Chihuahua, May 31, 1810, archive 2320.

Felipe Vijil to Gov. Mariano de la Peña, Valencia, November 30, 1812, archive 2469.

Lt. Col. Pedro María de Allande to Lt. José María de Arce, Santa Fé, November 20, 1816, archive 2681.

ii. *Twitchell Collection*

Guía for Juan C. Armijo, Santa Fé, August 1, 1844, archive 7771.

Guía for Mariano Chávez, Santa Fé, August 2, 1844, archive 7775.

Register of Guías, Santa Fé, August 3, 1844, Nos. 24–30, archive 7778.

Ambrosio Armijo, request for *guía* for son José Armijo, Santa Fé, September 10, 1844, archive 7823.

Register of Guías, Santa Fé, September 2–September 5, 1845, Nos. 6–23, archive 8244.

Ambrosio Armijo to Administrador de la Aduana Fronteriza, Santa Fé, September 1, 1845, archive 8231.

Guía for Ambrosio Armijo, Santa Fé, September 10, 1845, archive 8256.

Comandante de la Partida to Alferez Ramón Sena, Santa Fé, October 21, 1845, archive 8321.

Guía form, archive 7757.

iii. *Read Collection*

Record of naturalization of David Waldo of Virginia, Taos, June 17, 1831 (copy), Folder A.

List of Americans in Santa Fé in 1825 (copy), Folder A.

Manuel Alvarez, Memorial to Congress, Washington, February, 1842 (copy), Folder A.

Certificate of United States citizenship of Manuel Alvarez, St. Louis, Mo., April 9, 1842, Folder B.

Appointment of Manuel Alvarez as Commercial Agent, Washington, March 18, 1845, Folder A.

Manuel Alvarez to Secretary of the Treasury Robert J. Walker, Independence, Mo., June 18, 1845, Alvarez Letter Book.

Chief Clerk of the Department of State to Senator T. B. Catron, Washington, October 18, 1913, Folder D.

iv. *Alvarez Papers*

Account Book, 1839–45 file.

David Waldo to Manuel Alvarez, Independence, Mo., April 20, 1841, 1839–45 file.

Carta de Seguridad for Sgt. Pedro Sandoval, Chihuahua, March 1, 1842, 1839–45 file.

Charles Bent to Manuel Alvarez, Taos, November 12, 1844, 1839–45 file.

Distancias de Santa Fé a Chihuahua, Note Book.

Edwin Norris to Albert Speyer, New York, July 24, 1845, 1839–45 file.

P. Harmony, Nephews & Company to Manuel Alvarez, New York, February 10, 1847, 1856 file.

Francis B. Rhodes & Company, invoice, New York, May 7, 1844, 1839–45 file.

Solomon Houck to Manuel Alvarez, Valverde, November 30, 1846, 1846 file.

f. *The Bancroft Library, Berkeley, California*

Juan Agustin Morfi [?]. "Desórdenes que se advierten en Nuevo México y medios que se juzgan oportunos a repararlo para mejorar su constitución y hacer feliz aquel reyno" [Documentos para la historia de Nuevo México, I, 381–438] (transcript).

Pedro de Tamaron y Romeral. "Visita del Obispado de Durango, 1759–63" (transcript).

Documents for the History of Chihuahua. 2 vols. in 1 (transcript).

J. J. Warner. Reminiscences of Early California.

g. *Biblioteca Nacional, Mexico City*

Testimony of Juan Hartus Vallejo, Juan González de Retana, Nicolás Bustrín, and Antonio Sánchez, Parral and Mexico City, February 23–September 26, 1714, Archivo Fransciscano, Custodio de Nuevo México, Legajo 6, Expediente 5.

h. *William J. Glasgow Papers* (Private Collection), *El Paso, Texas*

Edward J. Glasgow. Narrative of Some Events in the Life of Edward James Glasgow (ca. 1900).

II. OFFICIAL DOCUMENTS

Abert, James William. "Report of Lt. J. W. Abert on His Examination of New Mexico in the Years 1846–47," 30 Cong., 1 sess., *House Exec. Doc. No. 31*, pp. 417–548. Washington, 1848.

American State Papers. 38 vols. Washington, 1832–61.

Colección de documentos inéditos relativos al descubrimiento, conquista y colonización de las posesiones españolas en América. Compiled by Joaquín F. Pacheco, Francisco de Cárdenas, and Luís Torres de Mendoza. 42 vols. Madrid, 1864–84.

Legislación mexicana ó colección completa de las disposiciones legislativas expedidas desde la independencia de la república. Compiled by Manuel Dublán and José María Lozano. 42 vols. in 54. Mexico City, 1876–1912.

The Magoffin Papers. [*Publications of the Historical Society of New Mexico, No. 24.*] Santa Fé, 1921.

Memoria de la Hacienda Nacional de la República de México [Annual report: title varies]. Mexico City, 1837–46.

Recopilación de leyes de los reynos de las Indias. 4 vols. Madrid, 1681.

U. S. 30 Cong., 1 sess., *House Exec. Doc. No. 31.*

———. 30 Cong., 1 sess., *House Report No. 458.*

———. 18 Cong., 1 sess., *Senate Doc. No. 7.*

———. 28 Cong., 1 sess., *Senate Exec. Doc. No. 1.*

———. 30 Cong., 1 sess., *Senate Exec. Doc. No. 1.*

———. 30 Cong., 1 sess., *Senate Misc. Doc. No. 26.*

III. CONTEMPORARY DIARIES AND LETTERS

Aull, James and Robert. "Letters of James and Robert Aull," edited by Ralph P. Bieber, *Missouri Historical Society Collection,* Vol. V (St. Louis, 1927–28), 267–327.

Bieber, Ralph P. (ed.). *Marching with the Army of the West: The Journals of Abraham R. Johnston, 1846; Marcellus Ball Edwards, 1846–47; and Philip Gooch Ferguson, 1847–48.* Glendale, Calif., 1936.

Bolton, Herbert Eugene (ed.). *Spanish Explorations in the Southwest, 1542–1706.* New York, 1930.

Fowler, Jacob. *The Journal of Jacob Fowler.* Edited by Elliott Coues. New York, 1898.

Gibson, George Rutledge. *Journey of a Soldier under Kearny and Doniphan, 1846–1847.* Edited by Ralph P. Bieber. Glendale, Calif., 1935.

Gregg, Josiah. *The Diary and Letters of Josiah Gregg.* Edited by Maurice Garland Fulton. 2 vols. Norman, 1941–44.

Gregg, Kate L. (ed.). *The Road to Santa Fé: The Journal and Diaries of George Champlin Sibley and Others Pertaining to the Surveying and Marking of a Road from the Missouri Frontier to the Settlements of New Mexico, 1825–1827.* Albuquerque, 1952.

Hackett, Charles Wilson (ed.). *The Revolt of the Pueblo Indians and Otermin's Attempted Reconquest, 1680–82.* 2 vols. Albuquerque, 1942.

Hammond, George P. and Agapito Rey (eds.). *Don Juan de Oñate, Colonizer of New Mexico, 1595–1628.* 1 vol. in 2. Albuquerque, 1953.

———. *The Expeditions into New Mexico Made by Antonio de Espejo, 1582–83.* Los Angeles, 1929.

———. "The Rodríguez Expedition into New Mexico, 1581–82." *New Mexico Historical Review,* Vol. II, Nos. 3, 4 (July, October, 1927), 239–68, 334–64.

Houck, Louis (ed.). *The Spanish Regime in Missouri.* 2 vols. Chicago, 1909.

"The Journals of Captain Thomas Becknell from Boone's Lick to Santa Fé and from Santa Cruz to Green River." *Missouri Historical Review,* Vol. IV, No. 2 (January, 1910), 65–84.

Lafora, Nicolás de. *Relación del viaje que hizo a los presidios internos situados en la frontera de la América Septentrional.* Edited by Vito Alessio Robles. Mexico City, 1939.

Magoffin, Susan Shelby. *Down the Santa Fé Trail and into Mexico*: *The Diary of Susan Shelby Magoffin, 1846–47.* Edited by Stella M. Drumm. New Haven, 1926.

Marmaduke, Meredith Miles. "The Santa Fé Trail: M. M. Marmaduke Journal," edited by F. A. Sampson, *Missouri Historical Review,* Vol. VI, No. 1 (October, 1911), 1–10.

Pike, Zebulon Montgomery. *The Expeditions of Zebulon Montgomery Pike.* Edited by Elliott Coues. 3 vols. New York, 1895.

Polk, James K. *The Diary of James K. Polk.* Edited by Milo Milton Quaife. 4 vols. Chicago, 1910.

Richardson, William H. "William H. Richardson's Journal of Doniphan's Expedition," *Missouri Historical Review,* Vol. XII, Nos. 2, 3, 4 (January, April, July, 1928), 193–236, 331–60, 511–42.

Storrs, Augustus, to Thomas Hart Benton, Franklin, Mo., November, 1824, *Niles' Weekly Register,* Vol. XXVII (January 15, 1825), 312–16.

Thomas, Alfred Barnaby (ed.). *After Coronado*: *Spanish Exploration Northeast of New Mexico, 1696–1727.* Norman, 1935.

———. *Forgotten Frontiers*: *A Study of the Spanish Indian Policy of Don Juan Bautista de Anza, Governor of New Mexico, 1777–1787.* Norman, 1932.

————. *Teodoro de Croix and the Northern Frontier of New Spain, 1776–1783*. Norman, 1941.

"A Trade Invoice of 1638," *New Mexico Historical Review*, Vol. X, No. 3 (July, 1937), 242–46.

Webb, James Josiah. "The Papers of James J. Webb, Santa Fé Merchant, 1844–1861," edited by Ralph P. Bieber, *Washington University Studies*, Vol. XI, No. 2 (St. Louis, 1924), 255–305.

Wetmore, Alphonso. "Major Alphonso Wetmore's Diary of a Journey to Santa Fe, 1828," edited by F. F. Stephens, *Missouri Historical Review*, Vol. VIII, No. 4 (July, 1914), 177–97.

————, to Secretary of War Lewis Cass, Franklin, Mo., October 11, 1831, *ibid.*, 179–84.

Winship, George P. (ed.). *The Coronado Expeditions, 1540–1542* [*Fourteenth Annual Report of the Bureau of American Ethnology*]. Washington, 1894.

IV. CONTEMPORARY MEMOIRS AND NARRATIVES

Bartlett, John Russell. *Personal Narrative of Explorations and Incidents in Texas, New Mexico, California, Sonora, and Chihuahua, Connected with the United States Boundary Commission During the Years 1850, 1851, 1852 and 1853.* 2 vols. New York, 1854.

Benavides, Alonso de. *Fray Alonso de Benavides' Revised Memorial of 1634.* Edited by Frederick Webb Hodge, George P. Hammond, and Agapito Rey. Albuquerque, 1945.

Benton, Thomas Hart. *Thirty Years' View.* 2 vols. New York, 1854.

Carroll, H. Bailey and J. Villasana Haggard (eds.). *Three New Mexican Chronicles.* Albuquerque, 1942.

Connelley, William E. (ed.). *Doniphan's Expedition and the Conquest of New Mexico and California.* Topeka, 1907.

Cooke, Philip St. George. *The Conquest of New Mexico and California.* New York, 1878.

Coyner, David H. *The Lost Trappers.* Cincinnati, 1859.

Davis, William Watts Hardy. *El Gringo, or New Mexico and Her People*. New York, 1857.

Edwards, Frank S. *A Campaign in New Mexico with Colonel Doniphan*. Philadelphia, 1847.

Farnham, Thomas Jefferson. *Mexico: Its Geography, People, and Institutions*. New York, 1846.

Furber, George C. *Twelve Months' Volunteer*. Cincinnati, 1850.

García Conde, Pedro. "Ensayo estadístico sobre el estado de Chihuahua," *Boletín de la Sociedad Mexicana de Geografía*, Vol. V (Mexico City, 1857), 293–95.

Gregg, Josiah. *Commerce of the Prairies*. Edited by Max L. Moorhead. Norman, 1954.

Hafen, Leroy R. (ed.). *Ruxton of the Rockies*. Norman, 1950.

Hardy, R. W. H. *Travels in the Interior of Mexico*. London, 1829.

Hobbs, James. *Wild Life in the Far West: Personal Adventures of a Border Mountain Man*. Waterford, Conn., 1875.

Hughes, John T. *Doniphan's Expedition*. Cincinnati, 1848.

Kendall, George Wilkins. *Narrative of the Texan Santa Fé Expedition*. 2 vols. New York, 1844.

Pattie, James Ohio. *The Personal Narrative of James O. Pattie of Kentucky*. Edited by Timothy Flint. Cincinnati, 1833.

Ruxton, George Frederick Augustus. *Adventures in Mexico and the Rocky Mountains*. New York, 1847.

———. *Life in the Far West*. New York, 1849.

———. *Life in the Far West*. Edited by Leroy R. Hafen. Norman. 1951.

Villagrá, Gaspar Pérez de. *History of New Mexico*. Edited by Frederick Webb Hodge and Gilberto Espinosa. Los Angeles, 1933.

Webb, James Josiah. *Adventures in the Santa Fé Trade, 1844–47*. Edited by Ralph P. Bieber. Glendale, Calif., 1931.

Wislizenus, Adolph. *Memoir of a Tour to Northern Mexico Connected with Col. Doniphan's Expedition, in 1846 and 1847*. [30 Cong., 1 sess., *Senate Misc. Doc. No. 26*.] Washington, 1848.

V. CONTEMPORARY NEWSPAPERS

Los Angeles *Express,* October 16, 1873.

Los Angeles *Herald,* October 23, 1873.

Niles' Weekly Register (Baltimore), January 15, October 8, October 15, December 24, 1825.

San Francisco *Review,* September 28, 1883; August 2, 1884.

VI. RECENT STUDIES

Almada, Francisco R. *Geografía del estado de Chihuahua.* Chihuahua, 1945.

Anderson, Hattie M. "Frontier Economic Problems in Missouri," *Missouri Historical Review,* Vol. XXXIV, No. 2 (January, 1940), 182–203.

Atherton, Lewis E. "Business Techniques in the Santa Fé Trade," *Missouri Historical Review,* Vol. XXXIV, No. 3 (April, 1940), 335–41.

———. "James and Robert Aull—A Frontier Mercantile Firm," *ibid.,* Vol. XXX, No. 1 (October, 1935), 3–27.

Bailey, Jessie B. *Diego de Vargas and the Reconquest of New Mexico.* Albuquerque, 1940.

Bancroft, Hubert Howe. *History of New Mexico and Arizona.* San Francisco, 1889.

———. *History of the North Mexican States and Texas.* 2 vols. San Francisco, 1884.

Bloom, Lansing. "Ledgers of a Santa Fé Trader," *New Mexico Historical Review,* Vol. XXI, No. 2 (April, 1946), 135–39.

Bork, Albert William. *Nuevos aspectos del comercio entre Nuevo México y Misuri, 1822–1846.* Mexico City, 1944.

Chittenden, Hiram Martin. *The American Fur-Trade of the Far West.* 3 vols. New York, 1902.

Cleland, Robert Glass. *This Reckless Breed of Men: The Trappers and Fur Traders of the Southwest.* New York, 1950.

Cox, Isaac Joslin. *The Early Exploration of Louisiana.* Cincinnati, 1906.

Culmer, Frederick A. (ed.). "Selling Mules Down South in 1835," *Missouri Historical Review*, Vol. XXIV, No. 4 (July, 1930), 537–49.

Daly, H. W. *Manual of Pack Transportation*. Washington, 1917.

Dorsey, Dorothy B. "The Panic and Depression of 1837–43," *Missouri Historical Review*, Vol. XXX, No. 2 (January, 1936), 132–61.

Foreman, Grant. *Advancing the Frontier, 1830–1860*. Norman, 1933.

González Flores, Enrique. *Chihuahua de la independencia a la revolución*. Mexico City, 1949.

Hollon, W. Eugene. *The Lost Pathfinder: Zebulon Montgomery Pike*. Norman, 1949.

Hughes, Anne E. "The Beginning of Spanish Settlement in the El Paso District," *University of California Publications in History*, Vol. I (Berkeley, 1914), 293–333.

Hull, Dorothy. "Castaño de Sosa's Expedition to New Mexico in 1590," *Old Santa Fé*, Vol. III, No. 12 (October, 1916), 307–32.

Literary History of the United States. Edited by Robert E. Spiller, Willard Thorp, Thomas H. Johnson, and Henry Seidel Canby. 2 vols. New York, 1949.

Lounsbury, Ralph G. "Materials in the National Archives for the History of New Mexico Before 1848," *New Mexico Historical Review*, Vol. XXI, No. 3 (July, 1946), 247–56.

Manning, William Ray. *Early Diplomatic Relations Between the United States and Mexico*. Baltimore, 1916.

Mecham, John Lloyd. *Francisco de Ibarra and Nueva Viscaya*. Durham, N. C., 1927.

"Missouri Jack Passes His Physical," *Missouri Historical Review*, Vol. XXXVI, No. 3 (April, 1942), 341–42.

Omwake, John, and others. *The Conestoga Six-Horse Bell Teams of Eastern Pennsylvania*. Cincinnati, 1930.

Perrine, Fred S. "Military Escort on the Santa Fé Trail," *New Mexico Historical Review*, Vol. II, Nos. 2, 3 (April, July, 1927), 175–93; 269–304; Vol. III, No. 3 (July, 1928), 256–300.

Powell, Philip Wayne. *Soldiers, Indians, and Silver: The North-ward Advance of New Spain, 1550–1600*. Berkeley, 1952.

Riddle, Kenyon. *Records and Maps of the Old Santa Fé Trail*. Raton, N. M., 1949.

Scholes, France V. "The Supply Service of the New Mexican Missions in the Seventeenth Century," *New Mexico Historical Review*, Vol. V., Nos. 1, 2, 4 (January, April, October, 1930), 93–115, 186–210, 386–404.

Stephens, F. F. "Missouri and the Santa Fé Trade," *Missouri Historical Review*, Vol. X, No. 4 (July, 1916), 233–62; Vol. XI, Nos. 3, 4 (April, July, 1917), 289–312.

Stephens, Henry Morse, and Herbert Eugene Bolton (eds.). *The Pacific Ocean in History*. New York, 1917.

Thompson, James Westfall. *A History of Livestock Raising in the United States, 1607–1860*. Washington, 1942.

Twitchell, Ralph Emerson. *The Military Occupation of New Mexico, 1846–1851*. Denver, 1909.

———. *The Leading Facts of New Mexican History*. 5 vols. Cedar Rapids, 1911–17.

Young, Otis E. *The First Military Escort on the Santa Fé Trail, 1829*. Glendale, Calif., 1952.

Index